To Arnie,

THANK YOU

for your commitment,

support & caring for

peace with justice

to Palestinians

Bernard Sabella

April 15, 2018

A Life Worth Living

A Life Worth Living

The Story of a Palestinian Catholic

Bernard Sabella

EDITED BY
Carole Monica Burnett

RESOURCE *Publications* · Eugene, Oregon

A LIFE WORTH LIVING
The Story of a Palestinian Catholic

Resource Publications
An Imprint of Wipf and Stock Publishers
199 W. 8th Ave., Suite 3
Eugene, OR 97401

www.wipfandstock.com

PAPERBACK ISBN: 978-1-5326-1530-6
HARDCOVER ISBN: 978-1-5326-1532-0
EBOOK ISBN: 978-1-5326-1531-3

The partial quotation of Acts 2:11 in chapter 5 of this book is taken from the Revised Standard Version of the Bible, copyright 1952 [2nd edition, 1971] by the Division of Christian Education of the National Council of the Churches of Christ in the United States of America. Used by permission. All rights reserved.

All photographs are the property of the Sabella family.

Manufactured in the U.S.A.

Contents

Preface

WITH THE BIRTHS OF our granddaughters Natalie (2014) and Naya (2015) and the eager anticipation of a third grandchild (to arrive in 2017), I came to realize that as my life's chapter approaches its eventual end, other chapters and generations will follow. I felt that it was important to keep a record of what previous generations of the family have gone through and to portray life as it was in the Old City of Jerusalem in the fifties of the last century to the new generation of grandchildren. I also wanted to share my experiences and those of my wife and family as we grew up keeping to the Christian faith and traditions of the forefathers and also proud to be Palestinians, sharing in the woes and hopes of our people. Many in the Western world and elsewhere are not aware of the presence of Palestinian Christians, and I find it important to sensitize readers to this fact. This is my story and that of my multi-generational family as we have experienced it.

An important part of the experience of my immediate family was the years spent in higher studies in the U.S. Each of the members of our family has ingrained in them one or two memories of our U.S. sojourn for education that had become part of our growing up. Our U.S. experience allowed us to meet a wide range of people with different backgrounds, and it enriched us with educational tools that Mary, my wife, and I have employed as we shared in the education of young generations of Palestinians.

In what I have written, I did not focus strictly on the political dimension of the conflict situation in which we live, although one cannot avoid seeing that in our different stages of life we were, and continue to be, impacted by political developments. Palestinian society is not only its politics; aside from the difficult conflict with Israel, Palestinian society stands on its own with a rich culture, traditions, social relations, and a history on the land that spans over fourteen centuries. I see myself as a simple, average person with a unique life experience. When I set out to write, I was also motivated by the thought that simple, average persons are entitled to narrate their stories. People of exceptional talents and histories share their biographies with wider audiences; average, simple people share theirs with those of their immediate circles but also with a wider audience of those who seek to learn how an average, simple, Christian Palestinian experienced his life and that of his family.

I feel that without my telling the stories of the fifties as lived from a personal experiential perspective, they will forever be lost. Jerusalem's private schools in the fifties and sixties of the twentieth century were known as the educational institutions for forming future elites in the different areas of society, economy, education, and governance. Looking at my graduation photo taken in 1964, I can point to Muslim and Christian students who made an imprint on the society and its various domains. I can also recognize other high school graduates who have worked hard to see that their children will receive as good an education as they have received themselves. The love of education in Palestinian society was the pride of the people, and it was customary for parents to show pride when one of their children graduated from high school or went on further to university studies.

The essence of being Palestinian is not political, although politics overshadow all aspects of life. I have spoken about my political experience as a Member of the Palestinian Parliament. But I know that politics were not the dominating factor in my life as I loved teaching, which I continue to do whenever an opportunity arises. I also appreciated the opportunity to work with the Department of Service to Palestinian Refugees, which is associated with the churches in Palestine and elsewhere. The plight of Palestinian refugees continues today, with over five million of them; and without a solution to their ongoing difficult conditions, there can be no lasting peace between Israelis and Palestinians. The historic injustice of creating the Palestinian refugee problem, with the establishment of Israel, has contributed to much animosity and hostility between the two sides. Without justice for the Palestinian refugees, I cannot see how permanent peace between the Israelis and us can take place.

The growth of my own family impressed on me the cycles of life and the need to see that different stages of one's life carry different perspectives and experiences. I owe much to my family, Mary my wife in particular. She is a caring person with a predisposition to be exacting and perfect in what she does. Margo, our eldest, with Paul and Nani in Edinburgh are a source of pride for us. And so are Zack, our middle son, and his lovely wife Lisa and their energetic daughter Naya with one more on the way. Mona, our youngest, keeps working for human rights, and we are proud of her as she dedicates her life to lofty ideals for a world without human rights abuses.

I owe special thanks to those friends who read some of the parts of the book and added their inputs or corrected some information: Harry and Pat Wallace from Sydney, Australia; Monsignor Khaled Akasheh from the Vatican; Professor Paul Wright from the Institute of Holy Land Studies. I am also thankful for comments made by my immediate family on facts and information that needed to be updated or corrected. Mary, Zack, and Margo have given their inputs; Lisa, my daughter-in-law, has helped in pho-to-zipping and dispatching. My sister Hilda and brother Maurice offered their rich collection of family photos for me to select the appropriate ones. My brother Tony in Australia browsed through the manuscript and offered his valuable inputs. My sister Bernadette shared with me the account she had heard of Father's pardon by the Ottoman Jamal Pasha. I owe thanks to Father Kail Ellis of Villanova University, to Dr. Saliba Sarsar of Monmouth University, to my college roommate Louie Sell, a retired U.S. diplomat, and to Daoud Kuttab, a media pioneering person in Amman, Jordan, for having read the manuscript before it was sent to the publisher.

I am most thankful to my friend and editor Carole Monica Burnett. When I was starting on the manuscript, I contacted her for advice on who could edit my writing and help me with finding a publisher. She unhesitat-ingly volunteered for the demanding job, in spite of her own work require-ments. Without Monica, I could not have met the deadline for submitting the manuscript. She was an inspiration for me at times when I felt over-whelmed by so many other things; her insistence and perseverance in seeing to it that the book would be finished on time was an act not only of friend-ship but also of love for Palestine and its people.

Jerusalem, Sunday, August 27, 2017

1

Growing Up in a Refugee Family: Catholic and Palestinian

THE CARNIVAL DAYS PRECEDING Ash Wednesday were occasions of fun in our quarter of the Old City of Jerusalem in the fifties of the twentieth century. Boys and girls, with faces colored and with costumes from head to toe that could elicit laughter and awe, walked around the neighborhood for "trick or treat" favors or disfavors. In some ways our Christian-pagan celebration was similar to the way Americans celebrate Halloween and to the Jewish celebration of Purim. The origins of these celebrations may lie deep in the history of paganism, but we kids did not care a bit about origins and enjoyed strolling from home to home adorned with colorful faces and clothing, banging on drums and singing as we went along. Days of fun, however, especially since the fifties of the last century, were also a period of readjustment for our parents and families, who were dislocated and became refugees as a result of the 1948 Arab-Israeli war.

Dislocation and Dispossession

My parents were wedded in 1939 at the Terra Sancta Franciscan Church on Kings Street in West Jerusalem, a little way up the road from the American Consulate. When they got married, my mother, Marguerite, was barely seventeen while my father, Zachariah, was forty-one. The difference in age of almost a quarter of a century made Mom closer to our tastes and preferences than to my father's. But they did fare well, and Mother was a big support to Father throughout their lives. When I asked Mother one day why she had married Father, who was much older, her response was that he was a religious person and accordingly he was expected to treat her well and in addition to remember in his prayers the souls of both of her parents. In

1

particular her father, as she told me, approved the marriage, stating that "when I am long gone, your husband will remember me in prayers."

My father, a municipal employee in the British Mandate city of Jerusalem, worked hard in order to construct in 1937 the modest family home that saw my birth in 1945. I was third in the order of the family's children. Abel, nicknamed Abdallah, our grandfather's namesake on Father's side, was born in 1942; Hilda was born in 1943; Bernadette in 1946; and Maurice in 1947. After a year's hiatus Anton, or Tony, was born in 1949. In 1957 Mother gave birth to Therese. I still remember how I accompanied my mother to the maternity hospital by the Austrian Hospice in the Old City of Jerusalem in January 1961, when David, or Daoud, the youngest of the siblings, was born. Altogether we were five brothers and three sisters. Parents followed the practice, then prevalent in Palestinian society, of having as many children as possible. Some thought that the more children a family had, the better the prospects of parents in old age, because the children would take care of them. Thus the child-bearing business was seen as some sort of social security. Others thought that having many children, especially boys, would increase the respect of the society for the family and would enhance the status of the mother. These were attitudes of a traditional society that were not passed on to us as we contemplated forming our own families later on in life.

My parents were accustomed to giving foreign-sounding names, often French, to their newborns, perhaps as a way to affirm their identity as Roman Catholics, "Latins" in the local parlance, in a society where the majority was Muslim, with a variety of smaller communities of different Christian denominations. Some relate our French-sounding names to the time when the French Consulate in Jerusalem was in charge of the affairs of local Palestinian Catholics: the difficulty of French consular officers in spelling the Arabic names led the Catholics of Jerusalem to stick to French names. I do not subscribe to this narrative, as I think that naming children is a question of identity. In the case of my family, names of saints figured prominently as a tribute to saints to whom my father paid special devotion. When I was born on the eve of Epiphany, my mother registered my name on the birth certificate as Epiphan, which was most fitting. When Father arrived at the maternity ward, he did not like the name, and instead he prescribed that I would be known as Bernard, my alias, which stuck to me while Epiphan was used for more official and formal transactions. Father had a special devotional attraction to the Virgin Mary and was impressed by the life and example of Saint Bernard, who was known for his continuous and perhaps obsessive devotion to her.

I do not recall much of my first three years; babies and infants are not supposed to have a strong memory, or so popular imagination would have it. But I recall a yellow school bus going down the hilly road with my brother Abel and sister Hilda off to pre-kindergarten; a glimpse of that bus remains in my mind, the first imprint that I recollect from my infancy. The chicken coop that Aunt Leonie, Father's sister, who was living with us, used to tend (she loved animals by nature and had a special way with them) has also a place in my memory. Fascinated, I would stand by the pen and would gaze for a long time on what was going on inside it. I cannot characterize my family's quality of life or extent of happiness or unease between 1945 and 1948, but I know that the eventual dislocation and our becoming refugees in 1948 left a life-long impact on all of us, particularly on my father and mother.

As the fighting raged on around our home in Qatamon (now a West Jerusalem neighborhood), which was situated between a British military camp and a Jewish underground stronghold, my parents felt safer in moving away. Their decision to move was further strengthened by the bombing on the night of January 5, 1947, by a Jewish underground group, the Haganah, of the Semiramis Hotel, which killed seven members of the Abou Souan family, close friends of my parents, among the scores of killed and wounded. This Christian family, who owned the hotel, wanted close relatives and friends to come together to celebrate the New Year amidst mounting tensions in the neighborhood. They felt that having the gathering in a hotel rather than a private residence better assured the safety of those present. An older friend of mine who knew the Abou Souan family personally has told me that the night of the bombing was a particularly rainy one with heavy showers. As some of the Abou Souan family members were set to leave the hotel for their home, which was within walking distance, their host, the owner of the hotel, insisted that they stay and provided them with overnight accommodation. Those who stayed lost their lives in the bombing.

As the fighting intensified, my parents, with my Aunt Leonie and Cousin Joseph, who was then twenty-four years of age and lived with us, gathered up as many of their possessions as they could, locked the house, and took the bulky iron keys with them. They were hoping to find refuge in the Old City of Jerusalem for a couple of weeks and then to return after the fighting subsided. But their hope never materialized because Jerusalem was divided and the western neighborhoods, including Qatamon, became part of West Jerusalem, which was claimed by Israel as its capital. Our home, built in 1937, was expropriated by the Absentee Property Authority in Israel. In effect, this meant its transfer to newly arrived Jewish immigrants to Israel. When years later I mentioned to an American Jewish group during a lecture and discussion that my parents were some of the "great contributors" to the Zionist dream because their home was expropriated by the government of Israel, they took offense at my insinuation that the welcoming of Jewish arrivals into newly created Israel was at the expense of my parents and thousands of Palestinians like them who were dispossessed of their home.

My parents had no choice but to seek refuge somewhere; they eventually opted to go to Lebanon, where they settled in Ghazir, a small village by the Mediterranean. We lived in Ghazir for a whole year on the savings of my father, who had managed to withdraw his assets from the British Bank of the Middle East, which was previously known as the Ottoman Bank. Ghazir was a small community of Maronite faithful, many of whom attended daily Mass. Ghazir was home to the Maronite Patriarchal Seminary, where mostly young Lebanese Catholics of the Maronite rite were trained to become priests. My father, a devout Catholic, went to Mass every day, and this was the reason why the villagers of Ghazir loved him and welcomed us in their midst.

The tension between Lebanese and Palestinians was always high, particularly as thousands of Palestinian refugees, like my family, found their way to Lebanon following the eruption of Arab-Israeli fighting in 1948. This tension was not simply related to the difference in nationality but also to the fact that the majority of Lebanese Christians at the time were fearful that an influx of Palestinians, mostly Muslim, would unsettle the religious balance between Christians and Muslims in the country. This sensitivity still persists, unfortunately, and is dealt with by restricting Palestinians to the refugee camps in which they live, including the Palestinian Christian refugee camp of Dbayieh, north of Beirut, not far away from Ghazir. In addition Palestinians are barred from employment in almost seventy professions, such as medicine, in order to prevent them from integrating into the Lebanese setting. Some advocates for the right of Palestinians in Lebanon to job opportunities argue that if the Palestinian refugees remain poor and unemployed, the likelihood that they would leave Lebanon and go back to the West Bank would remain slim. If they are working and earning a decent income that would enable them to stand on their own two feet, then the likelihood that they would opt to go back to the West Bank and start anew would be much greater.

As Father's savings dwindled after a year's stay in Ghazir, and as he had no means of finding employment in Lebanon, the family moved on to Bethlehem. The trip from Ghazir to Bethlehem was accomplished with a hired taxi. The driver, a Syriac Orthodox Christian from Bethlehem, used to travel the Beirut-Amman-Jerusalem-and-Bethlehem road regularly. I remember that as we approached Bethlehem, a fight broke out between our driver, who was hot-headed, and some road construction workers who had asked him to stop. My father intervened and calmed the situation, but the screaming and yelling made me afraid.

Much later, in 1961, as we were attending Mass on the Monday following Easter Sunday in the Church of the Franciscans at Emmaus, a village mentioned in the Bible (Luke 24), in which the benediction of the bread took place, Aunt Leonie spotted a Lebanese woman who was the daughter of the family with whom we stayed in Ghazir in 1948. I remember Aunt Leonie citing a famous Arabic saying: *Jabal 'ala Jabal la yaltaqi—Insan 'ala Insan Yaltaqi* ("A mountain never meets a mountain, but a man meets a man"). This was an apt proverb, as members of the two families had not met for more than twelve years. The meeting was possible because prior to the June 1967 war, Lebanese pilgrims and others from Syria, Jordan, and Egypt came to Jerusalem to celebrate Holy Week and Easter Sunday.

In Bethlehem, the family rented one room, which I still pass by on my way to the Nativity Church through the narrow serpentine alleys of Bethlehem, and we lived there, the nine of us. But the problem of employment for my father remained since Bethlehem of the early fifties was more like a village than a flourishing town and even the small number of pilgrims and tourists who arrived, although in general wealthier than present-day pilgrims and tourists, did not contribute much to improve the economic prospects and prosperity of the village where Jesus Christ was born. Besides, the arrival of thousands of refugees as a consequence of the 1948 war meant that the economic and social pressures on Bethlehem were tremendous. The newly arrived refugees were housed in three camps around Bethlehem: Dheisheh, Al 'Izzeh, and Ayda. The impact of the arrival of the refugees, mostly Muslim with a minority of Christians, meant that the demographic composition of Bethlehem was likely to change from a Christian majority into a Muslim majority.

Years later, I heard stories about the opportunities provided by pilgrims arriving at the Nativity Church in the early fifties. Apparently, Manger Square in front of the Church of the Nativity was the ideal place for young local boys to spot promising pilgrims who might lend a hand of support or provide the needed channels to realize dreams, especially of furthering education abroad. When I was teaching at Bethlehem University in Bethlehem (not to be confused with Bethlehem, Pennsylvania), a colleague of mine, a professor of physics and an expert teacher, told me how he had ended up in college in the U.S. One day in the early fifties he spotted a group of American pilgrims with a couple of priests. He approached one of the priests and started a conversation with him. As the conversation went on, the priest became interested in the story of the young boy who was speaking very good English and who conveyed to him his wish to go to college in the U.S. Certainly my professor friend stressed again and again the inability of his family to cover the expenses that would be incurred by study in the U.S. To the surprise and jubilation of my friend, as he told me, the priest turned out to be the president of a college with a degree program in Physics. Eventually my friend ended up studying at that college and went on to earn a PhD in the U.S. Because of his attachment to Bethlehem and to his family, my friend came back and started teaching at junior colleges and high schools until the opportunity to teach at university level became available with the founding of Bethlehem University in 1973.

The second story of opportunity arising in Manger Square had a different ending. A distant Sabella cousin who earnestly wanted to continue his education abroad saw a group of English-speaking pilgrims and tourists crossing the Square. As he approached them and struck up a conversation with them, the head of the group, a Monsignor, picked up on the boy's wish to continue his university studies. The group, as it turned out, had come all the way from Australia, "down under," to venerate the birthplace of Jesus Christ in Bethlehem. The Monsignor promised to help out; but first my cousin had to fill out an application for the university of his choice, and upon acceptance the logistical matters would then be sorted out. In the early fifties, the only means of communication between Jordan and Australia was via airmail. So my cousin applied for admission by writing back and forth until it was clear that he could indeed go to Australia. The Monsignor, nevertheless, was worried about the living arrangements of my cousin and how he would fare so distant from his family. The suggestion arose that the best solution was for the whole family to apply for immigration to Australia, and so they did. When my wife Mary and I visited Australia in 2002, I met with my distant cousins and their families; one was a very successful businessman investing every penny he could get his hands on, and the other had become a world-renowned chiropractor with clients from near and far. They were indeed happy with their new homes and their accomplishments.

These two stories illustrate well the aspiration of Palestinians to pursue education. Some overzealous Palestinians would argue that we are one of the most educated nations on earth. While I do not discount that we Palestinians do take pride in continuing our education, I am doubtful that we are actually the most educated. But education, unlike other earthly goods, does stay with a person, even despite dislocation and dispossession; if one is educated, one remains educated. Hence education becomes some sort of security or safety net, so to speak, particularly at times of great crises and dislocations.

When my father told my mother that he had been offered employment in the Municipality of Jerusalem on the east side of the city, which had become part of Jordan following the 1948 war, the decision was to move immediately to the Old City of Jerusalem. Moving to Jerusalem meant that the family had to find a place to live. Through church contacts my father was informed that we could move for free into two rooms of a large house that had several compartments in the Old City belonging to the Franciscan Custody of the Holy Land. The Franciscans, a religious order founded by Saint Francis of Assisi in the thirteenth century, have had a presence in the Holy Land ever since their inception. Their mission is to take care of the Holy Places and to minister also to the indigenous Catholic faithful in Jerusalem, Bethlehem, Nazareth, Cana, and Jaffa. The house, known as Dar Moussa Effendi (the "Home of Sir Moussa"—"Effendi" being an Ottoman Turkish title equivalent to "Sir" to address people of social standing, and Moussa having been at one time the mayor of Jerusalem), was close to the Church of the Holy Sepulcher—which endeared it to my devout father, who would be able to attend daily Mass in the Church, come rain or shine.

Dar Moussa Effendi was built around the turn of the twentieth century by an elder of the Husseini family, an old and well established Jerusalem Palestinian Muslim family. One should remember that Jerusalem outside the walls did not have much construction at the turn of the twentieth century, and most well established families built their mansions within the walls of the Old City. Once construction accelerated outside the walls in the first two to three decades of the twentieth century, many of the well-to-do families were inclined to sell their mansions within the walls to invest in more spacious and accessible accommodations outside the walls. Conscious of the need of their parishioners for housing within the walls of the Old City, the Franciscan Custody wisely bought the property as it did other properties in the Old City during the decades of the British Mandate of Palestine, which lasted from 1920 to 1948. There were seven or eight Palestinian Christian refugee families from the 1948 war living in the Dar. The Old City homes of wealthy and prominent Jerusalemites were usually single-family homes. Upon purchase by the Franciscans, the Dar, or "Home of Sir Moussa," was divided into smaller apartments whereby more than one family could share the home.

The problem with this compartmentalization was that the two rooms we were assigned did not have either a toilet or a kitchen and certainly no running water or electricity. At a certain time, as I recall, the Franciscans allowed my parents to cover with aluminum sheets the space just in front of the two rooms and to use it as a provisionary kitchen. I remember this clearly, as my bed opened up to the newly improvised kitchen, and when in winter the Jerusalem rain came down heavily, I was awakened by the raindrops hitting the aluminum sheets and making some sort of musical orchestra, which, in the ears of a young boy trying to sleep and be ready for school the next day, was not always appreciated. But somehow the raindrops on the aluminum sheets gave me reassurance that rain in Jerusalem was a sign of hope, given the arid conditions that made rain a cherished gift, and an affirmation that we were not forgotten even if we were poor and had only the clothes on us. For years we used the toilet downstairs, some dozen of steps down from our two rooms. Now that our apartments are fitted with at least one or two toilets, I cannot imagine how we managed with such a situation, especially at night. But we did manage, and our environment taught us how to adapt.

The earthenware jar, a substitute for running water in those days, which was used for drinking water, was placed in a corner of the kitchen with a stainless steel cup atop a wooden protective top, hygienic (as we would say today) for all of us to use; sometimes cousins and other kids drank from it as we were all playing in the *Hosh*, or the home's courtyard, and needed to replenish our body fluids, especially on hot summer days. We were not worried about drinking from the same cup, as the most important thing was to drink. Our drinking water was hauled by a water carrier who, using a sheepskin as a container, would fill up the earthenware jar from a water source in the Christian Quarter, about ten minutes' walk from our home, which was supervised by the Municipality. Suleiman Mansour, a local Palestinian artist of international renown from the village of Birzeit near Ramallah, immortalized the water carrier in a painting depicting an old man carrying in a sheepskin the whole Old City of Jerusalem with its mosques and churches. Every time I contemplate the painting, I am reminded of the days when the water carrier was as important to us as running water is today for many of us.

We had a cistern that collected rain water and that served the other needs of the household such as washing clothes and bathing. When the washing lady came from Sur Baher, a nearby village on the road to Bethlehem, every Wednesday or Thursday to help Mother, she hauled the water needed for her task from the cistern. Sometimes neighbors helped out in hauling water, but the hard work was left to the women, Mother included, for most of the time. The washing lady was an older Muslim lady, and Mom treated her with all the respect due to her, including offering her a hearty breakfast and insisting on her sharing our noon meal. When Mother passed away in 1973, this elderly lady, still alive and active, came from her village to pay the last respects.

A story that I have heard my mother and this washing lady talking about was the marriage of the washing lady's husband to a new bride. According to Islamic religious law a man can marry up to four wives if he is equally fair to each one of them. It was rare for Palestinian Muslim families to be polygamous, as most remained monogamous. It was not simply a question of the fairness of the husband to more than one wife, but the economic and social necessities discouraged marriage to more than one wife. When Mother inquired about why the husband, who was already married to two wives, needed to marry once again, the washing lady explained that both she and the second wife wanted their husband to get married to a new bride in order to ensure progeny. Both wives were unable to bear children, so the two set out to search for a suitable bride for their husband because, as the washing lady told my mom, he was a good man and deserved to have offspring. Eventually they succeeded in procuring a young bride for their husband, and they both treated her as their protégée rather than as a marital competitor. This story reminds one of Old Testament stories of marriage and other intricate relationships, such as the triangular relationship of Abraham, Sarah, and Hagar, in which love is not necessarily the most crucial element in making choices, even the most intimate of choices.

The water from the cistern was also beneficial for our weekly baths on Saturdays, when the water was placed in an aluminum container, used previously to store olive oil or Arabic butter, and heated by a kerosene primus stove, the same primus that was instrumental for many years in cooking our meals. I always had an irrational fear that the primus would explode, causing bodily harm, or that the aluminum container that sat atop the primus would bear down on the primus and cause some accident that would hurt someone. A rounded aluminum washtub was used, and Mom or Aunt Leonie rubbed us hard with olive oil soap from Nablus, north of Jerusalem, as they poured hot water from a stainless steel cup over heads and bodies. We always felt clean for the whole week after the Saturday bath. Generations of Palestinians argue that the Nabulsi soap is the best soap in the world. Nowadays the soap continues to be made in Nablus, biblical Shechem.

It was customary for Aunt Leonie to ask me at the end of the bath, as she was wrapping me in a towel, to pray for the health, happiness, and welfare of Father, Mother, Uncle, and all other family members. It was Aunt Leonie who also instructed me to cross myself when I spotted the crescent moon and to wish for the month ahead to be one of success and continued health. There was also a custom related to the loss and replacement of our teeth in childhood. Whenever one of us siblings lost a tooth, we were instructed by the elders to place it under our pillow for the night with the hope that we would be rewarded the following morning. Most of us kids followed the instruction as well as that which encouraged us to throw the tooth towards the sun while asking it to give us a new and better tooth.

Cleanliness, nevertheless, was not altogether guaranteed by the weekly bath. A year or two after I was enrolled in school, a lice problem occurred, and we had to undergo an impromptu inspection every day by the school principal to ascertain that we were not affected. Because of my worry over lice, I went to my cousin Awni, a barber (who later migrated to the U.S. and lived south of San Diego, where he achieved success), who convinced me that I should shave off all of my hair. When the shaving was done, I felt naked and somehow ashamed of my new appearance. When I arrived home, the kids of the neighborhood started chanting: Ar'ah 'Ar'ah Hantiteh—Bidha Zeit wa Kibriteh ("Bald Bald Head—In Need of Olive Oil and a Match Box"). My instinctive reaction was to hide behind the water cistern with its square, stone, elevated, protective edge and to seek the aid of my mother and aunt and other motherly figures. Some consoled me that by shaving off my hair, I would assure stronger hair buds for a lifetime. I never knew what the folkloric saying "Bald Bald Head" meant. Likely the match box, Kibriteh, was added because it rhymed in Arabic with Hantiteh.

Aunt Mary

Aunt Mary, Father's other sister, like us and like the more than fifty thousand Palestinian Christians among the 726,000 Palestinian refugees, ended up displaced. She had a room next to us while our maternal cousins, the Dickhas, also refugees, were living across from us. Aunt Mary, a widow of a postal employee whose bald-headed photo adorned the wall at the entrance to her room, had her own home on the Jerusalem-Bethlehem road but had to flee to the Old City when the fighting flared up in 1948. Aunt Mary and Aunt Leonie finally caught up with each other, and they often used to speak and discuss matters in German, which they had learned as young girls at Schmidt's School in East Jerusalem. Speaking German enabled them to open up freely to each other and to comment unhindered on developments around them, particularly at home. I still remember the fascination I felt when I looked over some of the school's notebooks that Aunt Mary had kept from her school days. Written in beautiful handwriting, clean and very methodical, I thought the notebook was a piece of art and not simply schoolwork. My mother, Marguerite, did not understand a word of German, and she suspected that her two sisters-in-law were talking about her, if not outright conspiring. But relations between Mother and Aunt Leonie were mostly cooperative as they divided the chores of the house and as

Aunt Leonie undertook to do shopping and other errands, especially in the Christmas and Easter seasons.

Aunt Mary was a person of independent will and strong determination with some means. She did not accept charity and believed that she had to earn her living. In the early fifties, when the Anglican Bishop's School, Madraset Al Mutran, in Amman needed a housekeeper for the boys who were boarding students, Aunt Mary accepted the job when it was offered to her. She traveled to Amman in spite of the rather primitive road system of the times. She worked in the Bishop's School for some years until the early sixties, but she kept her room next to us. With the savings she had inherited from her late husband, Daoud, she decided to invest some with her paternal cousin in Beirut, Nicola, who had become a successful businessman selling American car parts after his family was forced out of their original city of Haifa during the 1948 war. From this investment Aunt Mary continued to receive handy returns until the 1967 Arab-Israeli war, which made communication between Jerusalem and Beirut impossible. Unfortunately for Cousin Nicola, he had to suffer once again the repercussions of conflict and war when the 1975 civil war in Lebanon wiped out his business and reduced his millions of Lebanese pounds into a mere handful of U.S. dollars. Aunt Mary, nevertheless, was determined to rely only on herself. She found employment for some years at the American Spafford Foundation in Harrat Al Sa'diyah (Sa'diyah Quarter), just inside the Damascus Gate in the Old City of Jerusalem. The Old City was divided into four quarters: the Armenian, the Christian, the Jewish, and the Muslim. Sa'diyah Quarter comprised the bulk of the Muslim Quarter and included Al Wad Street leading to Al Haram Al Sharif (the Noble Sanctuary) and to the Wailing Wall. Spafford was well known for its health care services to infants and its outreach to the handicapped and other needy of the Holy City. The Spafford Foundation had been founded by the nineteenth-century American Christian migrants who made up the American Colony in Jerusalem, which later became a plush hotel and meeting place for politicians, businessmen, aspiring intellectuals, and peace activists, among others. Aunt Mary enjoyed working and was determined to chart her own course amidst the various challenges and vicissitudes of life. Refraining from excessive smoking, she would enjoy only one cigarette a day as she prepared to go to bed at night.

As a young adult in the second half of the sixties, when I was enrolled at Franklin and Marshall College in Lancaster, Pennsylvania, I was invited to dinner at the college president's residence. I was seated next to a gentleman professor who specialized in art and who, it turned out, was related to the Spafford and Whiting families, the founders of the American Colony in Jerusalem. Once he knew of my rather modest background, he shunned me for the whole evening. I thought that the original sojourners who were central to the legend of the American Colony and later on the Spafford Foundation would not have approved of his demeanor.

Aunt Mary impressed on me the need to learn Hebrew when I returned from university in the U.S. in 1971. She argued that all successful shopkeepers in the Old City knew Hebrew, and this accounted for their business successes with Hebrew-speaking Israeli shoppers. The first few years of the Israeli occupation of East Jerusalem and the rest of the Palestinian Territories after the 1967 war were considered by some, on both Israeli and Palestinian sides, as the "honeymoon" years because contact between the two sides was possible without the checkpoints, travel restrictions, curfews, separation wall, and other population control methods of recent times. I recall asking Aunt Mary what she thought of the Israelis in general; her response was mixed. On the one hand, we could live together, as some of the Israelis were friendly and wanted simply to live in peace. But, on the other hand, she was not convinced that the Israeli authorities were just or fair, as they had not compensated her and others for the loss of their homes as a result of the 1948 war. She told me how her own home was occupied by a newly arrived Israeli family, and she wondered whether it was just to compel her to live in confined one-room lodgings while others were enjoying her former home. She felt that the Israelis, or at least their government, had not learned the lesson of history that injustice will only brew dissent, conflict, and further confrontation.

When Aunt Mary was in her eighties, she fell down and broke her pelvis. She was treated in an Israeli hospital and later had to undergo rehabilitation, also in an Israeli institution. One day when I was visiting her, I asked her again what she thought of the Israelis. She told me that they were good people because they treated her as they would treat their own. The lesson became clear to me that the way we feel about others depends in the end on how others treat us. This summarizes all political wisdom on how we can arrive at peace and make reconciliation possible in our troubled and divided land. In fact, this is a lesson that our world today ought to grasp, especially as movements of people across continents have become more feasible and more frequent. Inequalities and unjust treatment, whether real or perceived, lead to conflict and eventual confrontation.

When Aunt Mary passed away in the eighties, I was in the U.S. pursuing higher education and therefore could not pay my respects and bid her the last farewell. I often visit her grave at the Mount Sion Roman Catholic cemetery, which is not far away from the grave of Oskar Schindler, who saved the lives of 1,200 Jews during the Holocaust by employing them in his ammunition and enamelware factories. The burials of Aunt Mary, my parents, and significant others of my family next to Schindler always evoked in me questions about the rationality or irrationality of encounters and closeness above and below ground. Here was a man who had devoted an important part of his life to saving Jews, and had taken serious risks in so doing, now lying in eternal rest next to Christian Palestinians, most of whom were refugees or offspring of refugees from the 1948 Arab-Israeli war.

A Poor and Blessed Family

We were a poor but not an overly unhappy family during the fifties. We did not have wealth; instead, we had lots of siblings, cousins, and friends. It was usually my father who did the routine daily shopping for the necessary food items. Many of the fruits and greens he bought were from farm women who came to the city from the villages and rural areas surrounding Jerusalem very early in the mornings to sell their produce in the streets by our house. Everyone who ventured into the Old City of Jerusalem in the early morning during those days would see and hear these colorfully dressed farm women advertising their produce and its price. Father would go from one seller to another until all that was needed for a day's food was secured. It was only on Sundays that we had a meal with meat; usually our Sunday dinners consisted of squash, vine leaves, and tomatoes, all stuffed with rice and minced meat. It was the best meal of the week, as on other days we had a vegetarian diet, which was quite healthy but sometimes wanting in taste. *Mish Kol Yom 'Adas* ("Not Every Day Lentils!") was a popular saying that we often repeated when we objected to the vegetarian menu offered day after day. It is also a universal Palestinian saying justifying a meal that is rich in meat and other salty and sweet delicacies.

Shopping for the festive meals of Christmas and Easter was the task set for Aunt Leonie. She knew where to buy the best turkeys or, if family finances did not allow it, to get chickens, minced meat, and the additional provisions for a fitting family meal. I often accompanied her on her shopping sprees, not only for food but also for clothing and shoes. In contrast to the habits of a consumer society, our shopping for nonfood items was occasional, centered on Christmas and Easter. The skills of bargaining endeared Aunt Leonie to the merchants with whom she would spend up to half an hour choosing the clothing and other items and arguing over the price. The periodic shopping sprees saw us getting new shoes; usually the shoes we were wearing had been repaired several times but still did not prevent rainwater from soaking our feet and socks as we walked back and forth to

school. Nowadays when I am apt to buy new pairs of shoes, showing dis-
comfort with my old but still usable shoes, my eldest daughter Marguerite
tells me that my inclination has been caused by my experience with leaking
shoes when I was a kid. Pants, shirts, underwear, pajamas, and other needed
clothes were also bought with the idea that they should last for a year or
more. Ours was a society that valued money because we did not have much
of it, and it was a selective society in regard to buying consumables of all
kinds. A poor society is not altogether an unhealthy society.

Because we were refugees, we received goods from UNRWA, the
United Nations Relief and Works Agency. Established to provide aid for
Palestinian refugees, UNRWA used to distribute food parcels and bags of
used clothing (*Bu'aj* in Arabic) near St. Stephen's Gate by the Church of
Saint Anne near the eastern wall of the Old City of Jerusalem. Once or
twice I took upon myself as a young boy the responsibility of collecting the
food parcels and the bag of used clothing. We were asked to stand in line,
and a man with a long belt made us respect the queue by using it at will
to hit the ground and at times to hit people. The parcels and bags remind
me nowadays of the distribution going on in neighboring countries to the
Syrian refugees who have left their country following the breakout of civil
war there, which has lasted now for over five years. The rudimentary parcels of food were a guilt-removing exercise for the world community, but
mostly for the Western powers, which did nothing to prevent the injustice
done to Palestine and its refugees or to handle its political and other consequences adequately. In today's world some still blame this failure as one
of the causes for the spread of terrorism and for the bitter feelings toward
Western governments. The bags of clothing came mostly from ordinary
American women who, on cleaning their closets, decided to donate the
used clothes to charity. We were thrilled with these donated clothes, as they
enabled us to pick one or two clothing items that fit a member of our family. The other clothes that were not deemed suitable were either discarded
or sold to the old-clothes dealer, who advertised his presence especially on
days following the distribution of bags of clothes.

Another indication of our distress and need for help was the weekly
distribution of loaves of bread (*Tulam*) that the Franciscan bakery inside
Saint Savior Convent used to prepare. Scores of needy Jerusalemites would
line up, waiting their turn to reach the well-protected double-glass window,
access to which was through a revolving iron gate. Whenever I stood in line
waiting for the *Tulam*, I thought to myself that it may have been easier to
get through the gates of heaven than inside the Franciscan bakery. The glass
window had an opening in its lower side that was wide enough to allow us to
extract the loaves of bread assigned according to family size and need. I was

not particularly excited about the exercise, nor was I quite happy with the feeling that we were dependent even for our basic necessities on the charity and mercy of others. Not that mercy and charity are not good qualities by themselves, but when you are on the receiving end, you often ask, "Why?" and "How can I overcome and stand on my own two feet without need for help or charity from others?"

Holy Days

Christmas to us was quite simple. On Christmas Eve, Mother and Aunt Leonie would prepare a festive evening meal. When the whole family gathered for the Christmas Eve meal, I felt inspired to prepare a written five-minute speech thanking parents, expressing love to them and to my siblings, while mentioning one or two of their idiosyncrasies, which evoked laughter, and welcoming any family and outside guests who may have joined the dinner table.

Father always asked me to go and get sweet and dry red and white wine bottles from the Kamar Grocery at the entrance to the Christian Quarter. I remember quite well that the price of a bottle of Cremisan wine would not exceed the equivalent of forty-four U.S. cents in the local currency. The wine tasted good, but, irrespective of the quality—which was advertised as having "natural, agreeable, and full-bodied relishing flavor," by the Italian Silesian Brothers, who had produced the wine since 1885—its purpose for us was to enliven the evening and to mark it as different from other evenings. The Cremisan wine cellars and convent are not far from Bethlehem, but unfortunately the lands surrounding them are now set for confiscation by the Israeli authorities for the construction of the Separation Wall. Today a good Cremisan red wine bottle would cost no less than ten U.S. dollars each. Palestinian society has never been known as prone to drinking. Perhaps this is due to the influence of Islam, which prohibits alcohol, although many of the drinkers in our society are Muslims. During the holy month of Ramadan, which is a fasting month, Muslim drinkers refrain from imbibing alcohol out of respect for the sanctity of the month and for the sensitivity of those fasting.

Early on Christmas morning, with five of us kids lying in our beds next to each other, we would awaken to the presents from "Papa Noel," the same as Santa Claus, in whom we believed and put our trust. Our presents were simple: a small piece of Jordanian money (20 fils = 8 U.S. cents), known for its tiny size, with a bag of chocolate and other sweets wrapped in see-through colorful wraps and at least one clothing item newly acquired. I felt at the top of the world with these gifts, and I was indeed overjoyed and thankful for "Papa Noel," knowing quite well that these were prepared by Mom and Aunt Leonie. The rest of the day we spent on a shopping spree in the narrow streets surrounding our home, and years later, we started a sort of family and youth tradition by all going to Bethlehem. In Bethlehem itself, we started our visit with the Shepherds' Field in the small town of Beit Sahour, just one or two kilometers down the hills from Bethlehem, and then we began our walking trek to Bethlehem to venerate the Infant Babe of the Grotto. These were lovely days full of good and positive memories with the zest of young people whose world needed to be developed and whose hopes and expectations were indeed broader than the realities in which they lived.

On one Christmas Eve, I accompanied Dad to the Church of the Nativity in Bethlehem for midnight Mass. In the fifties of the last century it was easy to gain access to the midnight Mass, unlike today when you need special invitation cards, which you have to request from the Franciscan office weeks, if not months, ahead in order to secure entrance. Midnight Mass was then an occasion to pray and to reflect and to identify with the birth of the Infant Babe of the Grotto. At present, Christmas midnight Mass has turned into a media event and has lost its luster of years past. The whole idea behind the Mass is to celebrate in prayerful reflection the birth of Jesus. The joy and public expressions on the occasion should be left to Manger Square, just in front of the basilica. Some heed this guideline as they invite choirs from all over the world to perform in Manger Square on the Eve and Day of Christmas. Crowds of Palestinians—Muslims and Christians alike—together with pilgrims and tourists from all over the world, congregate in Manger Square as they listen to the choirs, and for a break some avail themselves of the well-known hummus and falafel of Afteem, which is a small restaurant with a cavernous appearance. A few steps down from Manger Square, it was established back in 1949 or 1950 by a Palestinian Christian refugee from Lod (Lydda) on the Mediterranean.

In the fifties when we headed to Saint Catherine Church in Bethlehem, where midnight Mass was celebrated, most in the church were there for fervent prayers, often in silence and meditation. The atmosphere elicited warmth, and, regardless of one's degree of religiosity, it obliged worshippers to bow their heads in prayer and reflection. The sense of religious togetherness and identity, connecting the different nationalities and religious orders present, was overwhelming. Father would not be satisfied with the midnight Mass only, where the Latin (Roman Catholic) Patriarch of the Holy Land officiated, but would go on to attend Mass or a number of them in the Grotto itself, where Jesus Christ is believed to have been born of the Virgin Mary. By the time we had returned to Jerusalem by bus along the narrow, winding, long, and hilly road that bypassed the direct Israeli road to the west (which was inaccessible because of closed borders between Jordan and Israel), it was already seven or eight o'clock in the morning, and we would hit the sack, as they say.

Christmas heralded joy to the little town of Bethlehem whereas Easter brought the pilgrims and the commotion to Jerusalem during Holy Week. The Lenten season began with the Carnival weekend, when those who were intent on fasting had the last chance, until Easter Sunday, to satisfy their taste buds with rich meaty dishes and delicious sweets. As I mentioned at the beginning of this narrative, we children were dressed in colorful outfits, our faces painted with different clownish colors, and as we went from home to home in the Christian Quarter, we banged on drums and produced noise with other musical instruments. We were hoping to collect enough chocolates, bonbons, and other sweets to last us for a long time. This was fun and transported the other kids and me into a magical world of bonding with each other and dealing with grownups on our own childish grounds. Mother, aunts, and all the women in the Dar with experience in preparing the special Carnival dishes came together on the Thursday preceding the Carnival weekend in a joyous atmosphere to prepare *sanbousek* (tiny pieces of minced meat enveloped by dough) and *mutabak* (sheets of folded thin dough with sweet white cheese and sugary minced walnuts within). We savored these delicacies, which took hours of preparation. Mothers and other women had the opportunity then to reaffirm the culinary tradition inherited from older generations, thus reflecting community continuity and spirit. This tasty tradition has now almost disappeared, with only a limited number of families still practicing it.

Lent was kept consciously by most families, including us children. We abstained from eating meat on Wednesdays and Fridays (although my family normally had meat only on Sundays, as I mentioned), and undertook to perform small "acts of sacrifice" here and there.

With the arrival of the first Easter pilgrims, especially those from Cyprus, Egypt, Lebanon, Syria, and other neighboring countries, the atmosphere of Easter started to fill the city. We kids went to the Damascus Gate in order to welcome and guide the pilgrims to their accommodations at homes rented out by locals inside the Old City. This pilgrimage-related commercial enterprise helped to secure some needed income particularly for Easter week. My own family never rented out a room because we did not have the additional space. But we used the occasion of the arrival of pilgrims from Cyprus to buy the special brandy, known for its quality, that the pilgrims brought with them to cover some of their pilgrimage expenses. Stands that sold all sorts of souvenir items mushroomed in the streets and alleys of the Christian Quarter leading to the Church of the Holy Sepulcher. Candles of all sizes, designs, and colors were offered in stalls and shops, and local children, on Easter vacation from school, employed their freshly learned foreign words and phrases to entice pilgrims to buy souvenir items and candles and to barter with them over brandy and other possible items of trade carried by the pilgrims. I never set out my own stand for souvenir items, but I did work as a boy helper in a couple of souvenir shops by the Church of the Holy Sepulcher. Besides the commercial use for the newly acquired words of English and other languages, we also used to help pilgrims and tourists to maneuver their ways within the Old City. I remember many a morning when, on the way to school, a tourist would ask me how to reach the Holy Sepulcher. I would instruct him or her as to the route to follow and then would proceed to accompany him or her to the required destination, whenever I felt that the poor tourist did not understand my instructions. Commerce was never my choice of vocation or career, possibly because we were taught at home that "money was not everything" and that there were other things in life that money could not buy.

Some of my friends who were in love with imported chocolate and who naturally could not afford its price took advantage of the overcrowding in the Christian Quarter during Holy Week to snatch some samples from the grocery shops that sold imported chocolates and other sweet delicacies. It was easier to do during the Easter season because a multitude of shoppers would congregate in the Samara mini-market, not far away from the Franciscan Girls' Orphanage. I often argued with my friends that shoplifting was not fair in principle and was also unfair to the owners of the groceries. Their response, which was never justifiable to me, was that the grocery store owners made more than enough profit from the locals and from the pilgrims, especially during Easter time. My friends enjoyed the chocolates and went about their business as if no sin or transgression had been committed. One of my friends who used to shoplift ended up finishing his medical studies in France and joined the medical profession in Amman, Jordan. He has had a reputation as a good and conscientious surgeon; apparently the fleeting transgression of shoplifting in Jerusalem has not influenced the course of his life negatively.

Easter Week started with Palm Sunday. Some families in Jerusalem's Christian Quarter specialized in preparing palm branches in tree-like designs with pockets to hold flowers. These were sought by local families, especially those blessed with small children, and they were decorated with flowers and colored ribbons in preparation for the Palm Sunday church service, which was truly a community event centered on children, infants, and the newly born. At the end of the service, a procession within the church, and outside if weather permitted, took place with parents holding their children and the decorated palm branches. It was an occasion for those who had cameras to take photos of infants and children holding the decorated palm branches. Olive tree branches, a symbol of peace and reconciliation, were distributed by the officiating priests to parishioners at the end of the procession. These olive tree branches blessed our homes from year to year and reminded us that we were a link in many generations of indigenous Christians who had kept the faith without interruption.

On the afternoon of Palm Sunday the community took part in the traditional procession that started in Bethphage, a village on the eastern slopes of the Mount of Olives, where Christ had asked his disciples to fetch a donkey for him to mount and ride into Jerusalem. The procession passed from the Mount of Olives, winding down past St. Stephen's Gate to the Church of St. Anne just inside the Old City wall. Palm branches, symbolizing victory, were carried by all. At the termination of the procession, the branches were shaken as the Latin Patriarch, the highest officiating Roman Catholic ecclesiastic in the land, entered the church. The sound produced by the shaking of the palm branches was reminiscent of that of the crowd that gathered around Jesus and greeted him as he entered Jerusalem.

After the procession, another of those events that attested to the prevailing Muslim-Christian cooperation and harmony took place as Christian and Muslim Boy Scout groups, which helped keep order in the procession, circled the walls of the Old City in their colorful uniforms and with flags as they played bagpipe renditions of popular nationalistic tunes. Bagpipe music among Palestinians had been incorporated into our musical lore during the British Mandate period between 1920 and 1948. The Scottish contingents in the armed forces of the British Empire inspired our adoption of their preference for bagpipes, and we have continued this adopted tradition into modern times since it has become part of Palestinian Christian religious rituals and celebrations.

Not only were we thrilled by the Palm Sunday procession, especially the bagpipe music of the Boy Scout troops, but we enjoyed the social aspects of the occasion also. Jerusalem had scores of Christian private schools: German, Spanish, Italian, French, Armenian, Syriac, Coptic, Catholic, Greek Orthodox, Lutheran, and Anglican. The Palm Sunday procession was an occasion for boys and girls from these various schools to meet and socialize, which added fun to the event. The conservative community of those days could not prevent us from intermingling at this solemn religious celebration. Interactions between boys and girls in those days were rather restricted. It was unthinkable to have a friend of the opposite sex, as social norms and traditions insisted that such a relationship should be officially sanctioned in the engagement preceding marriage.

For the grownups the procession was a message to the city and the world that Palestinian Christians had a presence in Jerusalem, which they reaffirmed by their participation in it. When the procession was initiated in the thirties of the twentieth century, my father took an active part together with a cohort of his friends in first organizing the event. The idea of the procession caught on, and both the religious and the civil authorities since that time have respected the tradition of a yearly Palm Sunday procession from Bethphage to Saint Anne's Church within the Old City walls.

On Good Friday Christians from Jerusalem and throughout Jordan as well as thousands of pilgrims from all over the world showed expressions of mourning and grief as they walked through the Via Dolorosa or the Way of the Cross. The procession through the fourteen Stations of the Cross was terminated at Calvary and was accompanied throughout by the Franciscan parish church choir and the Arab Catholic Boy Scout troop, which kept order. I will never forget the Lebanese women who walked barefoot along the Via Dolorosa, some of whom insisted on maneuvering some of the difficult cobblestoned streets on their knees. In one of these years, probably in 1964, we were overwhelmed by the fact that no other than the famous Lebanese singer Fairouz arrived to walk through the Via Dolorosa. As a result of her visit she came up with some songs for Jerusalem that have immortalized not only the city and its sanctity but also the pain and suffering of its population following the 1948 war. Upon arrival at the Holy Sepulcher Church I saw women and men with tears in their eyes as they knelt down at the Unction or Anointing Stone, on which the body of Christ was anointed prior to his burial, facing the entrance to the Church. I felt humbled by the strong and unconditional faith of these pilgrims, particularly so because, living close to the Church and having had frequent opportunities to visit it with its various chapels and shrines, I had become less sensitive to the emotion-laden symbolism of these holy sites.

Sabt an-Nour, or the "Saturday of Holy Fire" (literally, "Holy Light"), was the day when the Resurrection of Christ was commemorated in the ceremony of "Holy Fire," organized jointly by the Greek Orthodox and Armenian churches, which took place in the Sepulcher, or edicule, enclosing Christ's tomb. Cypriot, Greek, and Coptic pilgrims slept overnight by the Sepulcher in order to have the honor and privilege to be the first to receive and hold the holy fire. Locals started joining them in the early hours of the morning as the Church, its front square, and its upper roofs became packed with crowds. All carried bundles of candles and glass lanterns. Around noontime, the Greek Orthodox Patriarch and his entourage proceeded from his residence to the Holy Sepulcher, through a staircase leading from the roof to the interior of the Church.

Meanwhile, Christian youths gathered in one of the squares of the Christian Quarter and proceeded through the narrow alleys to the Church. On their way, they alternated in carrying one of their group on their shoulders as he led them in shouting slogans. Among these, one could hear: *Ya 'Adrah Aleiki Al Salam—Min Masihiyeh wa Islam* ("O Virgin [Mary], peace be unto you—From Christians and Muslims alike"), and *Ihnah Al Nasarah wil Shame' Bidanah—Lamar Giries Al Khader Saleinah* ("We Christians and the candles in our hands—For St. Geries [St. George], Al-Khader, we pray"). As the youths entered the Church, they circled the Holy Sepulcher repeating: *Hatha Qaber Sayidnah—Sayidnah Issa Al Massih—Bidammo ishtaranah—Ihna al Yom Faraha* ("This is the tomb of Our Lord—Our Lord is Jesus Christ—Christ has bought us—With his precious blood he has redeemed us—We are today happy"). After circling the Sepulcher three times, they gave their place to members of old Arab Palestinian Orthodox families of Jerusalem who, as a tradition, carried embroidered banners and family emblems fit for the occasion and made their own procession as they awaited the arrival of the Patriarch.

The Patriarch and his entourage found their way from the Catholicon Church, east of the Sepulcher, and proceeded to the small chapel holding the tomb of Christ. The Patriarch took off his thick outer robe and entrusted his throne to an aide as he entered the small chapel in order to perform the ritual of the Holy Fire. The crowd, which heretofore had shown excitement, fell silent in anticipation of the appearance of the Holy Fire. The Patriarch stayed for half an hour or so in prayer and meditation, and then around 2:00 to 2:10 pm, the "Light" appeared and was quickly passed through holes in the walls of the chapel from one bundle of candles to another. Glass lanterns were lit as well, and the more zealous among the faithful passed their hands over the blaze of the candles and then crossed themselves in benediction. The Light spread instantly to the environs of the Church, and the whole place, inside and out, was ablaze. Joyful ululations were heard, bells rang out, and the Holy Fire was already on its way to other places across the country and on to Amman, Athens, Nicosia, Beirut, and even more distant locations.

The bands of the Greek Orthodox and other Boy Scout troops, including Muslims, who waited for the Light to appear on the roof of the Church, started playing as the troops proceeded all together through the narrow alleys of the Christian Quarter. They were met by the group of youngsters now carrying lit candles and lanterns, as they again shouted their slogans, which intermingled with the band music. The atmosphere was always one of public joy and celebration, and local Christians greeted each other with the traditional Easter greeting: *Al Masih qam* ("Christ is risen") and its response: *Haqqan qam* ("He is indeed risen"). I was never keen on being in the middle of crowds, but as a boy I did attend once or twice the ceremony of the Holy Fire inside the Church. The feeling of people pressing on one another and the lit candles passing between hands with some disregard for physical safety made me quite nervous.

The "Khader and Kurd Bakeries" in the Christian Quarter, both owned by Muslim Palestinians, celebrated Easter in their own way as they produced rectangular and round loaves of bread with a colored Easter egg in the middle of each loaf of bread. This was especially touching to us local Christians who did regular business with these bakeries throughout the year. This gesture by the two Muslim bakeries reflected the bonds across the religious communities with Muslims and Christians sharing in each other's festivities, holidays, and happy and sad occasions. Christians reciprocated by helping to wash the Aqsa Mosque and visiting with Muslim dignitaries whenever there were religious feasts or other events that needed a show of solidarity. In Ramadan some Christian families invited their Muslim friends to break the fast with them. We had no idea then that religion could be a dividing boundary as we lived together and opened up to each other's traditions, which encouraged mutual respect for the values and moral imperatives in our respective religions.

The Abyssinians or the Orthodox Ethiopians had their own way of celebrating Easter. Since we lived near their community, it had become a sort of tradition for the boys and girls in our family to go and celebrate on Easter Eve with them. At our school we had some Ethiopian students whose families had settled down in Jerusalem, and they had become Arabized, speaking Arabic and integrating with the larger Jerusalem society. Mother and a woman of Ethiopian origin, living not far away, visited with each other and exchanged remarks on the difficulties, the challenges, and the better things of life. I would follow their exchanges, as usually Mother made me accompany her on such visits. This was an additional reason for me to take part in the prayers and celebrations of the Abyssinian Ethiopian community.

The Abyssinian priests and some scores of Ethiopian pilgrims coming especially for the occasion would gather on the roof of Saint Helena's Chapel, one of the chapels of the Holy Sepulcher, where Ethiopian monks lived. A procession with the purpose of searching for the body of Christ was always set to start at eight o'clock in the evening, but it was usually delayed for half an hour or so in order to allow for the intricate preparations. The priests wore colorful robes, and a couple of them had drums with one or two playing a sistrum, a small musical instrument that originated in ancient Egypt and that belongs to the percussion family. The sistrums were constantly being shaken to keep us alert and to ward off the evil spirits during the search for the body of Christ. The procession moved four times past the cupola of the church as drums were banged and as beautifully colored umbrellas were spun over the priest carrying the Gospel. Chanting in the sacred language of Ethiopia (Geʻez) had a different rhythm than chanting in Arabic, to which we were accustomed, and it accompanied the procession from beginning to end. The procession concluded with not finding the body, hence affirming that Christ had indeed risen. In more modern times, it has become rather difficult to gain access to the procession because hundreds of Ethiopians who have come to Israel to work and acquired residency permits participate in the traditional and colorful procession. The roof of Saint Helena Chapel becomes so overcrowded that police are obliged to turn away many of those who would like to participate.

Beloved Churches

For me as a young boy, the Church of the Holy Sepulcher was not only my pleasant backyard where I often went, but it also left some not-so-pleasant memories. I remember the fire that raged for a whole day in November 1949 and that damaged the roof of the great dome of the Church. As my older siblings and I drifted towards the Church from our nearby home, we saw many Jordanian soldiers who were helping out in extinguishing the fire. King Abdullah of Jordan, a scion of the Hashemite Dynasty, which is originally from Hejaz, now in Saudi Arabia, became the first Emir (Prince) of the Dynasty in Jordan. He was the founder of modern Jordan. Emir Abdullah took a personal interest in seeing that the fire was brought under control and later on worked with the different church authorities to ensure that the roof was expediently and safely restored. Some later narratives spoke of the King himself arriving at the Church to help out with extinguishing the fire.

Historically, the Church of the Holy Sepulcher had suffered from various kinds of damage and calamities, whether from earthquakes, military incursions, or fires. The fact that three different denominations or church communities—Greek Orthodox, Franciscans, and Armenians—were in charge of the place made it difficult at times to agree on the rehabilitation of the Church or the restoration of important sites within it. Recently the present King Abdullah of Jordan, the great-grandson of the founder of Jordan, announced that he would contribute from his personal funds to the restoration of the small chapel in the Holy Sepulcher that holds Christ's tomb. Nowadays, fortunately, there is more awareness of the need to maintain the buildings of the Church, and hence agreement among the different owner churches is much easier to gain when renovations and maintenance schemes are called for.

It is worth mentioning that two Muslim families hold the keys of the Holy Sepulcher, and they are in charge together to ensure the opening and closing of the Church at set times. I have been aware of this fact since my boyhood since I witnessed many times the closing of the Church in the evenings and during the special vigils and ceremonies of Holy Week. Of late, I have become acquainted with the person from the Nusseibeh family who is in charge of opening and closing the gate of the Church—a fine gentleman who carries out his duties conscientiously and who is sensitive to the holiness of the place and the responsibilities he bears. Another family, named Judeh, actually has the keys, and a couple of members of this family have to be present when opening and closing are done by my friend from the Nusseibeh family. If this sounds complicated, it is because life in Jerusalem and in the Holy Land has never been simple. As one lives and grows in the city, one becomes accustomed to things that newcomers, visitors, and pilgrims would find incomprehensible.

Jerusalem abounds with churches. Some place the number of churches in the city at seventy; others are less generous, as they put the number closer to fifty. In either case the twelve thousand Christians who lived in the city had a wide choice from which to select the service of the church that they would like to attend. The church that I felt myself most attached to was the "Pater Noster" or "Our Father" on the Mount of Olives. It is a Carmelite convent for nuns that was established sometime in the nineteenth century by a French princess. I felt awed by the sight of the "Our Father" prayer in different languages and dialects, each having its own rectangular plaque with ceramic tiles on which the prayer was handwritten in beautiful and precise calligraphy. The "Our Father" spoke to me in Arabic, Aramaic (the language spoken by Christ), Hebrew, Armenian, English, French, Native American languages, and the various dialects of Africa, Latin America, Australia, New Zealand, and Europe, among scores of other dialects from all over the world. Perhaps it was because I had always found the *Abana* ("Our Father") prayer to be an affirmation of my own belief that I grew naturally attached to the church of the Pater Noster. The simplicity of the church and its location on this biblical site, the Mount of Olives, always made me think of the early Christians and how they practiced their new faith.

Assassination and its Aftermath

One of the events in the early fifties that I have never forgotten was the Friday, July 20, 1951, assassination of King Abdullah of Jordan by Mustafa Shukri Ashshu, a twenty-one-year-old tailor from Jerusalem, as the King entered the Aqsa Mosque to pray the noon prayers. Ashshu was shot dead by the King's guards after his successful attempt on the King's life. I still remember sitting around the table for lunch as Mother was serving us scrambled eggs and hummus, the traditional Palestinian mashed chickpea dish, and falafel, deep-fried ground chickpeas, when shots were heard from the direction of Al Aqsa Mosque, which was not far from our house down the road. All of a sudden the city closed down completely, Jordanian soldiers appeared on the streets, and a curfew was declared. It was hours later that the death of King Abdullah, founder of the Hashemite Kingdom of Jordan, was officially announced.

The conspirators were all Palestinians; they included a Roman Catholic priest, the late Father Ibrahim Ayyad from Beit Sahour (of "Shepherds' Field" fame). They used to meet in the coffee shop by our house, the same coffee shop that saw Bedouins and sheep farmers negotiate sales over a cup of bitter Arabic coffee. Some of the conspirators worked out the details of the assassination of the King in that same small coffee shop, which extended its seating area to the narrow street leading to our home. We would pass by them and wonder what these people were talking and arguing about. All the conspirators were arrested and sentenced to different prison sentences, except Father Ayyad, who was deported because of his religious standing. The photos of all the conspirators appeared following the assassination of the King on the front page of the local paper with their names and places of residence printed underneath each of the photos. The reason for the King's assassination, according to the conspirators and their supporters, was his position on the partition of Palestine between a Jewish home and an Arab state. There was a general feeling among Palestinians that the King had given away too many of the political demands of the Arabs of Palestine. While he was known as an astute and discreet politician and diplomat, the overall political and military conditions of the times did not allow him to do much toward helping Palestinians to get a much better deal in the division of Palestine between Arabs and Jews in 1948. King Abdullah was known for his practicality, which he had passed on to his grandson, King Hussein of Jordan, who as a young boy was with his grandfather in the Mosque and escaped a stray bullet when it ricocheted from a medal on his chest.

During the days of curfew, which lasted for a couple of weeks following the assassination of the King, we used to while away our time by congregating around a wooden box with a hole in its lower surface, and taking turns in showing through the hole the photos with which my maternal uncle David had been entrusted by George, his British soldier friend of British Mandate times. These were fascinating black-and-white photos, hundreds of them, which reflected the events and developments during the period of the British Mandate, including the battles of World War II. Each of us kids improvised narratives and stories as the photos were shown, one following another. I do not know what eventually happened to these photos, which are a treasure of historical documentation. Perhaps they lie hidden among the corners and closets of the Old City home where we moved after the 1948 war and where my sister Hilda and brothers currently reside. We also used to while away time by shows ingeniously created with a white cloth screen and a source of light behind it with characters, hand movements, and other tricks shown on the improvised screen. The narrations that came with the images on the screen made the kids, a score of us, laugh and follow the stories very attentively. Sometimes my father and other adult figures in the Dar would join us and add their sense of humor and their own tricks to the admiration and awe of all of the children.

Cousins

During those days of curfew, or a short time later, our cousins the Abeds and their mother Frida from Ramallah, a town to the north of Jerusalem, came to stay with us as they were preparing to leave for the U.S. to join my maternal uncle Jack, who had left before them. While they were with us in Jerusalem, we had much fun together as we gathered every evening to play games or to go around the neighborhood visiting the Church of the Holy Sepulcher and buying some sweets and other tasty treats from the shops by the Church. When they left, we were saddened by their departure because most likely we would not have a chance to see them again.

Aunt Frida was an unforgettable character. She hailed from a prominent Ramallah family that had chosen to migrate to the U.S. in the thirties. All her brothers and their families had moved to New York City, to Brooklyn specifically, where they became very successful businessmen specializing in textile products. Their Ramallah Trading Company sat for many years not far away from the Empire State Building, and their business extended all over the United States, especially its eastern and southern states. The Ramallah home where they lived still stands today but is occupied by new owners. There we accumulated many happy memories as we visited on Sundays. We started our visit with attending Mass at the Holy Family Catholic Church not far away from Aunt Frida's home, and then when we walked back through the main street of Ramallah, we had ample time to greet friends, visit bookstores, or simply wander around.

On summer days in downtown Ramallah, we could not resist the Rukab Ice Cream, advertised as truly and authentically American ice cream although its origin in the 1940s when the parlor opened was from a Greek recipe that the mother of the owner had handed down to her son. Some of the members of the Rukab family, like Aunt Frida's family, chose to migrate to the U.S. A member of the Rukab family had the ingenuity to learn the secret of making ice cream in the American way. He decided to return home to Ramallah in the early fifties, where he opened an ice cream parlor that still stands on the main street of the town. Rukab Ice Cream has been appreciatively savored also by American students and tourists who have passed by Ramallah then and now.

The meals served by Aunt Frida were typically Palestinian. She offered *labaneh* ("cream cheese"), *zeit wa za'ater* ("olive oil and thyme"), hummus, pickled olives, and small cucumbers with freshly picked tomatoes and home-baked bread with watermelons as dessert. She would also prepare the dried fruits, raisins and figs, which she kept in a special wooden shed within the house, as a suitable dessert. During summer time, when these fruits were abundant, the Ramallah families dried them and stored them in the shed within the home, for use during the winter months. She was a very prudent woman, but her fame among my cousins, as I discovered later on when I visited them in their Long Island home, was due to her paintings, which hung in their home. Since her childhood she had been inclined toward painting in her native town of Ramallah.

The town of Ramallah was a Palestinian Christian town whose original inhabitants professed the faith of their forefathers. A visit to Ramallah, then as now, would feature the conspicuous variety of its churches. There were the Roman Catholic, the Greek Orthodox, the Anglican, and the Lutheran churches among others. All of these churches were administered by local Arab Palestinian Christian clergy. Once in a while there were expatriate Western clergy who helped out, and those who had stayed in the country for a long time had learned Arabic and become closely identified with their churches and congregants. Ramallah Christians, like other Palestinian Christians, were not converts or descendants of converts; in fact, they prided themselves on having roots that extended back to the original Christians of the Land. It sounds inappropriate when a Westerner asks a Palestinian Christian or another sort of Arab Christian when he or she was converted to Christianity, punctuating this question with the exclamation "Praise the Lord!" Most likely the Palestinian and Arab Christian answer would be, "We have been praising the Lord for centuries, from the time before Christianity spread all over the Western world!"

Ramallah then was more like a provincial village, its people knowing each other by first name. The family played an important part in the life of the town, and a number of families, who developed businesses and started enterprises, came to have prominence. I remember that when we sat in the early afternoon in the small courtyard in front of Aunt Frida's home, we had a view of fields of fruit trees and other greeneries as far as the eye could see. Her stone house was similar in its architecture to other Palestinian homes, which were built with thick walls of stones that retained the warmth in winter and the coolness in summer. The home was very simple but functional. Because Aunt Frida's home was located centrally, we could hear the churches' bells as well as the muezzin's call for prayers that came from El Bireh, the twin town of Ramallah, whose inhabitants were mostly Muslims.

The serenity, quiet, and calm of Ramallah in those days contrast sharply with Ramallah at present. Unfortunately many of the original families have migrated to the U.S., and those left today have become a minority as Ramallah takes on more and more the countenance of a diverse and somewhat chaotic city. Nevertheless, one cannot cling to the past as the necessities of life force us to deal with the consequences of changes taking place all around us.

Even though Aunt Frida's family belonged to the Greek Orthodox Church, a nephew of hers, Monsignor George Khader, had become a Roman Catholic priest at the youthful age of twenty-two. He visited our home in the Old City sometime in the late fifties or early sixties with the brother of Aunt Frida, Issa, who wanted to say hello to my Mom and to assure her that her brother Jack, who was employed at the Ramallah Trading Company in New York City, and his family were doing all right. In spite of their different church affiliations, Issa, a very successful businessman, decided to donate to the Holy Family (Catholic) Church in Ramallah all of the seating stalls now found in the church. Every time I visit this beautiful parish church, I am reminded of his generosity.

Father George Khader, Aunt Frida's nephew, was expected to have a promising future in the Church as some thought that he would eventually become a bishop and possibly the Patriarch of the Latin Church in the Holy Land. This did not transpire because Monsignor George succumbed to a major heart attack at the age of forty-nine, two years after the June 1967 war, which saw him helping with the recovery and burial of the bodies of those killed and attending to the injured and their families. The Latin Patriarchate in Jerusalem sits right beside the walls of the Old City by the Jaffa Gate. It was there that some of the heavy fighting took place in the June war of 1967, and Father George was witness to the death, injury, and destruction that had occurred. Out of human compassion and a priestly vocation he set out to help in whatever way he could.

School Days

As we settled down in the Dar, it was time to enroll us children at school. I recall one September morning in 1951 when my father accompanied me, at the age of six, to the Frères School at the New Gate. We walked through the Christian Quarter up the hill to the school. The uneven, rough, cobblestoned streets of the Old City of Jerusalem were difficult to maneuver, but I held on to Father's hand, and in this way we finally arrived at the Frères. I was overwhelmed by the structure of the school building, at the top of which on a special stone pedestal sat a heavy statue of Saint Jean Baptiste de la Salle, the French founder of the Frères, or the Brothers of the Christian Schools, and the patron saint of teachers in the Catholic Church. Ever since that first day I worried continually about the possibility that the statue would one day cause a disaster if an earthquake struck or for any other reason it moved from its place. It was customary for us at school to line up by class every morning and after breaks in order to go to our classrooms. We were not only blessed by the statue, but it seemed to me that we were at risk also from its mere presence since I always had a terrible feeling that the statue was liable to fall down and crash on someone's head.

My first day at school was traumatic rather than exciting. More than thirty students were packed into the classroom, and some of our teachers had no clue about pedagogic methods to deal with the trauma of a new school environment to small creatures. What added to the trauma was the stick that some of our teachers carried as a sign of authority and which they used to make slapping sounds. None of the individual attention needed was given, as the classroom was overcrowded and the teachers were clearly overwhelmed by the numbers of students as well as by their own lack of appropriate educational training.

Although the Frères School was supposed to be "elitist," I soon discovered that there were two kinds of students: those who could afford the tuition fees and hence were more privileged, and those like me, children of refugees whose parents could not afford the fees and hence were schooled gratis or received some kind of financial support. But to be fair to the Brothers and teachers, we never felt a difference in treatment except when the paying students would have a meal because most of them were boarding students, some of whom had come from Amman and other parts of the country across the River Jordan. We were all offered a cup of terrible-tasting milk on our mid-morning break, which we had to drink regardless of our taste buds. The cup of milk was offered *gratis* by UNRWA because it was assumed that we did not have access at home to the milk we needed.

Father's salary came to 9.75 Jordanian dinars a month, roughly forty U.S. dollars, which in those days was not enough to break even for a family of ten. Joseph, my cousin, found a job with UNRWA, the United Nations Relief and Works Agency, which was set up by the General Assembly of the UN in December of 1949 to carry out direct relief and works programs for the more than 700,000 Palestinian refugees who had had to flee their villages and towns when the 1948 war erupted. Some of these refugees were forcibly evicted or put in such a precarious situation that they decided to flee for their personal safety and that of their children. Many of the refugees ended up being housed in impromptu communities of tents, and they needed attention and provisions. The refugees were spread out across the region from Lebanon to Syria to the East and West Banks of the Jordan and in the Gaza Strip. Caring for the refugees meant that the UN needed to set up an organization that would provide them with the basic health, education, food, and employment services.

Among the efforts to assist and support the newly arrived refugees was that of three Anglican canons at the St. George Anglican Bishopric in Jerusalem. Witnessing the conditions under which the refugees were living, particularly in the harsh winters of 1949 and 1950, the three canons decided to call on prominent figures among the indigenous Christian communities to come together in order to offer what they could to alleviate the misery of the refugees and their quite difficult circumstances. As a result of the efforts of the three canons, ecumenical committees were established in Jordan, Lebanon, the Gaza Strip, and Nazareth in Israel to address the concerns and needs of the refugees and displaced. These committees became known together as the Department of Service to Palestinian Refugees, and when the Middle East Council of Churches was established in 1974, the Department became part of it. The Department continues its work today, and in 1997 I became its executive secretary or director, a commitment to which I remain faithful.

Because my cousin Joseph knew English very well, he was recruited by UNRWA to supervise the social services in Jerusalem and the West Bank. The job paid him well, but by then he was independent except for sharing meals with us while living with my Aunt Leonie in a room next door. Joseph's sad story was that he was born in Lima, Peru, where his parents had migrated sometime in the 1920s. When he was a baby of a few months, his mom, Hannah or Anne, fell down from the roof of their home and sustained injuries that kept her in critical condition for two weeks, after which she succumbed to her wounds. Joseph's father, aware that he could not care for the baby, made the trip back to Jerusalem and entrusted Joseph to the care of Aunt Leonie. Until he was fifteen years of age, Joseph thought that she was his natural mother. When news arrived from Lima that his father had passed away, Aunt Leonie had to tell him the story of his being in her custody, which led him to mourning and grief.

The decision of Joseph's parents to migrate to "Amerika," as all of North, Central, and South America were known to the locals in Palestine, was not unique. Hundreds of families from the Bethlehem area and some from Jerusalem, including at least three of our own family, had migrated to Chile early in the twentieth century, some as early as 1900 or around that date. The push of the political situation at the end of the Ottoman Empire, the conscription of eldest sons to the Ottoman army between 1914 and 1918, the locust invasion in 1915 that devoured "the green and the dry" (*Al Akhdar Wal Yabis*), and the overall bad economic situation, including a famine that had hit the country, were all factors that encouraged many Palestinians to seek refuge in the Americas.

Joseph was fortunate to have had Aunt Leonie by his side; she took care of nurturing and accompanying him throughout his childhood, youth, and adult life. Our family relationship with Joseph would extend a lifetime as he eventually wedded Bernadette, my younger sister, in 1964. Even though Joseph and Bernadette were first cousins, this did not prevent the exchange of marital vows. In our Palestinian culture, among both Muslims and Christians alike, it was acceptable for first cousins to marry each other. In fact, in traditional Palestinian and Arab society there is a folkloric saying: *Ibn Al 'Am Binazzel Bint Ammo 'An al Faras* ("Male paternal cousin can force his female cousin to come down from the bridal mare"). It was a custom in many villages and towns that when a wedding took place, the bride would ride on a mare or stallion with her family and tribal kin accompanying her to the home of her prospective bridegroom. The gist of the saying is that the paternal cousin takes precedence over strangers in wedding his first cousin. First-cousin marriage was not encouraged, but if it happened, it was not necessarily frowned upon. It needed a special dispensation from the parish priest, who blessed it in a religious ceremony similar to other marriages.

Thanks to the support given by UNRWA to cover the tuition fees of refugee children, the financial burden on my parents' budget was lessened, and despite the crowded classrooms and poorly trained teachers, school was not altogether an unpleasant experience. Most students were not fond of the religious obligation of going to Mass every morning, but this experience made me discover the religiosity within me. I became known as a very religious student, and some even regarded me as a candidate for priesthood because of that. I should not underplay this candidacy: during a parish trip to the Latroun Monastery on the then-borderline between Jordan and Israel, which is now a highway between Jerusalem and Tel Aviv, I was struck by awe and admiration for the priests there who had dedicated themselves to silence, prayer, and work. My mother, who had accompanied us to the monastery, noticed that I was impressed by the Latroun priests, and she asked me if I would like to become a priest like them. I was not decided because, as strong as the religious inclination within me was, so was the attraction to the opposite sex. The two could not go together—or could they?

School elicited nightmares in the first few weeks. I dreamed that I would go to school in my pajamas or barefoot; the feeling of shame was too strong to ignore in the school environment of the early fifties. This may have been related to the culture, which some characterized as a shame culture; the Arabic word 'Eib translates to "shame." Without discussing the details of the effects of a shame culture on an individual, it can be characterized as a culture that enforces conformism, as also did the French educational pedagogy that was based on memorizing and that was promoted at our school. If you were not like the rest of us, then certainly something must be wrong with you. Thus one became self-conscious not simply about how to dress, what to say, and how to behave, but also about what one thought. In one way this culture offered protection within a collectively imposed subscription to particular values and expectations, but it also restricted opening up in a free and spontaneous manner to new experiences. It may also have encouraged conservatism, as novel ways of doing things, dressing, or expressing oneself were frowned upon and elicited ostracism by peers and by the society at large.

I admired the self-confidence of S., a young man with same-sex orientation, a well-known hair stylist who did not hide his sexual preference from the public. Whenever he entered the movie theater on Sunday afternoons, the hall would become abuzz with name-calling, but S. would not have any second thoughts about enjoying the movie unperturbed. Most likely he had overcome the effects of the shame culture.

The reliance on memorizing at school, part of the French pedagogical method, made us laugh at it, and we were apt to repeat the well-known Arabic idiom: Al Tikrar U'alem Al Himar ("Repetition teaches even the donkey"). In spite of this apparently flawed teaching methodology, our school was known for its excellence in teaching languages, English and French in addition to Arabic, the mother tongue. Our teachers were not graduates of teachers' colleges or universities, as most of them finished high school and then advanced in their fields through personal application. As we progressed through the school years, we developed respect for our teachers, and they became our role models. Whenever we were assigned homework, we spent hours after class either writing an essay on topics such as "Not all that glitters is gold" or memorizing the many stanzas of a long poem. We also took care in writing our homework because calligraphy was part of our writing-skills training; the A's, B's, and C's should conform to specific standards and, for example, should not extend above or below the double lines that divided the page.

What was amazing, though, was the fact that each class was a unique socializing environment that was almost separate from both the class above and the one below. My brother Maurice was two grades below mine, and his friends and environment were entirely different from mine. Even the socializing after school was different, with distinctive tastes and predispositions in politics and social life. Abel was in an upper class, a world completely different from mine, while Tony, who was in a much lower class, also had experiences and a cohort of companions that were completely set apart from my own. Age was the determining factor in one's experiences at school.

Many of our teachers were refugees themselves and hence had an understanding of the conditions of life under which all of us lived. They were kind for the most part but also demanding and uncompromising when it came to homework and other school obligations. Many of our teachers did not impress us as being particularly religious; in fact, we sensed that they had many doubts themselves about religion and its role in human affairs. I remember in particular a Greek Orthodox teacher, a Palestinian Christian native of Jerusalem, a pharmacist who was teaching us Chemistry. As I was known as a very religious person, he always criticized me and the hypocrisy of posing as religious and then not doing the things required of a conscientious person. I never knew what these required things were precisely, but one thing I knew: that if doing well in Chemistry was one of them, I was absolutely a failure because I could not solve the simplest equation. Eventually I had a dispensation from attending the Chemistry class, which was indeed a relief.

We tended to imitate our teachers as role models or to get involved in pursuits, such as sports or Arabic poetry or English literature, which avowedly were to the liking of particular teachers. The more we excelled in any one of these, the closer we were to our role model. So looking up to our teachers became a motivating educational tool, and it gave us self-confidence to know that we could excel in a topic or activity.

I was not known as being good in English; my performance was passable, but I could not match the other students who read English books profusely and hence excelled in both written and spoken English. When we

sat for the General Certificate Exam (GCE) of the University of London,
which private schools in Palestine and Jordan continue to offer, my English
teacher, Mr. Sarkis (Sarkis being a common Armenian name), God bless
his soul, anticipated that I would not make it. The surprise was that I got a
good grade on my English exam while other students who were considered
better than I was did not pass. I thought that the ideas I wrote down on my
GCE English essay must have done the trick, as probably they impressed
the English examiner who was grading our papers. The GCE was important
because a passing grade on it allowed us to go on to university studies.

At school I became fond of reading, especially books of Arabic literature. On the walls of the school there were shelves full of books, many
of them rare and almost all in Arabic with some in English and French.
From an early age I started reading Arabic novels, biographies, historical
narratives, and works of other literary genres that opened up my mind and
introduced me to worlds previously unfamiliar to me. One of the Brothers,
noticing my love for books, entrusted me with the task of arranging the
books properly and with the process of lending them out to other students.
This was one of the most gratifying jobs I have had in my entire life. In one
way, reading books voraciously was a means of escape, in a sense creating a
world that cannot be touched by others. What this hobby of reading in Arabic did for me was to enable me to find an affinity with Arabic literature and
to discover that the Arab and Muslim civilization was a highly admirable
one. It was through these readings that I came to accept others who were
different from me in religion and in other ways.

One feature of school life that caused me to ponder existentialist matters and the after-life was the everyday sight of the reproductions of paintings depicting Dante's *Inferno* that lined the walls of our school; the original
paintings probably have a considerable monetary value. These were terrifying paintings, and we were wont to joke about them as we passed them.
But our joking was really a reflection of our nervousness about the fate that
would await us if we were to end our lives down in hell. The paintings also
made my peers and me question whether God would really mete out such
harsh and terrible punishments on poor, unfortunate, sinful souls. Even if
the scenes of purgatory held more reassurance for those of us who went
to confession every Saturday afternoon and partook of Holy Communion
every Sunday morning, we all felt relieved when the school administration
decided to get rid of these reproductions altogether. Apparently someone
convinced the Brothers that God is also a God of mercy and compassion!

School and friendships consumed most of our growing-up years.
While I was not the most brilliant and high-achieving of students, I compensated by making friendships rather easily and reaching out to those with

promise. When grade and certificate distribution days arrived, all the school classes were assembled in the Grande Salle ("Large Hall"). I was never first or second in academic performance. Perhaps there were only a couple of years in which I made it to the first five of my class, not because of my application or innate intelligence but simply because the other students were not up to the challenge or simply because I was liked by my teachers. I still remember that on one or two rare occasions in the earlier classes or grades, I was awarded an honor medal for being the second in my class. The medal was similar to the Légion d'Honneur, a French medal, and wearing it for a few days as I walked back and forth to school through the Christian Quarter made me feel special and honored. During my years in the more advanced classes, however, when Brother Principal Felix handed out the certificates, he usually felt moved to scold me in front of the whole school and to remind me that my brother Abel was earning all the honors for his excellence and achievements in the various subjects while I was not showing similar inclinations.

In a way, my mediocre performance at school served as a protection against others who might place expectations on me. It was the high expectations placed on Abel that imposed various kinds of pressure on him; for example, he was invited by close and distant neighbors and acquaintances to go to their homes in order to help out with the tutoring of their children in French, English, Mathematics, or any of the other subjects in which he excelled. We would be ready to go to sleep at around eight o'clock in the evening when a knock on the door would be heard and some neighbor would be asking Abel for his input on an essay or a sentence in French or English. Abel was made to jump up to higher classes a couple of times because his performance was always ahead of the class in which he was found.

Family Matters

As I progressed through the school years, I became more aware of the deep impact that the 1948 war and the refugee experience had made on my parents and their generation. While sipping their early morning coffee, Father and Mother used to exchange views on what had happened to our family during the 1948 war. As I lay half-awake, I heard them talk about the Qatamon home and how unfair and unjust it was that we were all dispossessed of that small home that had been built and maintained with hard work and determination. My family was never a wealthy one, as Father's municipal work earned him just enough of a salary to allow us to lead an acceptably dignified life.

Since his youth Father had been deeply religious. During World War I, as Aunt Leonie told me, Father was conscripted into the Ottoman army and almost died. He recovered through the intercession of Reverend Father Issa Bandak of Bethlehem, a maternal cousin of my father, who knew Jamal Pasha, the Ottoman governor, personally and used to host him in the Hortus Conclusus, or Enclosed Garden Monastery, in Artas village, south of Bethlehem. As a result of Reverend Father Bandak's intercession, Father was released from his military obligation. By one account he was saved from a death sentence imposed because he took Ottoman army bread and distributed it to starving families in Jerusalem. Ever since his release, according to Aunt Leonie, Father had been attending daily Mass. Father was lucky to have been released since many elder sons, particularly of Christian families, had immigrated to distant lands, most often to Chile, El Salvador, and other Central and South American countries in order to avoid military conscription into the Ottoman army.

Reverend Father Bandak was the chaplain of the Hortus Conclusus and oversaw the beautiful sanctuary with Latin American nuns managing the place for sixty or so years. In 1901 a Uruguayan Monsignor had decided to build the sanctuary in honor of the Virgin Mary, for which donations came in particularly from several Latin American countries. In the sixties we used to go as a family to have picnics in the beautiful gardens surrounding the convent. There is a special feast day for the Virgin Mary on which whole parishes from Jerusalem and Bethlehem and from across the country congregated at the Hortus Conclusus to attend Mass and then to break bread together in the gardens. Artas village lies in a valley full of fruit trees and vegetables of all kinds, and it was a rewarding day for all of us to get away from Jerusalem and to be together in such a beautiful place.

Father was not a political figure; in fact, he was as distant from politics as anyone can be who does not trust either politics or politicians. Mother was more interested in politics; she was a quarter of a century younger than Father, and she expressed her dismay about Western policies that left the Palestinians unprotected and that were responsible in a way for the tragedy of the Palestinian refugees and the disintegration of Palestinian society to make room for the newly emerging Israeli society. But in spite of their sadness and desperation over what had happened to them and to other Palestinians, neither Father nor Mother ever expressed antagonistic feelings towards the Jews as a people; rather, they were set to start afresh with the little that was left to them and were determined to give us a good education that would stay with us throughout our lives. In retrospect, my parents sensed that their personal tragedy and that of the Palestinian people were symbiotically linked with the tragedy of the Jewish people. While they never spoke about what befell the Jews during World War II, I always sensed that in their discussions and exchanges they considered not only themselves and the rest of the Palestinians as victims but also the Jews as well. We were all caught up in the vicious grip of history that pitted one victim against another. Victimhood, nevertheless, was not to be accepted at our home as we struggled to make ends meet and to live as decently and in as dignified a manner as conditions then allowed.

The painful events of 1948 had taken their toll on my father. In the mid-fifties he started to suffer bouts of depression. Mother consulted with some doctors specializing in mental illness at the Bethlehem Hospital. At that time, the primitive and painful treatment for depression and other forms of mental illness was to give the patient electric shocks supposedly capable of altering elements in the brain and hence contributing to the patient's recovery. I still recall the worry and, I may say, the fear that Father expressed on the mornings of his weekly or bi-weekly sessions of electric shock. It must have been a traumatic experience to endure these ordeals, and when he and Mother arrived back in the evening from the tiresome, day-long trip to Bethlehem, he felt devastated. With the help of Mother and the support of Aunt Leonie and Uncle Rock (Father's brother who was living in Amman as many of the Palestinian refugees did), Father eventually recovered. As his work in the Municipality of Jerusalem progressed, we had to turn to the other preoccupations of living, other than how to overcome Dad's depression.

Years later, when I was teaching at Bethlehem University, I met the "psychiatrist" who was in charge of the electric shock therapy. He was adamant in his belief that the shock therapy was effective and that it usually brought about changes in the patient's cognition and behavior. He argued that those with obsessive-compulsive disorders like washing hands or repeating gestures benefited the most. I never examined this "psychiatrist's" opinion, nor did I consult with other professionals since in pre-1967 Jordan we did not have more than a couple of certified "psychiatrists," to whom patients were referred mostly for prescriptions—not for the kind of intensive one-hour sessions during which the more affluent in modern societies would engage in ritual weekly encounters for narrating their woes and frustrations.

Mental health was and remains a problem that traditional society has usually put aside as the will of God, believing that *Heik Allah Biddo* ("this is what God wants") and that humans cannot do much to alter the divine will. The sick person in traditional society remained at home and in the community, undergoing a convalescence that could have been in itself a way to adapt her or him to the surrounding environment. Counseling and other therapeutic measures to deal with mentally traumatized and affected people emerged in Palestine only in the seventies and eighties as a result primarily of the effects of a continuing Israeli occupation. As counseling became more accepted in the society, it became a method to deal with the ordinary stresses and strains. Palestinian universities, Bethlehem and Birzeit among others, led in offering counseling services to their students and thus contributed to the growing acceptance of therapeutic interventions apart from prescriptive drugs. Nowadays Palestinian universities offer degrees in social work, counseling, and mental health.

The therapy-through-talking approach had always been practiced in Palestinian society as friends, cousins, and siblings confided in each other about their problems, challenges, and dilemmas. I remember that I always sought advice on a weekly basis from a priest friend of mine. He was the same priest who later on in my life would officiate at our engagement, Mary's and mine. In these weekly sessions we spoke about both personal and social concerns, and my priest friend always encouraged me to seek answers in the example of Jesus Christ and in the reading of the Holy Bible. He was also well rooted in his native Palestinian Christian village of Taybeh, near Ramallah, and always proud of his heritage as a Palestinian and as a Christian. Later on I learned that there was also religiously oriented counseling, but I never used it except for my meetings with my priest friend. Today in Palestinian society psycho-social services are extended to thousands of people, particularly to those, like the Gazans, who are periodically traumatized by the effects of wars and continuing military confrontations. As the society moves from tradition to modernity, more and more people are faced with stress that requires counseling and psychological help. But resistance to such methods continues even among some of the more educated groups, as going to counseling is considered being "insane" and hence some of those who are in urgent need of counseling and psychological help refrain from seeking this help because they fear the stigma.

Once he had recovered from his depression, Father went back to his old ways. One of Dad's daily habits was his insistence on saying the Rosary. He would assemble all the kids of the Dar at around five or six o'clock in the evening and start reciting the Rosary. As kids we did not like the restriction that this imposed on our freedom of movement and on our disposition to while away time just playing and having fun. As we smiled and giggled during the obligatory evening prayers, Father remained serious in his pursuit of the daily devotion, which forced us in the end to comply with his desire and show respect toward the whole exercise.

Father was accustomed at the end of the Rosary recital to highlight two special requests from the Virgin Mary: the end of Communism in what was then the Soviet Union and the conversion of Jews and all non-believers to the true faith, namely, Christianity. Years later, Communism as we had known it in the fifties and sixties would cease to exist. Was Dad's invocation a small contributing factor to the change? And how would Dad, if he were alive today, rate Vladimir Putin in comparison with the Communist leaders of the Soviet Bloc? As to the conversion of Jews and other non-believers, I never understood why, with the amalgam of Christianity, including thirteen officially recognized churches in the Holy Land and smaller sects and cults, anyone would want to persuade Jews and other "non-believers" to affiliate themselves with Christianity. A Sunday visit to the Church of the Holy Sepulcher, filled with all kinds of noises, different sounds, and hymns at the prayer services of the six different Christian communities, would discourage anyone from wishing on others the difficult choice of joining one of those communities. Although, as a practicing Palestinian Catholic, I can understand the ministry of witnessing to others, I find myself enchanted with a world in which a multiplicity of faiths, cultures, and traditions coexist and hopefully endure in mutual acknowledgment and acceptance.

One Rosary recital, nevertheless, stood out, and I have recalled it ever since. One evening as we were reciting the Rosary, someone came in and told us that they had just heard on the transistor radio that John F. Kennedy, President of the United States, had been shot. Father immediately asked all of us to bow our heads and to say a special prayer for the President of the United States. Years later, when Robert Kennedy was shot by Sirhan Sirhan during the presidential race, the feelings of shock and disbelief overwhelmed us as we said prayers in memory of yet another Kennedy. What made our emotions even sharper than average was the fact that Sirhan Sirhan's family was living not far away from our own home, and Father, because of his work in the Municipality, probably also knew his father. But as a family we felt particularly sad that another promising candidate for the presidency of the strongest nation on earth was cut down before being able to fulfill his promise as a leader.

The Movies

Dad was not the most open-minded of fellows even though he had a good heart. One of the ills that he fought as we were growing up was the cinema. I discovered that Jerusalem had a movie theater in the mid-fifties. One day when I was hanging out with Fredo, my maternal cousin, he suggested that we go to see his father, who was an electrician of renown. (Later on he was selected for the team that set up the first Jordanian broadcasting station in

Amman.) We dropped by the electricity shop across from the W. F. Albright Institute of Archaeological Research on Salah Eddin Street, the main commercial thoroughfare of East Jerusalem outside the walls of the Old City, and while we were there, Fredo's dad, Francis, "Abu Mattia," told us that he had a surprise for us. He walked with us a few meters down the road to the new Al Hamra Theatre, and, knowing the ticket agent, we gained entrance for free and found ourselves walking down the aisle of a dark movie hall with the black-and-white giant screen lighting our way. Sitting down to watch the movie was like entering into a totally different world. I was taken aback by its magic as I watched attentively what was going on for an hour or so. Overwhelmed, I related my experience to Mom and my brothers and sisters.

The Al Hamra Theatre became a hub of Jerusalem society in the late fifties and throughout the sixties. On Sunday afternoons the youth of the city would attend the two movies advertised as *filman bi tathkarah wahidah* ("two films for one ticket"). Usually the main attraction would be a movie released sometime during the previous year; more than several months would have passed before the Al Hamra Theatre would receive a copy of a newly released film from abroad, and we would also see an older one reminiscent of the cowboy movie that was repeatedly shown at our school on special occasions (such as the annual holiday of Saint Jean Baptiste de la Salle on May fifteenth). Most viewers would come for the main film attraction, but as a bonus they stayed to watch the second movie. On Sunday evenings the Al Hamra Theatre was the venue for the middle-class families of Jerusalem to come and enjoy the main attraction. I still remember seeing parents of my classmates, both moms and dads, entering the theater on Sunday evenings in a mood of fun and expectation. At intermission viewers would go out to smoke a cigarette and have a soft drink while exchanging views on issues of interest to family and society.

The Al Hamra Theatre played an important role in our social life then. It was also a relaxing way to end the week in preparation for another. But there were forces opposed to the movie theater and its entertainment industry, considering it to be the den of the devil and of his evil designs. In spite of the fact that the grandma of Fredo, "Um Francis," Maltese in origin, would go to Mass on Sunday mornings and would not miss a movie on Sunday afternoons, there was no appreciation by the opposition forces for the example of this elderly, seventyish lady. I would know that Um Francis, the mother of Francis, was going to the movies when I saw her very well dressed, carrying her handbag, and set on her way. She was a fascinating woman ahead of her times, possibly because of the influence of her Maltese origin.

At our Frères School, Brother Principal had a totally different approach to the theater; on Monday mornings he would visit our classrooms and ask in a very shrewd manner who among us had seen the wonderful movie shown yesterday in the theater. Some of us would fall for his trick and raise their hands; he would reprimand us but acknowledge that at least we were honest about it. Then he would get a list of names and single out those who went to the movies on Sunday without admitting to it. Apparently he had sent his "eyes" to report to him on the students who got in to see the movie. There was a punishment fitting the sin, like writing a hundred times, "I will not go to the movies next Sunday," or having to listen to a lengthy sermon on how evil the cinema was.

At home, Father sided with the opposition forces while Mother loved the cinema. Aunt Leonie would back us when we decided to go to the movies, and she usually gave me the missing coins that I needed to buy a ticket. But Father was always on the lookout for us on Sunday evenings when we were coming back from the movie theater. He would be walking back and forth along the Khan Ez Zeit Street by our house, and once he spotted us, he would just move his head from side to side in disapproval. He would not say a word of rebuke, but his headshake was enough to make us feel guilty and uncomfortable.

One of the rare occasions on which the "pro" and "con" camps of the film industry reconciled was when Al Hamra Theatre showed a film on the passion of Christ, *King of Kings* or a similar movie, during Holy Week. Mother would explain to Father about the movie and convince him that films can also be good when they convey a positive message to the viewers. Father would only nod his head, and this was a sign that we could all go to the movies to see the religiously inspired film. This was some sort of victory to those in favor of movie theaters in Jerusalem. Another important milestone came in the early sixties when the movie theaters of Jerusalem showed films like *Marcelino, Pano e Vino* that encouraged private school principals, mostly Christian at the time, to allow certain classes to go *en masse* to the movies for the special showing.

Talking about the movie theater reminds me of the film showing undertaken by no other than a Franciscan friar on Sunday afternoons during the fifties. The hall in which the films were shown was part of the orphanage where hundreds of kids, some of them having lost parents in the 1948 war, were taken care of by the Franciscans. The Franciscans were *avant garde* on this score, and they offered some entertainment to the families of the Old City of Jerusalem who had experienced the trauma of the 1948 war. But my recollection of the film showing at the Franciscan orphanage was that most of the families who came brought with them quantities of roasted seeds,

especially watermelon seeds, which during the film were split uninterrupt-
edly in a well-practiced dental maneuver, unique to Palestinian and Arab
culture, and which resulted in a conspicuous mess on the floor of the hall, in
addition to the sound of the cracking of seeds throughout.

Social Life

Life in the fifties for the refugee families of Jerusalem reflected the will
to recreate the community that had been uprooted during the 1948 war.
Mother and other women of her generation hosted friends, neighbors, and
acquaintances to celebrate various festivities, both personal, such as birth-
days, and public, such as Christmas and Easter. The pre-1948 Palestinian
Christian community that lived predominantly west of the city had an active routine of social interchange that saw many families visiting with each
other for all kinds of occasions. In fact, Mother told me that they did not
need a special occasion to come together, and it was customary in the evening for a knock to be heard on the door that heralded the arrival of friends
and neighbors for an evening of fun and togetherness. The insistence in the
early fifties by the refugee families of Jerusalem on recreating a semblance
of the social scene that had existed before the 1948 war was, in many ways,
an affirmation of continuity and a refusal of the marginalization that was
usually the lot of refugees.

One woman friend of Mother's who particularly drew my attention
was a blonde woman in her forties who visited us in our Old City home
once in a while. I came to understand that she was the wife of a cousin of
my mother from Bethlehem and that she was originally from an Orthodox
Jewish background. She had fallen in love with a man from Bethlehem prior
to 1948, and somehow they had managed to get married despite great opposition from her family. Since she spoke Arabic, she was fully integrated
into the Bethlehemite Palestinian context. Later on I learned that one of her
daughters had decided to become a nun and had moved from Bethlehem to
Rome for the purpose. In one of her visits to Mom, she explained that some
of the Orthodox Jewish men of her family had followed her daughter to
Rome and forced her to leave the convent and to go back with them to their
Orthodox Jewish community in West Jerusalem.

The visits of this Bethlehemite cousin of Mom also opened my eyes to
some narratives that they shared on the social life in Jerusalem during the
British Mandate. Once I heard them speak of the time when expectant Jewish, Muslim, and Christian mothers in the maternity hospital that used to
be in the building behind the offices of the Municipality of Jerusalem would

vow to breastfeed each other's babies in case one of them could not. Mothers who had just given birth to babies were accustomed to asking each other's help in breastfeeding without thinking about religion or national background. Those who were breastfed according to these arrangements became half-brothers and half-sisters to those whose mothers had provided help. Those half-siblings could not marry each other when they grew up because the breastfeeding made them close family members. I was impressed with this cousin of Mom, who appeared to be living her life genuinely without regrets and clearly enjoying her social life without being hampered by her original background.

In spite of the fact that we were children of refugees, our activities and social life in the Old City of Jerusalem in the fifties and sixties were full of zest with some joy and happiness. What theatrical and musical skills we learned at school we passed on to our parents on Thursdays, when we had a free afternoon in accord with the French schools' weekly schedule, or on Saturday evenings. A group of my friends and peers would congregate at our home, and then we would announce to our mothers and neighbors that we were set to present a play to them. We would arrange the seats in one of the rooms and put up an improvised white screen, and, once ready, we would invite the moms and all present to take their seats. As the white screen came down, the play started, usually a comic one that made both players and audience laugh out loud at the various silly scenes and representations. It was fun in those days, when television had not yet been introduced and no one dreamed of the technological developments that characterize most people's lives today.

In fact, we did not have electricity at home until the mid-fifties. I still remember the day when electricity became available and how fascinated we all became with the electric lamp. It was like a miracle. A few months later Father bought a radio, and it was customary for Mother to switch on the radio in the early hours of the morning to listen to the news in Arabic from the BBC, which was then broadcasting from Cyprus. The radio became our means of following the developments around us and in the whole wide world. I was awed by the power of the radio, and even now I prefer radio to other means of communication. Before the introduction of electricity we used to do our homework with the help of a kerosene lamp; on some evenings we would sit for hours by the lamp in order to be ready for another school day with all our homework assignments done.

With electricity running, Mom decided it was time to buy a refrigerator, and I still remember going to the Nasrawi "General Electric" Shop, just outside the walls of the Old City by Damascus Gate, to choose a refrigerator. Mom had saved some money and in fact sold some of her gold and other jewelry from her wedding day, as she was wont to do whenever we needed some cash, in order to afford the price of the refrigerator. When she realized that what she had saved, together with the money exchanged for her jewelry, would suffice only for a first installment, she struck a deal with Mr. Nasrawi to pay the rest in monthly installments. It was word-of-mouth and a handshake that sealed the deal.

I do not recall how I became a barber's helper during my summer holidays in the late fifties. I was then thirteen or fourteen years of age and wanted to earn some cash perhaps to help out a little with the family's finances. What encouraged me to settle on this specific vocation was the fact that my maternal cousin Abraham was the barber. He probably invited me to help at his barbershop with the goal of teaching me the skills needed to become a qualified barber. The barbershop was not far away from my school at the New Gate and offered its own social ambiance: the clients knew each other, and many had commercial, service, and other occupational and purely social ties.

Some of the clients at the barbershop worked at the Commercial Printing Press of Tewfik Habesch, then the largest printing press apart from the Franciscan printing press and those belonging to other church and mosque printers in Jerusalem. The Habesch printing press, just across from the Frères School, was one of the original presses that operated during the British Mandate times and, at that time in its previous location, was used for some of the printing needs of the British mandatory government. Later on it served the Jordanian government with its various ministries. After the 1948 war broke out, the printing press ended up on the western side of the city with no possible access to it. All was lost, or so it appeared, but the owner of the printing press, Tewfik Habesch, an elder of the indigenous Palestinian Roman Catholic community, decided to rebuild it from scratch. He rented the premises across from our school to launch the printing press and to keep it running in spite of all odds. The workers at the Habesch press were regular clients of my cousin's barbershop. During their visits they exchanged views, discussing living conditions, wages, wives, children, and women, not in that order specifically. All of them were hard-working people earning enough to support their families. Their average monthly salaries ranged from five to a maximum of ten Jordanian dinars, or twenty to forty U.S. dollars at the exchange rate of the times. Yet they never complained and went on with their work, devoted to their many family and social obligations.

One particular client, a Sabella and a neighbor of ours in the Dar, was an avid smoker. Although his limited income did not allow him to cover the expenses of a large family, he continued to buy cigarettes and was living in relative comfort. I came to know that he had a brother in Amman who, following the refugee experience of 1948, had gone to Amman and had become a major importer, with Jordanian partners, of steel and other building materials. Amman in the fifties became a booming town with the arrival of thousands of Palestinian refugees. All sorts of construction were in demand, and importers of steel and other needed materials attained prosperity. So the millionaire brother of our Sabella neighbor provided him with a monthly stipend in addition to the meager salary received from his work in the printing press. This lofty tradition of doling out to family members in need is still ongoing in Palestinian society, but with the changing times and economic constraints, the tradition is fading out.

In the barbershop I was also introduced to the people and shops around it. In the coffee shop of Wahbeh Wahbeh, God bless his soul, not far away from the closed New Gate, games of dominoes were in vogue. (The New Gate, which is directly across from the Pontifical Notre Dame Center of Jerusalem, was closed between 1948 and 1967 as it lay on the no man's land or the armistice borderline between East and West Jerusalem.) The shopkeepers of the neighborhood would gather when business was slow and simply pour all their energies and souls into the dominoes games. Yells and screams, amidst sips of coffee or tea, were ordinary. It was fun watching them and hoping that my cousin or a friend of his would come out on top. The socializing effect of the barbershop did not stop at this. My cousin Abraham used to be the barber of the Franciscan convent just a few steps from the barbershop. He also was the "official" barber for the Jordanian army officers stationed at David's Tower not far from the Jaffa Gate. Abraham was well placed, and he knew the secrets of Jerusalem and the country. One time I was amazed when a new Jordanian government was in the making, and before any news of it was published, he knew who the prime minister and most of the ministers would be.

But the fascinating experience I had at the barbershop was an introduction to the art of olive wood carving. A local skilled carver and artist, Rudolph Saadeh, God bless his soul, whose shop or studio sat opposite my cousin's barbershop, was always improvising and creating inspiring pieces of art from olive wood. I dropped by his workshop during my free time from my barbershop duties and maintained the habit of visiting his workshop even when I was no longer a barber's boy. I was always taken aback by how a raw piece of wood became a superb object of art under his magical hands. When in 1964 the World Exposition, or World Fair, was held in New York City, I saw Mr. Saadeh working for hours on end for many days and weeks, carving out a replica of the ancient city of Petra's *Al Khazneh* ("The Treasury"). He had been commissioned by the government of Jordan to do the carving in order to place it as a centerpiece in the Jordan pavilion in the 1964 Expo. As things developed, I would see the same piece as it was finished in Jerusalem and also as exhibited at the New York World Expo.

Growing up in the Old City of Jerusalem in the fifties of the last century also meant that we had no guidance on intimate topics of body development or relations with the fair sex. A couple of incidents opened my eyes to the topic of sexuality. One involved the photos bought by a classmate from a shopkeeper on the way to school. These photos, in black and white, were of nude women in different poses. They were shown around during class breaks, and students took turns in examining them thoroughly. But learning about the opposite sex took place in exchanges with other students with a lot of fantasizing. Listening to grownups talking about their sexual preferences, especially in the barbershop, often left me unprepared to grasp the content of their talk. In particular, whenever one of the clients spoke explicitly about his romantic adventures, this left me with many questions that no one was ready to answer. Sex in the conservative Old City of Jerusalem in the fifties was a taboo topic at school and at home. Accordingly, generations of young people, both girls and boys, grew up with only minimal understanding of the emotional and physical sides of intimacy and closeness. Even nowadays most schools, private as well as public, do not offer any instruction or guidance on this important topic.

While our Frères School was an all-male school at the time, we had opportunities to connect with girls in neighboring schools through JEC, Jeunesse Étudiante Chrétienne (or Young Christian Students). This was a religiously oriented student organization that held different social and religious activities, including annual retreats, summer camps, and even regional gatherings of students usually held in Lebanon during the summers. Its motto was "See-Judge-Act," but aside from learning how to assess a situation and hence to plan action, one of the redeeming functions of JEC was to allow us to meet with female members of our age and to exchange views and plan with them the various social activities and other events. JEC allowed us to develop "leadership" skills as we were entrusted with organizing the various events ourselves and with making presentations in a sort of debating society, supporting our arguments with proper explanations and proofs. This was fun. We were guided by Father Michel Sabbah, a young priest from Nazareth who would be appointed by the Holy See years later to become the first Palestinian Patriarch of the Roman Catholic Church in the Palestinian Territory, Israel, Jordan, and Cyprus. JEC was not a society for indoctrination; rather, it aimed to help us to open up to others and to learn how we young students could run our own organization and plan its activities with some guidance but without the interference of adults.

Papal Visit

I do not recall if JEC had any role in the preparations for welcoming Pope Paul VI to Jerusalem in 1964. Schoolchildren were asked to dress in their formal school attire and to line up outside the Damascus Gate on January 4, 1964, the day of the Pope's arrival, and to greet His Holiness with Jordanian and Vatican flags. The weather was cold and rainy with some winds that would make children huddle together for warmth. We stood for hours by the Damascus Gate as the helicopter piloted by Jordan's King Hussein flew above the Pope's motorcade. The walls of Jerusalem were decorated colorfully with Vatican and Jordanian flags, and there was an atmosphere of jubilation and warmth in spite of the cold, windy weather and the dark clouds that hovered above us. Two huge photographs in black and white of the Pope and of King Hussein adorned the wall next to the Damascus Gate. Jordanian soldiers with their colorful costumes and their stern-looking faces lined the streets leading to the Damascus Gate, a point of entry into the Old City. Boy Scout bands played their loud music while more religious groups preferred to say the Rosary or to chant hymns that expressed devotion to what the Old City of Jerusalem symbolized to them and to their faith. A jubilant time, indeed! It moved both believer and non-believer and cemented the feeling that all inhabitants of the Old City, Muslims and Christians alike, were one as they took care to give the most fitting reception to their esteemed guest.

When the Pope visited the Holy Sepulcher, I was busy working as a helper in a small souvenir shop. From early morning, Jordanian soldiers lined the streets of the Christian Quarter, and when the Pope was set to pass by, I could not see his face because of the crowds surrounding him and because he was of a short stature. Instead, I saw his small, rounded cap moving up and down as he was hurried by his security guards towards the Church of the Holy Sepulcher. Pope Paul VI always stood out in my memory and in that of my generation as a great Pope and a daring one, especially because he initiated the visits of Popes outside of Vatican City to reach out to the world. He started this initiative in the divided Holy Land that was, and remains until the present, in need of a conciliatory gesture or plan. The declared purpose of his visit was to meet with the Greek Orthodox Patriarch of Constantinople, Patriarch Athenagoras, and to deliberate with him on the prospects for Christian unity after hundreds of years of separation.

I was deeply excited by his visit, especially when my elder sister Hilda, who attended the school run by the Sisters of Sion—a Catholic order of nuns that had been founded for the purpose of converting Jews to Christianity and that included a number of Jewish women who had converted and had become nuns—asked me if I could help her best friend to present an essay for their Arabic class on the visit of Pope Paul VI. I volunteered to write the piece, in which I expressed feelings of sentimental attachment to the Pope and what it meant for us to have His Holiness staying for a couple of nights in our city. I wrote it with enthusiasm because I wanted the piece to impress not only the Arabic teacher but also—as important, if not more so—my sister's best friend. When, after the Pope's visit, I asked my sister how well the piece on the Pope had been received by the Arabic teacher, Hilda told me that the teacher had scolded her best friend because she thought the piece was plagiarized and that her best friend could not have written it. Although I was somewhat flattered, I felt sorry for my sister's best friend, as she was put in a bad situation. I loved the feeling of piety and the Pope's readiness to open up and to reach out to others, as witnessed in his mingling with the crowds during his visit.

The Pope, after listening to elders of the Palestinian Christian community, decided that it was time to start a university in the Holy Land with the intent of stopping the emigration of young people. This was the idea behind the establishment of Bethlehem University in 1973, and it continues to be known as the Pontifical University of Bethlehem in acknowledgment of the role played by Pope Paul VI. Another institution that owes its existence to the Pope's visit is Tantur, or the Ecumenical Institute for Theological Research, which sits on a beautiful hill on the Jerusalem-Bethlehem road. The idea behind the Institute emerged from the time of the famed Second Vatican Council in 1963 and was once again entertained following the meeting of the Pope with the Greek Orthodox Patriarch of Constantinople, Athenagoras, on January 5, 1964, on the Mount of Olives in Jerusalem. The Institute was entrusted to Notre Dame University with its famed President Father Ted Hesburgh, and this university continues to oversee the Institute. A third institution that was started at the behest of the Pope was the Ephpheta Paul VI Pontifical Institute for Audio-Phonetic Rehabilitation in Bethlehem. This is a specialized institution that continues to serve Palestinian children who have problems with audio-phonetics. One day when I was teaching at Bethlehem University, I was advised to have a hearing test at Ephpheta, where it was recommended that I should check again on my hearing at regular intervals. Unfortunately I never did this, and my wife Mary always reprimanded me for this failure as she continually argued that I was hard of hearing. Or was it a ploy of mine, as of other husbands who would hear only selectively when their dear wives were talking to them!?

Completing School and Discovering America

School "characters" are very difficult to forget. One of my friends, Shakib, who later migrated to Canada and still sends me Christmas cards faithfully every year, was known for playing tricks on teachers. When Mr. Issa, our history teacher, would line the students up to recite in rotation the lesson learned on the previous day, Shakib would pin the lesson on the back of the student before him and would just read it out, to our amusement, which we tried to suppress in our effort not to laugh out loud. He would repeat this with the Arabic teacher and the very long poems we were supposed to learn by heart. My other friend Moussa, who, like me, was awarded a scholarship to go to college in the United States, was known for his habit of leaving school without permission to play billiards down the road in the Christian Quarter. He contributed to the persistent problem of smoking in the lavatories, and when caught he was cautioned and punished, but to no avail.

One of our part-time teachers in English and Accounting (though neither was his specialty) eventually left Jerusalem in the late 1960s for Canada, where he became a professor of Islamic Civilization at a prestigious university in Montreal. The most unforgettable anecdote was his encounter with George, who was troublesome and always improvised problems when the "professor" was conducting class: on one occasion, when George was disrupting class with his utterances and disorderly behavior, our distinguished teacher called him to come closer to his desk and scolded him in front of the whole class with these scathing words: "Listen, George, you would still need a thousand years to become an insect! So please know your place and be quiet." I do not recall if George received a good slap in the face, as was customary during school years, when physical punishment was an acceptable way to mend the behavior of unruly students. What our part-time teacher said to George was very insulting indeed, but our teachers had to cope with the variety of behaviors that really needed a school counselor to deal with them. In those days, the teacher was a father image, a counselor, a confidant, and a therapist, and fulfilled all the roles in which others should have provided support.

Our last years of school in the early sixties coincided with the rise of Arab nationalism and the powerful figure of Nasser in Egypt. Whenever Nasser delivered a speech, which would typically last for hours, the streets of Jerusalem were deserted as people congregated by their radios. The Jordanian authorities, which were not in agreement with Nasser, forbade listening to his speeches and warned that anyone caught would be appropriately punished. This threat was to no avail, as most Palestinians identified with Nasser and loved the way he delivered his speeches. In fact, although I personally

did not agree with everything he said, hearing him was a pleasure, as he was
a powerful orator. Whenever I listened to him, I was reminded of the speech
given by Julius Caesar in the Shakespeare play, which we memorized, the
speech delivered in the Roman senate before his assassination. Following
Nasser's speeches, many of the students would gather in the alleys of Jerusalem and discuss for hours the significance of what he had said and the
pros and cons of his position. His generally anti-Western and anti-Israel
positions found resonance with Palestinians and Arabs who felt strongly
that an injustice of enormous magnitude had occurred in 1948 and that the
Western powers sought only the cooperation of Arab leaders who would
suppress the aspirations of their people and go along with Western policies
without any questioning. The spirit of defiance toward the West that Nasser
expressed endeared him to millions of his citizens and others in the broader
Arab and Muslim worlds.

Aside from the spirit of defiance, the fact that Nasser was an excellent
orator appealed to the love that Palestinians and other Arabs felt for the
Arabic language. Arabic is the language of the Holy Qur'an, the holy book
of Islam, and as such it is close to the hearts not only of Muslims but also of
all those whose original mother tongue is Arabic. As I grew up, I came to
realize that the early Christians in the Arabian Peninsula, Iraq, Syria, and
Lebanon, among other countries of the Near East, had made contributions
to the Arabic language and literature. I came to read the books of the Jesuit
Father Louis Sheikho, an Iraqi, who wrote on Christian poets before and after Islam and also on Christianity and its literary contributions in the period
prior to the appearance of Islam. I also came to appreciate that, were it not
for the work of the Syriac Orthodox translators from Greek to Arabic of the
philosophical discourses of the ancient Greek masters during Abbasid rule
in Iraq in the ninth century, much of Greek philosophy would have been
lost forever.

In support of Arab Christian scholars and academics who say that they
have been part and parcel of Arab civilization from its inception onward,
there is indeed historical proof for the contributions of indigenous Arab
Christians to the rise and development of Arab and Muslim civilization.
This is something that most Westerners do not know, particularly in the
present days of confrontation, terror, and mutual recriminations, and many,
unfortunately, do not care to know. While many of the contributions of Arabic civilization to the knowledge that we all have today have been surpassed
by modern developments, still, as a Palestinian Christian, I take pride in the
accomplishments of Arabic and Muslim civilization as I stress the need for
us to catch up with the modern developments and to be on a par with the
advances that are making a difference in the quality of life of our modern

world. Nevertheless I am always awed and rewarded whenever I read a good history book or a literary work pertaining to past eras of Arabic and Muslim civilization.

In 1964, my last year of school, the United States Information Service, known by its acronym, USIS, announced a writing competition on the life and ideals of Abraham Lincoln. I had read about Lincoln both in English and in Arabic during my school years as I frequented the American library both in Jerusalem and in Amman. I loved Lincoln's character, especially the fact that as a young lad he would study by a kerosene lamp and that he would walk for miles to borrow a book; he was a self-made man and, one can add, a self-taught man who overcame immense challenges and constraints to become eventually the sixteenth President of the United States of America and to lead his nation during its most crucial years. I was selected by my school to participate in the country-wide competition. My English teacher, Mr. Sarkis, an Armenian living in the Armenian Quarter of the Old City who was particularly liked by all students without exception, had always wanted me to improve my English, and he was not sure that I would succeed in the competition.

A month later, after I had submitted my essay, USIS announced the ten winning entries, of which five would be eventually chosen after a dinner party honoring all the winners. At the dinner tables each pair of winners was seated together with two American officials working either with USIS or with the U.S. Embassy. My intuition told me that this was a screening and not simply a dinner to honor winners. I did the best that I could with my English to impress my two American interlocutors. When the names of the five winners were published a week later in the local newspapers, I was among them.

The prize of the competition was a one-month, all-expenses-paid trip to the United States in order to visit New Salem in Illinois, where Abraham Lincoln settled for a number of years and worked as a shopkeeper and postmaster and eventually owned a general store. In addition we were to visit a number of other locations, including Utah and Washington, D.C., where the Lincoln Memorial was one of the impressive monuments adorning the American capital. A teacher was chosen to accompany us, who was no other than Mr. Issa B., the same part-time English and Accounting teacher at our school who had scolded George. The other four students came from all over the country. The prize was a dream come true because most of us students at the Frères School wanted to visit the U.S. in order to continue our education there and to look into prospects of immigrating. For me, coming from a family that could not make ends meet every month, an opportunity to visit the United States at such an early age was an excitingly overwhelming event.

It was a fun-filled visit, and as we toured New Salem Historic Village, we were impressed with the simplicity of the place as it took us more than 130 years back in history. What I admired most was the fact that Americans put great emphasis on their historical heritage and preserved it for future generations. When we visited Harvard University, we met with an Arabic teacher, a Palestinian by birth, who told us that we should perhaps emulate the Americans in their love for their heritage and in putting up statues and monuments to immortalize events and people. I am not sure now about immortalizing history in sculpted iron or bronze statues, as the choice of whom and what to immortalize often ends up being the choice of a few who are prejudiced in favor of a certain narrative of history and heritage. True, there are events and leaders that have or merit the consensus of the population in ranking them as leading events and public figures, and hence building statues or memorials to honor them would not be a problem. But what about those minor figures and events whose contributions have been inflated by some in order that whole populations would honor them, without truly having the consensus for it?

One of the highlights of the trip was visiting the New York World Fair of 1964, which gave me the opportunity to see in the Jordan pavilion the finished sculpted olive wood replica of Petra's *Al Khazneh* ("The Treasury") by Rudolph Saadeh, whose workshop stood across from my cousin's barbershop at the New Gate. I was overjoyed as multitudes of American and other visitors were admiring his work together with the stained glass windows that were a reminder of the Stations of the Cross in the Via Dolorosa.

In upstate New York, in Rochester in particular, I was able to take off a couple of days from the official tour and to visit, together with Uncle Jack, who lived in Long Beach on Long Island, some cousins of my father who had migrated from Jerusalem to the U.S. in the fifties. They had settled in Rochester and worked for the Kodak Company. It was fun to get acquainted with them, and they asked about the family in Jerusalem, Amman, and Beirut. Clearly they had adapted to the American way of life in dress and other ways, and had had no difficulty whatsoever in integrating into the local society and in upholding American values. One particular paternal cousin I still remember was Rosalyn, who, when she welcomed us, seemed to me to be entirely American both in physical appearance and dress.

The tour took us to Salt Lake City, which strikingly resembled the topography of Jericho and its surrounding areas. The Great Salt Lake itself reminded me of the Dead Sea, but Salt Lake City was a bustling town in the eyes of a young boy coming from a traditionally quiet and mostly dormant Jerusalem. We were introduced to the Church of Jesus Christ of Latter-day Saints (Mormon Church), which I had never known existed.

I was most impressed with the social services that it offered to people in need, especially in the outlying areas of Salt Lake City in preparation for the cold months of winter. We were introduced to one of the twelve elders who comprised the governing board of the Church and served as the source of wisdom and interpretation of the Holy Writings. We visited the historic Temple Square and were impressed with the majestic buildings, including the Tabernacle where the world-famous Mormon Tabernacle Choir made their home and offered their performances, which attracted people from near and far. I was introduced to the Book of Mormon and received a copy, which I brought back with me to Jerusalem. I saw a similarity between the Mormon principle of polygyny practiced in the nineteenth century and that allowed in Islam. But I was made to understand that, except for very special cases, polygyny is no longer practiced among Mormons.

What impressed me also about the Mormons was their sense of discipline, their cleanliness, and their pursuit of lofty spiritual goals rather than earthly and temporary gains. At the same time their subscription to these lofty goals did not prevent the Mormon faithful from pursuing careers and becoming successful businessmen and entrepreneurs. Apparently self-discipline can be a recipe for success in business and other earthly undertakings as well as for spiritual rewards.

I learned in the visit to Salt Lake City the meaning of "litter," which I did not know before arriving there. Having finished a hefty hamburger, which I tasted for the first time in the United States, and while being driven around in the city, I took the liberty of throwing all the trash out the car window. The moment I did this, a car with four elderly ladies, most likely in their late seventies and early eighties, all turned their heads towards me and gazed at me in disbelief. I asked the driver what I did wrong, and he informed me that I had just littered the highway, which I was not supposed to do, and he pointed to a sign stating: "Do Not Litter—Fine $50." This incident stayed with me in part because I felt guilty for the consternation I caused the four elderly ladies and for the polluting. One learns unexpected lessons in unexpected situations.

2

College Years:
The American Interlude, Part One

Opportunities and Choices

BACK IN JERUSALEM FROM the dazzling, month-long visit to the U.S., I was offered a teaching job at the Terra Sancta School run by the Franciscans. I taught English and History for the seventh to ninth grades. There was no need for teaching certification, and word-of-mouth together with my high school grades was enough to land me a teaching job at one of the many private high schools in the city. The Terra Sancta School was a boys' school, mostly attended by Christian students and specifically by sons of the Roman Catholic ("Latin") community of Jerusalem.

The students had absolutely no sense of discipline, and they were all over me. I could not handle their chaotic approach to education. What added to my pressures was the fact that the Reverend Principal of the School had built-in microphones in all classrooms, so any "loud" disturbance in the classroom would almost automatically present him with an invitation to visit the classroom and to check personally on developments there. One time, when I was explaining a history lesson, my knowledgeable presentation apparently appealed to my students; silence fell in the classroom for some time. All of a sudden, the principal arrived at the classroom to ascertain that all was well and that nothing serious had happened to me. But my inability to handle the unruly class resulted in the termination of my short teaching experience at the school.

As I was looking for another teaching job, the Brother Principal of my high school alma mater offered me an opportunity. For high school graduates of the sixties there were no available job opportunities except in teaching, government and municipal employment, or private and service sectors where the salaries were minimal. The only way a family could have survived financially was to put its resources together, so all the working members of the family would pool their salaries in order to make ends meet. I remember clearly that with the wages earned by my father, my brother Abel, and my sister Hilda, we were able to manage. In addition my uncle Rock, my father's brother, who visited with us periodically from Amman, would offer my dad some needed financial supplements.

In my new teaching job, I was to teach Arabic, English, and, to my amazement or dismay, French. When I explained to the Brother Principal my limitations in French, his response was that I would be teaching it to the first and second grades and hence this very elementary level did not require full mastery of the language. The teaching experience at the Frères was different from that at the Terra Sancta School; the administration was always supportive of the teacher in front of the students, even when in private the teacher was made to understand his faults or mistakes. The sense of discipline emanated more from the pedagogical nature of the educational process rather than from the stern approach of the patriarchal figure that was so distinctive of the principal of the Terra Sancta School. I was commended as a teacher in the Frères School, and because of my Arabic skills, the school administration was willing to offer me a scholarship to study Arabic at the University of Jordan in Amman, which had been established in 1964. This was in 1966, and they expected me, if I accepted the offer, to come back and teach Arabic at the school for a number of years. I was also thinking of studying law at St. Joseph Jesuit University in Beirut, Lebanon. I always thought that becoming a lawyer would enable me to use the argumentative discourses, assessed as "superb," that I had presented with the other students—discourses that were enhanced by my excelling in Arabic language and literature. But when I asked my father about what he thought of my different university options, he told me that law would likely lead me to ways that were not always honest because some lawyers, according to him, were prone to twist the truth and not honor the "truth and only the truth."

My month-long visit to the U.S. in 1964 changed the course of my future university plans by introducing me to key people in the United States Information Service (USIS) who alerted me to scholarships and possible university openings for undergraduate study in the United States. Scholarships for undergraduate studies were rare, but some U.S. colleges and universities wanted to enroll international students as a way to promote their international stature. They offered full scholarships to foreign students. These were considered as part of the aid provided by the American people for the development of different countries across the globe. In my case, it was Jordan (because the West Bank was governed by Jordan at this time), and the scholarship would be part of the U.S. aid package to the country.

Hence, if awarded a scholarship, I would have to serve the Ministry of Education in Jordan two years for every one year of scholarship awarded.

Among the American institutions of higher education offering undergraduate scholarships was Franklin and Marshall College (F&M) in Lancaster, Pennsylvania. It was in late summer 1966 that I received the letter from F&M informing me that I was the recipient of a full four-year scholarship. I read the letter in the Al Hamra Theatre as I was about to see an Egyptian comedy movie with some friends and other "comic" figures of Jerusalem. Among these comic figures were friends from my peer group at school who were always laughing and joking. I felt as if I were in heaven as I was overwhelmed by joy while examining the letter. Back home in the evening, I shared the good news with my family. Father and Mother were very happy with this development. Father in particular was relieved that the new opportunity in the U.S. would take me away from studying law at the Jesuit University in Beirut, which would have been quite expensive for him and the family. Nevertheless, Father wondered about how to provide for my spending money. I explained to him that I could also work part-time in the States and that should be enough to cover my needs. Still he insisted that there was not enough cash with him to cover the initial expenses for the journey from Jerusalem to Lancaster, Pennsylvania, where F&M is located, although USIS was covering my return flight ticket and helping out with some expenses of the initial trip.

When I explained my family's financial dilemma to Father Laurent, a French Canadian priest from Montreal who was studying the Old Testament at the École Biblique ("Biblical School," run by the Dominicans near the Damascus Gate), he reassured me that he would come up with some funds to help me with the trip to the United States. Father Laurent studied Arabic with me—not that I was a good teacher, but for lack of a more proficient expert, I was recommended to him. When I relayed to my father the generous offer of my Arabic language student, he was not convinced, and he said that he would believe it when he would see the money. Father's attitude reminded me of St. Thomas, who wanted to touch the wounds on the body of Jesus to ascertain that indeed he was the Master. Father Laurent did come up with a hefty $500 that not only helped me find my way to Lancaster, Pennsylvania, but also enabled my father, mother, and a couple of my siblings to travel by car to Beirut in order to see me off when I boarded the flight from Beirut Airport to New York.

As the plane took off, I remembered fondly the support given by my family, by Father Laurent, and by my Aunt Leonie. In particular I was thrilled when Aunt Leonie, in her late sixties, invited me to go see *The Sound of Music* with her at Al Hamra Theatre as a farewell gesture on her part before I traveled to the U.S. She chose the best two seats in the house, bought me ice cream, which I loved, and made me feel like a charming prince who had just been assured succession to the throne. This was all a wonderful experience for me and gave me the feeling that the best a person could hope for was a warmly caring family. Aunt Leonie, I recalled with some emotion as the plane was high in the sky, had saved my life once when a piece of meat got stuck in my throat and I could not breathe for some moments. I was then twelve or thirteen, and were it not for her quick reaction to my emergency, I would not have survived. She asked me to open my mouth as wide as I could and then she maneuvered her fingers to pull the piece of meat out. We did not know about the Heimlich maneuver at the time; it was her improvised technique that saved me. This terrifying experience stayed with me for some time and made me extra careful and, in fact, a slow eater ever since.

A Newcomer in America

On arrival in New York I was met by my uncle Jack, who took me to his home. I had difficulty in understanding the slang of my cousins. Whenever my five cousins spoke, I was too shy to ask for more clarity or for an interpretation. It sounded to me as if they swallowed half of the words; they countered that this was the way New Yorkers spoke. My cousins did not know any Arabic because they had forgotten all about it and were quite comfortable in the accommodating environment of Long Beach, Long Island. They had become Americanized. Aunt Frida, Uncle Jack's wife, was a magnificent hostess. Her Palestinian food whetted my appetite and provided the emotional link that I needed during the early days of the transition from the old country to the new world. Conversing in Arabic with her gave me some solace from the uncertainty I felt whenever I listened to my cousins' slang. Driving around Long Beach, my cousin Lucy was noticeably conscientious about stopping at the "Stop" signs. I asked her why she did that even when clearly there were no cars crossing either way. In response she gave me a lesson on how one should respect laws, even when apparently these laws do not cover all eventualities. Apart from the cultural differences, what I liked about my Long Beach cousins was their determination to chart their course of life to suit their preferences and expectations and to develop themselves through hard work and pursuit of further education.

It so happened that my eldest cousin, Essa, God bless his soul, was in his third year at Villanova University, and Uncle Jack was to drive him there over the weekend. Villanova is three quarters of an hour's drive from Lancaster, Pennsylvania, which was convenient for giving me a ride to my

college. After a brief introduction to the Villanova campus, we dropped
Cousin Essa off. Villanova University was established in the 1840s by the
Catholic Order of Saint Augustine.

The model of many current-day universities was initially borrowed
from the Muslim world, where students would surround a learned man in
one of the corners of the mosque to listen to him. Usually the learned man
was known for his specialty in one area of the Holy Writings and traditions
of Islam, similar to the specializations found nowadays in the universities
and colleges. Since the Middle Ages, when European and Arabic cultures
came into contact, excellence in education has become the hallmark of
Western societies, and the United States has indeed been a pioneer in higher
education. I realize that many are not happy with the standards and quality
of university education nowadays in contrast to the past; nevertheless, its
status as the capital of higher education, impacting the minds of millions
of American and international students, is something that I believe that
American society should strive to maintain proudly.

I would have an opportunity to visit Villanova University once again
in December of 2016. Oh yes, time flies, and one's life is but the blink of
an eye, as a departed friend of mine, God bless his soul, once told me. The
occasion for the second visit was a conference organized by Augustinian
Father Kail Ellis on "Christians in the Contemporary Middle East." Father
Ellis, of Lebanese descent, was always interested in the developments taking
place in the Middle East and accordingly was intent on following up these
developments with gatherings of academics and intellectuals who could
enlighten audiences at his University and elsewhere on what was happening. Such a conference, "Christians in the Contemporary Middle East," took
place in early December 2016. Father Ellis invited me to submit a paper on
"Christian Contributions to Art, Culture and Literature in the Arab-Islamic
World."[1]

In Lancaster, Uncle Jack dropped me off to find myself in a bare dorm
room with only the essentials. I was one of the first students to arrive at
college, a day or two before the arrival of the rest of the student population.
This made me rather anxious because I did not know what to expect. I had
brought with me an Arabic Bible. Having earned the reputation of being religious, I could not travel without the Bible. Besides, my father had given me
a Rosary and asked me to be faithful in reciting it daily. My mother, for my
protection, had pinned a Saint Cyprian amulet to my underclothes. The amulet of St. Cyprian, who converted to Christianity in the third century and
became Bishop of Antioch (not to be confused with the renowned Bishop of

---

1. Sabella, "Christian Contributions," 2016.

Carthage of the same century), was very popular with my mother's generation. Particularly the amulet was thought to protect babies and children and was treasured because of the high infant mortality rates of the times. In the amulet was included a prayer composed by the saint himself, in which he intercedes through the Virgin Mary for the protection of the bearer from all evil and ill, including all sorts of magic and amulets! I was all set to face the new world and to prove to everyone, but most importantly to myself, that I was courageous and up to the challenge.

The first few nights at the F&M dorm were difficult. It was hard to fall asleep even with readings from the Bible. I often heard Aunt Leonie's voice ringing in my ears. My friend Moussa from the Frères High School, God bless his soul, then on a similar scholarship in some small college in Ohio, called me on the unique rectangular black and shining metal pay phone with slots for coins and related how he was in tears almost every night. I always thought Moussa was a tough guy, judging from his smoking and running away from school to play billiards, but apparently when one was like a fish out of water, it was normal to fall back on the good people and things from back home that one never thought would be missed.

As the college slowly came to life with students assembling to register, I met international students assigned to rooms across from me and twinned with American roommates, with the encouragement of all kinds of welcoming activities, and I discovered that transition could be an invigorating time as well. As we sat talking about our backgrounds and our academic interests, I soon realized that some of my roommates did not share the same beliefs as I did. In fact, I was shocked to hear a foreign student expressing his disbelief in the Almighty. I was also awed by the independence shown by American students and how distant from their own parents and families some of them appeared to be. I soon discovered that some of these students were at college because they had asked for loans that they would pay back themselves after graduation. Self-reliance was a prized value, and unless one could prove oneself worthy of success, particularly in the American context, then his or her chances for achieving it would be weak indeed.

But what amounted to a real culture shock was the discussion I had with some of my American roommates about a legal case in which a daughter asked the court to oblige her parents to pay for her university studies. In the Jerusalem Palestinian culture we would never have thought of filing a lawsuit against our parents for any reason whatsoever. Respect for elders and for parents particularly was the hallmark of the relationship between children and their parents. I can never forget an occasion in Beit Sahour, a Palestinian Christian town known as the "Shepherds' Field" town, when a renowned American-educated professor of Psychology at Bethlehem

University approached his father and kissed his hand in a public gesture of respect and acknowledgment. While in my family we never kissed Father's hand, still the respect we had for both Father and Mother cemented our belonging to the family and simplified many things in life.

Social Encounters

F&M was one of the last university-level institutions in the U.S. that were all-male. This surprised me because I was expecting a mixed university population, but I adapted to the new reality that reminded me so keenly of my own high school back in Jerusalem. One of the realities of the college that forced me to examine my relationships to others was the fact that a considerable percentage of the student body came from middle- and upper-middle-class Jewish families from the greater metropolitan areas of Philadelphia and New York. Coming from the Old City of Jerusalem, which was part of Jordan, I had never encountered an Israeli or a Jewish person, except for the lady friend of Mom's who was married to a cousin of the family from Bethlehem. Coming to terms with the complex backgrounds of Jewish students was a learning experience. Some were warm friends; others acted in a condescending and hostile manner; still others wanted to exchange views and speak about what united and what divided us from each other. I liked most a Jewish friend who in my second year at F&M insisted that we go together to Baltimore, about an hour-and-a-half's drive from Lancaster, to explore the bars, discotheques, and "burlesque" shows of the city. He was introducing me to a dimension of American "entertainment" life that was unimaginable in the Old City of Jerusalem.

I never owned a car in Lancaster nor felt that there was any need for one since I came just to study and to pursue higher education. I was content in being sedentary and found great relief in my frequent walks to the center of the city, about half an hour's walk from the college, on Fridays and on the special days when there was a Farmers' Market. The farmers of Lancaster were a unique group of people; most likely some of them were descended from German ancestry, which explained their hard work and resolve. Others were religiously oriented and saw success in selling their farm produce as a benediction from God. This was similar to how my father saw his success or absence of misfortune—as in a cause-effect relationship corresponding to the extent of his religiosity and belief in divine intervention and care. I saw similarities between the Lancaster farmers and the conservative society of old Jerusalem and other Palestinian and Arab societies because these valued family, religion, and the traditions that kept people within a certain framework and that reinforced the old ways of doing things and relating to others. Naturally, in such an environment new faces and encounters were regarded warily; one did not confide in newcomers, for the simple reason that they were different.

On one of my frequent walks to downtown Lancaster I met by chance an old friend and peer from the Frères School, George S. I was overjoyed and asked him what he was doing in Lancaster, of all towns and cities in the United States. He explained to me that he had come to Lancaster to learn about watchmaking, repair, and maintenance. Lancaster was host to the Hamilton Watch Company, a unique and specialized watchmaking company started in the late nineteenth century. Ever since high school George's hobby had been watchmaking, which was a family tradition inherited from his father and grandfather. So it was natural for him to explore the possibilities of learning at Hamilton. He was aided by his brother, who worked in the Arabic language section of the Voice of America and who had interviewed me a couple of times during our month-long Abraham Lincoln tour in 1964.

Lancaster was a welcoming city altogether in spite of the traditional row between gown and town. One of the unique experiences that we international students enjoyed in the International House at Franklin and Marshall College was our relationship with the Shank family. The Shank family, which was of the Mennonite persuasion, consisted of a father, who was a hard-working carpenter, and a strong-willed mother with a number of children (I could never ascertain how many). On one of the Saturdays when we were sitting around in the dorm lounge, this family appeared from nowhere with a bushel of delicious apples. The delivery of this gift became a weekly ritual, and we awaited the arrival of the wooden basket of apples with eagerness. They introduced themselves and asked us to visit with them whenever we could, and they invited us to taste the apples. Tasting apples always brings me a sensory association; in this case the association was with family care, outreach, and the willingness to be friends and to act as surrogate family for the international students who missed loved ones back home. For me the association of apples with caring love dated back to the time in the early fifties when one evening I felt hungry but could not find anything to eat. Mother, sensing my hunger, produced as if miraculously a red apple, which seemed to be the most delicious apple I had ever tasted.

The relationship with the Shank family was central to my experience and, I am sure, to the experience of my fellow international students at F&M. We visited with them at their modest home in a rural area of Lancaster, where we broke bread with them. On one or two occasions we all huddled in the old Volkswagen van, which could take almost a dozen people, to go to special church services. I was surprised to discover in these church services that women sat on one side and men on the other side across from them. This seating arrangement made me think of other religious communities, not only Christian ones, in which separation between men and women was essential in the conduct of services. I never questioned the fact of separation, but I missed the rationale behind it. Was it related to the "purity" of men congregants and the need to preserve it during prayer services? Or was the seating arrangement a reflection of the stations in life accorded to men and to women and the division of labor between the genders? Or was it simply preserving the sanctity of tradition without altering or challenging it? It was not the intention of the Shank family to convert us; rather, it was a way to encourage us to feel at home. And certainly we did feel at home—as well as grateful to the Shank parents and to Anne and David, the eldest daughter and the youngest son.

Years later, when I was attending a conference of the Middle East Council of Churches in Cyprus, a young American man was sitting across from my family and me at the dinner table. As we introduced ourselves to each other, I asked him where he came from. It was from Lancaster, Pennsylvania, that he came. So I related to David (that was his name) the experience we had had with the Shank family. To my surprise and pleasure, David told me that it was his family who had established the contact with the International House and, yes, he was the same David whom I had met in Lancaster. We maintained contact for some time as David was working on his dissertation and preparing for the ministry, or so I recall.

News from Home

Studying at F&M was an exhilarating experience. In my freshman year I bought all the books required for my four or five courses. I started devouring the books one by one, staying up till the wee hours of the morning to finish the reading assignments, which reminded me of the educational philosophy of my high school. I thought that all my reading would surely impress my professors. Some were impressed, but others clearly let me know that it is not by reading books alone that one learns. I needed, according to them, a conceptual understanding of the ideas and narratives found in assigned books and not simply reading them.

Developing a broader conceptual base was certainly on my mind, but at the end of my freshman year I was also preoccupied by news from home, which spoke of mounting tensions between Egypt and Israel. The June war of 1967 saw me on a one-day visit to Philadelphia. Entering a diner to have a bite, I heard some of the customers speaking about bashing "those A-rabs"

1967

and "finishing them off." I was offended by the racist insinuations of these people, who saw the war only as a black-and-white media event and did not realize the complexities surrounding the enmity between Arab and Jew. On the streets of Philadelphia I saw dozens of young Orthodox Jews with small boxes in their hands, singing and dancing and collecting donations for the war efforts of Israel. Saddened, I thought of home, parents, and my beloved city of Jerusalem as the news spoke of the battle raging around the city.

In a couple of days I would know that new realities had been established and that my Old City of Jerusalem had been taken over by Israel. I was worried about the fate of my family as there was no immediate communication possible with them at that time. Eventually I heard from them and learned how they had huddled at a neighbor's home on the ground floor of the Dar. Luckily, Father had withdrawn some money from the bank on the Sunday before the war because he was intending to buy property outside the walled city. Fortunately, having cash available a day before the start of the June 1967 war enabled my family to take care of its needs and those of neighbors and friends during the weeks following the war. When calamities strike, whether natural or man-made, people tend to be strengthened by their coming together. This feeling of togetherness is essential to the task of survival, and it thus overrides monetary and other material considerations. Money ceases to be the focus as survival becomes the challenge.

Outdoor Adventures

The summer of 1967 saw me traveling by bus to the small town of Monterrey in Tennessee. There I had volunteered to be a youth leader or counselor in a summer camp in the beautiful and serene hills of central Tennessee between Knoxville and Nashville. The camp belonged to a family who had visited Jerusalem a year or two before my arrival at F&M. They had been guided by my father, who had learned the skills of a guide after his retirement from his Municipality work at the age of sixty-seven.

My father had studied hard for his guide license from the Jordan Tourism Ministry. I recall that he would be up till two or three o'clock in the morning poring over some guiding books, especially those by the Franciscan Father Hoade, who was known as an authority on the holy places and their history. Some of the American tourists who accompanied him suggested that he should write a book with all the information that he had acquired on the various holy sites. He was a dedicated perfectionist when it came to learning about the different sites, and he excelled in his work. One of the funniest stories he told us about guiding tourists was his accompaniment of an American family (who may or may not have been the same family as the summer camp owners) to the Grotto of the Nativity in Bethlehem. Father, a practicing believer, was accustomed to explaining to those tourists and pilgrims with him about the Grotto and then directing them to go down the semi-circular steps and to spend some time visiting, praying, and reflecting in the birthplace of Jesus Christ. He himself would devoutly remove the red fez that he wore on his head and would stand at the door leading to the Grotto bowing his head and holding the red fez in his hand. As he was resting and silently praying by the Grotto's door, waiting for the American family to finish their visit, a group of American tourists walked down by him and, following the lead of the first in the group, they each dropped dollars into my father's red fez, thinking that he was the doorkeeper to the Grotto. My father cherished the story but took care to return the tips.

At the camp in the summer of 1967 I got to meet the youngsters of upper-middle and upper-class American families. They were an impressive bunch of young people, willing to help and brimming with love for adventure and discovery. "The sky is the limit" seemed to me an appropriate description of the spirit that moved these young people. The summer camp nurtured their spirit of adventure and inquisitiveness and helped them to polish their outdoor skills. For two months, I slept in a log cabin with four to six of the youngsters, and we followed a regimen that made us so exhausted from the day's activities that by nightfall we were all ready to hit the sack.

During one of our outings in the woods, with me in charge of five or six youngsters, we needed to find our way out of a ravine. The only way to do it was to climb a steep hill. The youngsters toiled up the hill one by one, each climber warning the one below of the dangers and risks along the way. On one occasion a warning came down to us that there may be a rattlesnake in one of the crevices on the way up. So we exerted extra caution. As we reached the top, we could hear the sound of traffic on a highway nearby, but we still did not know which direction to take. Finally we arrived at a farm where a sign emphatically warned trespassers of the worst scenarios awaiting them. We entered into a discussion of why trespassers needed to be shot in order to ascertain one's right to property and why the owner or his aides couldn't check with the trespassers on the reason for their sin of trespassing. Eventually we found ourselves at a primitive post office beside a rudimentary rural road with a pay phone that enabled us to contact the camp and to get someone to come and pick us up.

I often thought about the idea of protecting private property and the right of an owner to shoot trespassers. Was the legal cover given to the owner of private property an acknowledgment from the state and society that he had earned the right to the property and hence also the right to protect it from unwanted intruders? Or is the obsession with protecting private property a reflection of a long historical transition from the time when property ownership was collective and the whole community owned it, in contrast to modern societies where ownership has become more individualized and private?

For me, getting lost in the dry ravine with the group of courageous young people was a learning experience: when in difficulty you have to find your way out and up. Help can come from younger people who have stamina, courage, and the will to overcome. But young people can make mistakes or end up in situations that are costly; I was saddened to know a year or two after the ravine incident that one of the brave youngsters had met his death in a rock-climbing accident when he and another fellow fell down a cliff together.

Of the youngsters in my summer camp charge, one insisted that I be introduced to his family in Knoxville, whose home was just across from the campus of the University of Tennessee. I visited with his family and became friends with both of his parents. When his mother had a serious illness and was expected to pass on, I presented her with some religious souvenirs from the Holy Land as a solace. I was moved when I learned that one of her last wishes was to have these items interred with her. His father, a liberal professional, attended my graduation at F&M, thus offering a touching personal sign of caring and friendship. Another fellow, with whom I still have some contact over Facebook, had invited me in one of the summers to go with his family to their summer home in Maine. This experience was exceptional. I will never forget the warm family atmosphere with the lobsters and the overwhelmingly beautiful vistas of the ocean. I learned there how to play Canasta and other card games during the evenings of family fun and togetherness. These were altogether glorious days in which I discovered dimensions of American life that would have been inaccessible to me without my American friends and hosts with their good will, generosity, and willingness to open up, thanks to the younger generation.

A Visit at Home in Jerusalem

In the summer of 1968 I went back again to the Monterrey camp but had let the camp directors know that I was planning to visit home to check on my family after the June war of 1967. They offered whatever help they could in order to facilitate my trip. But before my departure, the tragic and shocking assassination of Robert Kennedy occurred. One of the camp directors shyly asked me if I knew Sirhan Sirhan personally; I told him that his house was not far away from ours in the Old City of Jerusalem but that there were no interactions with his family.

The tragedy that befell some families in the Old City of Jerusalem after the 1948 Arab-Israeli war and then after the June 1967 war had resulted in international repercussions, and personal emotions in reaction to world events were vented, often in a violent and unchecked response for which there is absolutely no justification. The assassination of a promising young leader like Robert Kennedy diverted attention from important political processes within the U.S., hindering progress. Perhaps because of the Catholic background of my family, we felt particularly saddened and outraged by the assassination and were in prayerful solidarity with those who mourned.

Often U.S. politicians, especially those who run for presidential elections, make statements in support of Israel or even undertake visits to Israel. Some argue that these statements are intended to attract the Jewish vote and support in the U.S.; others tie these statements to the strategic alliance that links the U.S. to Israel. But Palestinians perceive these statements and visits as ignoring the injustice that befell the Palestinians in 1948. By playing up to Israel and its narrative, there is clearly unwillingness on the part of some U.S. politicians to see the conflict in a broader perspective of respect for human rights or to entertain consideration of any resolution to the conflict that includes the Palestinian narrative. In today's world, where communication plays an important role in transmitting words and deeds of politicians, caution must be exercised not to make statements that would be interpreted as broadening the gulf that separates people from each other. But let me insist once again that violence is not the way, and can never be, as history has shown again and again the failure of violence in bringing about reconciliation between conflicting parties, aside from the tremendous costs that individuals and groups pay with the perpetuation of violence.

Coming home in the summer of 1968 was a political and cultural shock to me. The Old City of Jerusalem had now changed hands since Jordan had lost the 1967 war. East Jerusalem, which had been under Jordanian jurisdiction, had fallen to Israel, together with the rest of the West Bank, Gaza Strip, Sinai Peninsula, and the Golan Heights, and had become occupied territory. The jubilation that I observed among some of my Jewish peers at F&M following Israel's swift and convincing victory was contrasted with the feeling of uncertainty expressed by my family members and by the greater East Jerusalem and Palestinian community. So what would happen now that Israel had taken over, and what would be our status with the new political and military realities?

More immediately I was anxious to hear how my family was faring in terms of living conditions. Mother explained that with the savings of Father they had managed relatively well during the days of the war and the weeks after. My younger brother Tony told me that he had sold postcards and other souvenir items at the Damascus Gate to Israelis as thousands of them flocked to the Old City of Jerusalem. He said that the Israelis visiting the Old City and other towns and cities of the West Bank were buying everything they could get their hands on. He explained the phenomenon by the fact that prices in Jordan were well below those in Israel and accordingly this was an opportunity to save some money on many of the products available in the newly occupied territory.

But what stood out during the visit was the story that Mother related about her visit to our Qatamon home, abandoned in 1948. Mom seized the first opportunity to visit the Qatamon home, as she wanted to see what had happened to it. The house was still there intact, and as mother approached the main door, the occupant came out and welcomed her. He told her that he recognized her from old photographs left in the house and that she was welcome to come in and have a coffee. It was too difficult for Mom to accept this offer, but she went in to inspect the house and to ascertain that it was well cared for. It was a painful experience that brought back memories and made Mom question the wisdom, if any, of having one's own home turned into a home for strangers who knew nothing of the home's history and its happy and sad times. Mom expressed this feeling on her way back to the Damascus Gate in an Israeli bus that was overcrowded. As she wore a golden cross around her neck, an Israeli speaking in Arabic told her, "You Christians are better than Muslims." She was shocked at the remark and responded by saying, "Listen, Mister, we have lived together with Muslims for decades, and nothing has ever transpired in our relationship like what happened between you and us. I am just coming back from my Qatamon home, and how do you think I feel when I see my home lived in by your compatriots and I am denied even repossessing it?"

For me these words expressed the sense of injustice that permeated the souls of not only my mother but of thousands of Palestinians who felt dispossessed through no personal fault of their own. To the present day, this sense of injustice has never been resolved. There can never be true reconciliation until the injustice that befell the Palestinians is dealt with in fairness and with respect to their right to dignity through redressing the injustice. It sounds like a difficult and, some would argue, an impossible formula, but it is important to strive towards such a formula since it would guarantee that the future of the Middle East would be one in which the core conflict between the Israelis and the Palestinians and other Arabs had been overcome once and for all. All parties, including the Israelis, should acknowledge their responsibility for what befell the Palestinians in 1948. Any political solution between Israelis and Palestinians that does not acknowledge this would be destined to fail. A working and practical solution to the plight of Palestinian refugees is still possible if all parties put their hearts in it.

My brother Maurice was working hard at being accepted by Salamanca University in Spain to study medicine. Spanish universities at the time did not require any fees, even from foreign students, if they qualified for admittance. Maurice started learning Spanish, and with the little he acquired he was admitted to Salamanca University, one of the medieval universities that had a good reputation for medicine. Other students from our school had applied to Spanish universities, a couple of whom were accepted together with Maurice. The insistence of Palestinians on continuing their university studies was characterized by some as a search for certainty. The acquisition of a university education and the skills it entailed was something that nobody could take away. Hence this human capital is retained and ensures some sense of stability in a world that seems not to offer it any more.

My eldest brother Abel seemed to have been traumatized by the June war. He was working in the souvenir shop inside the Franciscan convent, St. Savior, by the New Gate, helping out in packing and packaging orders for visiting pilgrims. His intelligence and outstanding performance in high school would have qualified him for further education and better job opportunities than packing and packaging. Some weeks after the war, he had to leave his job and to seek medical attention. It transpired that the war had made a deep psychological impact on him, causing him to need a relaxed and comfortable environment. My parents did the best they could to help him out, but eventually he shut himself up and economized on his communication with others. To this day he is being cared for by my sister Hilda and my brother Maurice in the same Dar in the Old City. In spite of the great expectations that everyone placed on Abel because of his school performance, he apparently could not handle the stress and strain of always performing and coming out on top. It is hard indeed to be expected to deliver, especially when those who imposed the high expectations do not realize how costly these could be to the person targeted.

I was saddened by what happened to Abel, and upon return to the United States I got busy reading the literature on psychological shocks and traumas, especially since I loved my eldest brother. I still remember the day when, sitting at the dinner table together, as was our custom at home, I had an argument with Abel about socialism. When he argued that socialism could be the road for us to take, I answered him, "But, Abel, if you were not sharing the loaf of bread in front of you with me, then how could you preach socialism?" My question apparently surprised him, and, being the sensitive soul he was, he did not mention socialism again at the dinner table.

Tony, some years my junior, was seeking ways to emigrate, and he told me that his eyes were set on Australia. He was not sure how things would turn out for young Palestinians in Jerusalem and elsewhere under Israeli occupation, and hence he wanted to find a new home somewhere else. Eventually, after years of effort, he succeeded in making his way to Australia, "down under," as an immigrant.

Emigration of Christians, especially the young among us, has been continual, particularly when the political, economic, and social conditions have acted as push factors for them to leave. This was the case under Ottoman rule in the early twentieth century when hundreds of Christian families moved out of the Bethlehem area and headed to Central and South America, to Chile and Honduras in particular. During the British Mandate times, in spite of the internecine conflict going on between Jews and Arabs, emigration of Christians and of Palestinians in general abated. The 1948 war saw a major wave of forced migration as over one third of the Christian population found themselves uprooted from their homes. These eventually found their way to neighboring Arab countries, Jordan especially, and many used their temporary stay in Amman, the capital of Jordan, as a way-station in their migration to North and South America. While the emigrants from the Bethlehem and Jerusalem areas moved to South America, the emigrants from Ramallah and north of Jerusalem migrated to the U.S. Some have attributed the attraction of the U.S. for the Ramallah emigrants to the fact that the Friends Schools, for girls and boys, were set up early on in Ramallah. Others have argued that because the original immigrants from Palestine arrived in specific countries, their relatives, friends, and families were more likely to follow them there. In the 1960s the conditions of life in Jordan and Israel encouraged many of the Christians to migrate, often in whole families, to Australia. Since that time, Australia has changed its policy on potential migrants from the Middle East, but then it was accepting Palestinians and others from the Middle East who qualified for Australian residency.

Tony's yearning to immigrate to Australia was in keeping with the general trends of immigration witnessed among the general Palestinian Christian population since earlier times. I was nevertheless grateful that Hilda, Bernadette, Maurice, Therese, and David, the youngest of my siblings, continued applying themselves to their studies and did not think of relocation. I felt that women in my family were generally more robust than the men in dealing with the aftermath of the traumatic June 1967 war.

Return to Franklin and Marshall

Back at F&M I had some chats with my Jewish and other friends about what I saw and felt while on the visit to Jerusalem. In the coffee shop by the famed Protest Tree, the venue for expressing our opinions on political, social, and sexual issues—which regretfully had to be cut down in the recent past because of an incurable tree disease—I heard one day a group of Jewish students arguing that Israel was now ready to confront even the Soviet Union. I approached them and said, "Was this your expectation of Israel and its rebirth: a mighty military power?" But being a Palestinian I was in no position to lecture them on Jewish values and how different the present political and military realities were from these values. Prof. Leibowitz, a biblical scholar and a respected religion teacher, was wont to warn his fellow Israelis right after the rapid victory of June 1967 that a prolonged occupation and rule over another people would eventually erode the lofty principles and values of Judaism and would destroy the purpose of creating the State of Israel. I admired the man because I saw him as a modern-day prophet whose love for his people made him speak up about his fears of the worst scenarios to come if a solution to occupation was not found.

In the "Religion and Literature" seminar course that I took in the spring semester after my return from Jerusalem, we had a lengthy discussion on the "God is dead" controversy. In my religiously conservative society there could be no contemplation of such a wicked statement. I related to the class, nevertheless, an incident that had happened to me when I was walking one night in the dark alleys of the Old City of Jerusalem. As I approached our home with my brother Tony, a half-drunken Palestinian was walking on the other side of the street from us. Tony recognized him at once and told me that the man was a communist. In exchanging conversation with him I inadvertently encouraged him by saying that we had to trust in God's will in order to remain steadfast and not to lose hope. To my amazement, this man responded in the manner of a drunken person as he moved from one side to the other, stating that God was nowhere to be found since he had been taken captive in an Israeli tank during the June war. I was dumbfounded at this man's statement, which reflected his disappointment and uncertainty about the Almighty's role in difficult and conflictual human affairs. Certainly this statement was not to be taken seriously, as Palestinians continued to trust in the Almighty and the controversy surrounding the "God is dead" argument did not make it into the discussions and exchanges of our daily and intellectual life back in Jerusalem.

An Iraqi Assyrian professor at F&M, who himself had attended F&M in 1946, a year after I was born, and later went on to earn a PhD at

Princeton University, offered a course on the politics of the Middle East and the complexities of the relationship between the West and the Middle East. In Baghdad, where his family lived, he had attended an American school whose principal was an alumnus of F&M and offered the more promising students, like Prof. Joseph, a scholarship to attend F&M. What made the course relevant to me was the fact that Prof. Joseph was the son of refugees from a genocide that the Assyrians suffered in Persia. I attended one of his courses and learned much about regional developments back home. He defended the Palestinians and presented their cause as a just cause in need of peaceful resolution. Most of his students were Jewish, but almost all were impressed with his objective interpretation of developments in the Middle East. I remember that on one of the weekends when students were holding celebrations of some sort, Prof. Joseph offered to present the Israeli version of Middle East history and the conflict with the neighboring Arabs for a sum to be contributed to the Student Fund. I listened to his magnanimous offer together with scores of students who applauded him warmly at the end of his presentations.

Another faculty member who impressed me was the young and handsome French professor, Prof. Bentley, whose death in an apartment fire at the age of thirty shocked all of us at F&M. I had just finished a course of French literature in English with Prof. Bentley and had read, among others, Malraux, Gide, and Albert Camus. In particular I was intrigued by *The Plague* of Camus and reflected on it in class discussions of the novel. Prof. Bentley gave us the final exam a couple of weeks before the tragic accident, and in the last session he gave us back our exams, on which he had indicated our final grades. He gave me an "A" for the course. When I asked him after class why he gave me this high grade, his answer was that, of all the students' written responses to the exam question posed on this novel of Camus, mine was the only essay to give a convincingly different answer. Prof. Bentley, God bless his soul, decided that I had earned an "A" grade in the course for this answer. I only wish that life were so easy!

This course grade of "A," although I was a "B" student overall, was repeated with Prof. Michalak, who taught the course on China and Japan. I took the course because I knew absolutely nothing about these two fascinating countries. My intention was to explore the society, culture, and politics of these two societies. Fascinated by the course, I embarked upon an examination of the reasons why Japan, a society that is based on the family, has succeeded in prospering economically while still maintaining its family and other traditions. Was it self-discipline? Or did the culture itself make it possible to save on unnecessary expenses and hence evolve into some sort of capitalist economy? Why have my own society and in fact the

Arab and Muslim region, in spite of family attachment and centrality, failed to develop such economic trends as existed in Japan at the time and were starting to be exhibited also in China? I was doing well in the course, asking these and similar questions, but my biggest surprise was when I received the final grade for the course. Prof. Michalak, a young, energetic member of the Department of Political Science, decided that I deserved an "A" grade. When I went to the International House, one of my Honduran friends told me that the professors liked me because I played up to them and hence they gave me the higher grades. When I asked Prof. Michalak why he gave me the "A" grade, his answer was similar to that given to me by Prof. Bentley: "You have earned it because on the question on Japan your answer was the only one that was exceptional and to the point."

Two challenging and quite different courses appealed to me at F&M. One was called "Egyptology and the Arts and Treasures of Ancient Egypt." Even though I came from a country geographically close to Egypt, I did not know anything about the great civilization with its riches that was the Pharaohs' Egypt. Accordingly I decided to register for the course, which turned out to be "photographic," meaning that the professor would show us one slide after another on the riches of ancient Egypt with corresponding comments and explanations highlighting contextual and historical background. This was an exciting course that challenged me to keep taking accurate notes and to activate my memory to remember what each photo symbolized together with the narrative behind it. I did well in the course when I earned a "C" grade, and I thanked the professor for his kind understanding of my limitations.

The other course was "Afro-American Literature," which I took in my third or fourth year. This was a pioneering course, taught by three or four professors, which looked at the development of Afro-American literature throughout the history of the presence of Black Americans on the continent. In reality this was a political course at a time when Black Americans were discovering the beauty of being black and taking pride in it. The professors, who were too permissive, told us at the beginning of the course that we could read the materials, submit term papers, and choose to take or not to take the final exam as well as to attend or not to attend classes. I took their advice, went to a number of lectures at the beginning of the semester, kept reading the material, and produced a term paper on the experience of Black Americans as expressed through religious hymns.

I was intrigued by the hymn that spoke of crossing the Jordan and finding salvation, signifying the hope that made Black Americans a persevering group in spite of all kinds of difficulties and odds. Another Afro-American hymn that spoke to me was the one that repeated, "Sometimes I feel like a motherless child." The feeling of being motherless was not simply a result of losing one's mother or of not knowing who one's mother was, as it reflected a broader existentialist feeling of loss, whether of homeland or of roots, and of enslavement and estrangement and the absence of protection for the individual and group, with the surrounding world not caring about what was happening. But I also learned about _The Fire Next Time_ (by James Baldwin), which reflected on the deep disappointments of Black Americans in a racially segregated society. I felt that the overall experience of Black Americans in the U.S. related to me and to the experience of my own people. The fire that was always burning in the hearts of the refugees and stateless people who left Palestine in 1948 was not extinguished, and there was trepidation that this fire may one day consume much more than simply the people who were living it. This was truly a learning experience, and I appreciated the fact that F&M at that time was pioneering and willing to experiment with various teaching techniques and topics in order to respond to the realities of the times. In fact, I have kept the paper that I wrote for the course, and once in a while I return to it for rejuvenation.

Two courses that enriched my knowledge, taught by Prof. Frederick Klein, were on American history. Manifest Destiny and the Civil War were the focus of readings, discussions, and lectures. Prof. Klein's lectures were stimulating if one was ready to listen attentively to his detailed narratives of historical events and their causes and effects. I admired the kindness of the man but also his vast knowledge of American history with anecdotal references to the minutest of details. He reminded me of my high school History teacher, who would tell us precisely what day and time Napoleon Bonaparte threw his hat over the Acre Wall. I concluded from attending the two courses on American history that history was the art of narrating and that narration could indeed explore dimensions of which most of us would never be aware. As Prof. Klein was absorbed in historical narration, he was occasionally in the habit of playing with his tie. When this happened, most of us students were concentrating on his tie as he rolled it upward and then let it roll back down, with some of us anticipating at what point the tie's direction would be reversed. But in spite of the tie-rolling performance, most students did come back to attend Prof. Klein's courses as I myself did because of the wealth of knowledge on American history that the man possessed.

Political Unrest

On one afternoon in the fall semester of 1968, while in a sociology class (sociology was my major at F&M), we heard a commotion out in front of Old Maine, where the class was being held. Looking out of the window, we spotted no other than Mohammed Ali, formerly Cassius Clay, as he was walking around the campus, invited by the college and a number of student groups, including Black American students. We were tempted to go down and say hello to him, but our professor, Prof. Eshelman, God bless his soul, advised us to rein in our emotions and to greet him later on, when he would have a scheduled meeting with the student body. At this meeting he demonstrated his boxing skills and expressed his political views on the Black experience, the Vietnam War, and other issues of inequality and racism in American society. These views were not particularly popular with the majority of Americans at the time. But the moral and ethical stature that Mohammed Ali developed, his opening up to others, his picking up on issues pertaining to human rights, that is, a society for all of its citizens, and his maintaining an affinity with America eventually endeared him to a wider American audience. The late sixties were the time when Black Americans discovered pride in "Black is Beautiful," and Mohammed Ali, among other promising Black American leaders, offered vision and hope. Inviting Mohammed Ali to the F&M campus was a sign of the times and an affirmation that all women and men were created equal.

F&M in the late sixties was not immune to the repercussions of the Vietnam War. The nightly news, which reported the number of American soldiers killed amidst a continuing conflict that was costly to all, only intensified the anti-war emotions among students. A Lancaster friend, whose father was a prominent lawyer in town and who had turned into a hippie, introduced me to Students for a Democratic Society (SDS). This was a leftist organization that opposed the Vietnam War and called for its quick termination. I attended a couple of meetings on campus just as a silent observer and to learn for myself how student activists were set to organize. Someone later told me that there were more "eyes" for the law enforcement agencies than actual SDS members or sympathizers at the meetings. But the SDS was part of a trend of a growing anti-war sentiment and movement sweeping across the campuses and among young people across the U.S.

When my hippie Lancaster friend got married, he invited me to his wedding in a nearby park, where he entered in his hippie clothes with his bride similarly dressed. It was a beautiful and simple event of exchanging vows, but I was sure that the middle-class parents of the happy couple, some of whom failed to attend, did not approve of the way the wedding was conducted or of the attire worn by the bride and bridegroom for the occasion.

Values are a reflection of the social bond of the group, and when one chooses to challenge these values, presumably one has chosen to become an outsider to the group. Others, nevertheless, placed the different values of young and old during the sixties in the context of a changing world and the role of America in it. There was also the questioning by young Americans of whether the capitalist system was the best for responding to the complexity of the social, economic, racial, and political challenges of American society. As the First Lady, Lady Bird Johnson, was determined to make of Washington, D.C., an international mecca of sorts, and as she worked to give the capital of the United States a facelift by planting gardens and flower beds all over, thousands were marching to the same city under the leadership of Martin Luther King, demanding equality, and thousands of others were insisting on the end of the Vietnam War. What had started as a protest movement on U.S. campuses ended up as a political consensus among the majority of the population on the need to pull out of Vietnam and to "bring the boys back home."

These were exciting and exhilarating times in the U.S., which reflected the vibrancy of American society seeking answers to the changing times. Clearly the society of the sixties was not happy, but admirably it was soul-searching. The role played on campus at F&M by my Jewish friends in leading the protests and actively participating in challenging the U.S. Administration's policies and actions on Vietnam was eye-opening to me. I was impressed with the insistence of my Jewish friends on the need to address the issues that divided Americans—not only the Vietnam War but also those pertaining to social and racial justice. I only wished that my Jewish friends had developed the same sentiments toward the injustice that befell the Palestinians following the 1948 war and would seek ways to redress the injustice. I used to argue with some of my friends that full justice in Palestine was not possible, but asked whether we could find a middle way. And could we give hope to thousands of Palestinian youth who were exasperated by their status as refugees with no hope for the future? These were issues that unfortunately continue at present to beg for answers.

Friendships

The F&M experience was truly enriching because of the opportunity for friendships with American roommates. My first-year roommate, Chris, was engrossed in the Green Room, which was the drama facility of the college.

Unfortunately, as he was driving back to the college one early morning after seeing a play in New York City, he had a car accident that necessitated the amputation of his left leg. I visited him in the hospital to wish him well and to uplift his spirits. This appalling accident forced him to withdraw from the college for one semester. This was the last I saw of Chris, but I followed his news and learned that he did come back to the college and eventually pursued an acting and media career.

My two other impressive American roommates and friends were Jack from Hershey, Pennsylvania, and Brian from Baltimore, Maryland. Jack and I developed a close relationship as we got to know one another and to appreciate our different backgrounds. I was invited several times to visit with his family in nearby Hershey and was warmly received by his father, who was part of the team that produced the world-famous Hershey chocolate "kisses." Jack's mother was a sweet lady who cared about Jack and showed her warmth in superb hospitality. It was a hard-working and caring family that sought to educate their children and open up prospects and opportunities for advancement for them. I liked this emphasis on education by Jack's family as it reminded me of my parents' insistence on sending us to the best high schools, both girls and boys, in order to provide the proper basis for further education and advancement. I kept in touch with Jack as I visited with him in Lancaster a couple of times after my graduation. We still maintain contact via social media, and we have remained faithful to the friendship we built back at F&M.

My other friend, Brian, pursued individual interests as he sought to understand the Middle East and its different cultures. I think he was for some time fascinated with those "foreign students" who seemed to be quite proficient in languages and who had had a different cultural and social experience from his own. As we bonded to each other, Brian invited me to his home, and we used to travel together across the Lancaster landscape and even for longer distances, as we did during my last summer at F&M, when we headed to Canada to visit with some friends there. As we drove through Bethlehem, Pennsylvania, early on a summer morning, Brian went through a red light, but luckily there was no traffic or police around. But as soon as we reached the highway, Brian told me that he would like to speed up to the maximum capacity of his car, 180 miles an hour or so, to get the feeling of how speedy the car could be and the feeling of speed itself. Luckily Brian was not on "speed" (the illegal drug), but he wanted to have the experience. I crossed myself and left it to the Almighty to guide my friend. On our trip to Canada, we went as far as Quebec City and Chicoutimi up north. I still remember how we arrived at Chicoutimi at around three or four in the morning and decided to take a nap in the car. At around eight or nine in the morning we moved to town and there met a young woman who, when we asked her where we could find student lodging, offered to host us at her home. This was a delightful gesture that pointed to the close-knit and welcoming environment that existed in the town of Chicoutimi. What surprised me, though, was the fact that when we dropped by the hotel in town on a Saturday evening, there was a tango-dancing party where most of the dancers were of Lebanese origin. The last time I saw Brian was in Jerusalem a couple of years ago when we had lunch together with our wives. Brian and his Jewish wife visited the Holy Land in order to learn for themselves about the sites that make of the Land a holy place indeed.

Among the foreign students with whom long-lasting friendships developed was Jürgen from Germany. An English language teacher in the beautiful and tranquil town of Baden Baden, he had come to the U.S. for a year of exchange in which he had hoped to be introduced to American culture and society. Jürgen and I developed an enduring friendship that has spanned our adult lives. He visited with my wife and me in Jerusalem and attended the weddings of two of our children: the one celebrated for Zack and Lisa in Jerusalem and the other for Margo and Paul in Edinburgh. We, in turn, visited with him in Baden Baden, where we were introduced to his eightyish mother, who knew of our friendship from F&M times. When Barbara and he decided to wed, Jürgen asked me to stand at his side, but Barbara wanted a male "maid of honor" at her side; so Mary, my wife, was Jürgen's maid of honor, or witness. We continue to visit with one another, and whenever I have an opportunity to see him while on a visit to Germany, I always seize it. Likewise, Barbara and Jürgen are keen on staying in contact with us in Jerusalem. Our latest meeting in June of 2017 took place in Strasbourg, France, the seat of the Council of Europe, where I represent Palestine in the Parliamentary Assembly of the Council. Mary accompanied me for the parliamentary meeting, and we all enjoyed a Brazilian meal while reminiscing about the good old days in Lancaster, Pennsylvania, and the other places where we have met and renewed our friendship.

At college Jürgen's roommate in the International House was Gordon from Chicago, but the two could not get along. The year Jürgen arrived at F&M, I was the dorm counselor of the International House, so I had to interact with each and every one of the residents and follow up on any problems or contingencies that may have arisen. Gordon confided in me his worldview and told me that his parents had warned him about striking up any friendships or relations with any of the international students, particularly those from the Middle East. He assured his parents that the Middle Easterners at the International House were a special category, different from the images that his parents held of Middle Easterners in general.

I was not flattered by this, nor was the somewhat condescending behavior of Gordon welcomed by his roommate or the other American and foreign students in the dorm. It was perhaps because of this antipathy that a group of residents of the International House, including the Swede Robert (who, years later, became a professor of psychology at a Midwestern university), decided in an impromptu manner to play a practical joke on Gordon. The trick made him believe that by a certain maneuver he could rerecord on the vinyl music record that was then popular any piece of music to his liking. The trick went on for days, and when I thought that enough was enough, I asked my peers in the dorm to put a stop to it. But the problem was how to convince Gordon that all was a practical joke created by his roommates and fellow dorm residents and that there was no basis in reality for this fabricated musical invention. It was my responsibility to do precisely this, and the poor guy almost had a nervous breakdown when he realized that it was all a practical joke indeed.

A real nervous breakdown nevertheless afflicted Amos, the tall and slim student from Sudan. Living across from me in the suite of four rooms, he started complaining that there were people out there against him. One day when we were having lunch in the cafeteria, he started shouting and accusing me of wanting to kill him. I realized immediately that he was having some sort of serious breakdown, and I immediately went to the Dean of Students and to the F&M infirmary to seek help. Amos received help and calmed down. He went on to finish his BA without any further disturbances.

A Yemeni student who went on to study medicine was having difficulty adjusting, and culturally he was in shock at being at F&M and in America. Having arrived from a tribal, traditional, conservative, and religious society in one that was individualistic, modern, liberal to an extent, and not outwardly religious, Mohammed had difficulty adjusting. Besides, he had a problem in following the lectures in class. I passed on to him what an upperclassman, whose family originally hailed from Ramallah, had told me when I started college at F&M: "Go to the professor, and explain to him or her your problem, and do not be shy about it." He followed this advice, and at least in a couple of classes he was able to record the lectures and to listen to them later on.

Another student who had difficulty with the language was Ahmed from Tulkarem, northwest of Nablus in the West Bank. His English was so minimal that the poor guy had to read the assignments line by line and word by word in order to understand the meanings of sentences. He had an English-Arabic dictionary by his side, which he used to translate into Arabic the many English words he could not comprehend. I looked one time at one of the pages he was reading and was shocked to see that practically every other word was translated into Arabic. This translation task took him hours to do, and some nights he was not able to go to sleep before sunrise because of his determination to finish a reading assignment for a morning class. I helped him somewhat, but, because of my own schedule and obligations, could not do it in a regular or intensive way. In any case, Ahmed had to move away in junior year because the weather in Lancaster affected a health condition that he had and he needed to be in a dry climate. Years later I received an internet message from one of his children informing me that Ahmed was alive and well and that he was practicing medicine in an Arab country. I communicated with him and wished that we could meet again one of these days to reminisce about our time in Lancaster. It was with Ahmed that one summer I spent a couple of nights in the television room of the Lancaster Theological Seminary, which is across from F&M, because no room was available in the dorms for these nights. This happened after my graduation from F&M, at the time of my impending move to the University of Virginia and when Ahmed was preparing to leave Lancaster for a drier climate.

An exceptional student was no other than Farhad from Iran. In the first few weeks following his arrival in Lancaster, he was busy trying to contact no other than the CIA, which he wanted so badly to join. He wrote letters and even submitted forms for this purpose, but to no avail. Someone advised him that if the CIA wanted him, they would contact him directly with no need for any initial communication on his part. He was a royalist since his father had worked with the Shah's government in Iran. His failure to join the CIA was compensated by his overwhelming success in sexual advances to the women he met in Lancaster, some of whom he invited to F&M for a visit. Some argued with him that he could not go on disregarding the sentiments of his fellow dorm mates by inviting women successively to his room. He calmed some of them down, but continued to be known throughout the four years of his stay at F&M as the "prince charming." He went on to work in Information Technology and joined a company on Wall Street, where he still works. Although I stay in contact with him periodically, I have never asked him if the CIA ever contacted him with a job offer.

From Honduras we had two students living in the International House, Carlos and José. Both came from very wealthy families and to an extent kept to themselves. Carlos used to tell me that the Palestinians who had migrated to Honduras over the years had taken over much of the economy, and their success was compared to the success of the Jewish community in the U.S. He encouraged me to visit Honduras and to look for a wife there from the Palestinian community, as the Honduran Palestinians would only intermarry with other Palestinians. I might get lucky, he suggested, and start both my own family and a successful business linked to my prospective wife's family. One summer we heard the sad news that José, always smiling and a shy, well-behaved young man, had died together with his father in a car accident on a mountain road in Honduras.

Speaking of marital prospects and related matters, I recall the privilege of getting to know Carolyn when she was on a visit to Jerusalem in the summer of 1966. I had invited her home to share a family meal with us. She was from Maryland, and when I told her that I had been accepted to F&M, she said that since Lancaster was not far away from Baltimore, we should certainly get together after I settled down at my college. When I arrived in Lancaster, I let Carolyn know, and in the first couple of weeks she came over. We enjoyed seeing *2001: A Space Odyssey* in the Fulton Theatre, the pride of Lancaster for its history of theatrical performances and symphony concerts. Our relationship was platonic. At one time I contemplated proposing, but Carolyn did not encourage me, as I sounded more confused than serious. I still remain in occasional contact with Carolyn, including one time when I visited Washington, D.C., in 2005. We continue to exchange Christmas greetings faithfully.

The second significant relationship was with Jane, who hailed from a nearby town close to Lancaster. I don't recall our first meeting, but we did have a friendship that lasted for over three years. Jane and I keep in touch occasionally over Facebook, and I have not had an opportunity to see her again in spite of the fact that I have visited the U.S. several times since my graduation from F&M in 1970. Friendships with the opposite sex were difficult for me to deal with because I came from a conservative and repressive society. It takes much more than the occasional encounter with the opposite sex to appreciate that a healthy relationship depends not only on physical attraction but also on being sensitive to a partner's expectations and readings on the relationship.

Travels

The office of the Dean of Students at F&M organized a couple of trips for the foreign students to see some aspects of American society. For one of these trips, we hired a van to go to Philadelphia on a Saturday evening for a cultural event intended for international students in the metropolitan area. We were accompanied by a young Assistant Professor of Anthropology, Carole, who on entering the van noticed that I crossed myself in preparation for the trip. Carole asked me the significance of the gesture that I had just performed, and I explained to her that back home, whenever we started on a ride or other events, we usually crossed ourselves for benediction and safety. As Akira, a student from Japan, was driving the van rather nervously, we found ourselves unexpectedly turning around on the highway facing the direction of oncoming traffic. Luckily there was no approaching traffic. After Akira managed to turn around to align the van with the flow of traffic, I advised him to pull over onto the shoulder of the road and asked another person to take over the driving. The new driver, a Portuguese student, did well indeed. Prof. Carole told me that perhaps it was crossing myself that had saved us from a serious car accident.

Akira was never happy with the F&M International House and with the college in general. He was from a family whose wealth came from its internationally acclaimed fashion business in Japan, and his mother often traveled to the U.S. for the high fashion shows in different cities. F&M was a middle- to upper-middle-class college, while the international students often came from modest backgrounds; this circumstance was not pleasing to Akira, who eventually decided to move on to a more prestigious college.

On April 4, 1968, we students arrived in Washington, D.C., in the early evening and settled down in our hotel rooms not far from the historic sights and monuments. Hours later we heard some commotion and saw fires burning in different places. The news of the assassination of the Reverend Martin Luther King Jr. in a Memphis hotel had saddened America and sent shock waves across the country. Some youths took to the streets, and there was absolute disorder, including looting, burning, and violent confrontations with the law enforcement agencies in several cities, including the capital city of the U.S. Rioting youth took over neighborhoods within blocks of the White House, which we were planning to visit the following day. With the scenes of rioting all around us, the decision was made to head back to Lancaster early the next morning.

Reverend King inspired all of us with his nonviolence and his insistence on equality for all. His dreams became the dreams of millions of people not only in the U.S. but all over the world. When I arranged the visit of the Reverend Jesse Jackson to Ramallah on July 31, 2002, during the Second Intifada, in my capacity as director of the Department of Service to Palestinian Refugees of the Middle East Council of Churches, the inspiration of Reverend King for nonviolence was felt and repeated by Reverend Jackson, who called for cessation of all violence between Israelis and Palestinians. As we crossed the infamous Qalandiya Checkpoint, Reverend Jackson instructed his group, among whom there were some Jewish rabbis and civil rights activists from the Chicago area, not to argue with the Israeli soldiers who would come onto the bus to check our identity cards. He emphasized that it was very important not to provoke a person carrying arms, including soldiers and others on duty. I learned an important lesson from Reverend Jackson: that any provocation of a person carrying arms could be considered as a reason to use the arms. This scenario has been also part of the story of Palestinians under Israeli rule, as the Israelis have usually carried arms and some were always ready to use them upon the slightest provocation.

In January 1969 Robert, an American roommate and friend, and I headed to Washington, D.C., to attend the Inauguration of President Richard Nixon and his Vice President Spiro Agnew (of "law and order" renown). While not a fan of any political party or candidate, I wanted to watch the Inauguration parade and to get the feeling of what it meant for Americans to have a new president elected every four years. Standing on a cold January morning on a Washington street while governors of various states passed by, I was thrilled to see these famous people in person. My friend Robert used to shout the first name of each governor who passed us, perhaps reflecting the fact that these governors had become famous or well-known publicly because of the votes given them by people like Robert. For me this was a practical lesson in democracy that I appreciated. We did not have the chance to catch a glimpse of the president as his motorcade went by, but we were happy that we took part in this important and significant event.

Examining Faith

At F&M I started to search for the meaning of religion. When Prof. Dewey, God bless his soul, of the Department of Religion mentioned in a lecture the proposition that religion could be as addictive as any addiction a person might have, this got me thinking. Why did I have to resort to religion and to prayer whenever I faced a crisis, or why did I have to attend Sunday Mass and felt guilty if I did not? Were the religious observances of my own father an addiction that helped him regulate his life and reduced the effects of the stress and strain of daily living and the traumas that he had experienced? What about inner peace, and could one have it without necessarily being religious?

These challenging questions on religion and its potentially addictive influence led me to scrutinize my own religiosity. It also helped me in the process of examining my own Roman Catholic background and of searching in other religions for comparisons and answers. Particularly impressed by the Quakers, I attended a service that was enormously different from the Sunday Mass to which I was accustomed. I started reading the Qur'an seriously and embarked on writing a couple of course papers on Islam. I wanted to learn about the religion of the majority of my own people and my own friends back home. Unfortunately I had not learned about Islam in my high school in Jerusalem, as any discussion of religion, especially others' religions, was not part of our school curriculum. I read about Unitarianism and had a discussion with some of its followers in order to understand their belief and how it reflected itself in practice. I picked up a couple of books on Buddhism and Confucianism and began exploring the principles that guided a majority of the world's population.

It was an element of growing up for me to open up to other religions and to realize that the truth was not in the sole possession of one religion in contrast to other religions, in spite of protestations to the contrary by this or that religious group. I learned that each religion had its own truth but that the proof of one's belief in its truth was in the practice of the lofty ideals and values enshrined in each and every religion. Differences in culture and religion add valuable flavor to life and offer a kaleidoscopic variety that otherwise would be absent if everyone subscribed to the same belief and world-view.

At a certain point, especially in my sophomore year, I felt that I needed some spiritual counseling. I rang up the local parish priest of the Roman Catholic church that sat a short distance down the road from the college. When I entered his office, the sixtyish priest welcomed me but shocked me the moment he spoke. He asked me if I were in need of financial help as if my visit were for that purpose. Perhaps my looks, someone suggested later, made the Reverend priest believe that the only reason for a visit to him by someone like me would have been for the financial side of life. Our meeting did not last long. I thanked him promptly and informed him that I often attended Mass on Sundays at his church. Afterwards I reflected on this visit with my friends in the dorm and wondered whether, if I had gone to a banker or financial officer of a lending institution, his first question to me would have been something like, "Son, are you in need of spiritual support?" This incident made me question the stereotypes that caused us to categorize people in certain ways and hence prohibited us from seeing people in their own right and without the presuppositions that made it impossible to communicate with them as human person to human person.

At Sunday Mass I was amazed at the number of congregants who partook of Holy Communion. I thought that this act should be ideal for the creation of a community spirit that would embrace all worshipers, including youngsters like myself. I was disappointed that this was not so, and it led me to think that partaking of Holy Communion was perceived more as adherence to an individual routine rather than an indication of willingness to be part of an encompassing communal church solidarity.

Another incident of a religious nature came one summer afternoon in my junior year as I was strolling across the F&M campus. I had by then adopted the mode of dress prevalent in the late sixties: T-shirt, blue jeans, and sandals with my hair presenting a hippie-like appearance. A tall man approached me with what appeared to be a Bible under his arm. He greeted me and asked whether I was a believer in Jesus Christ. I said indeed I was. Did I read the Bible? Yes, I told him, but in Arabic. With no comment from him on the Arabic Bible, he proceeded to ask me if I had been baptized. I told him yes, I had been, and that my parents had had me baptized when I was a baby. He was not satisfied with my answer, and he retorted that he was talking about being immersed in holy water. When I said that I had not been baptized that way, he affirmed that indeed I had not been baptized. He came back to ask me once again whether I was a believer in Jesus Christ. At this juncture I wanted to get this man off my back, so I started thinking of a strategy. When he repeated his question on whether I believed in Jesus Christ, I looked him in the eyes and came up with a response that I never forgot: "Would you believe me, sir, if I tell you that not only do I believe in Jesus Christ, but Jesus Christ and I practically grew up in the same neighborhood?" This man could not believe what I had just said, and he walked away thinking that I was some sort of deranged individual.

Summer Employment

During the last two summers at F&M I was hired to help out with national institutes that trained their members at the college. We were a small team and were free to come to work any time we wanted, but our duties involved writing checks and following up on reimbursements for the participating members, making sure that all details of lodging, food plans, and travel were well taken care of and that any problem was immediately addressed. While I came some days to the office at a very late hour, the person in charge of running the office always praised me as well as my American colleague for our performance. I remember him saying that if all graduates of F&M could handle successfully what we handled in the impromptu summer office, then F&M was indeed a successful learning institution.

Student Protests

The most memorable and exhausting experience that I had at F&M came in my last semester there when in the spring of 1970 the college administration decided not to rehire the "radical" professor of history Henry Mayer.

A hundred or so students took over the administration offices at East Hall; the timing of this action coincided with the events at Kent State University and student protests across the country against the Vietnam War and the plans to invade Cambodia. Since I was by then a "student leader," I could not allow myself not to take part in the sit-in or takeover. When I entered East Hall, I realized at once that the students were without a leader. I took it upon myself to lead, and together with some key students made a proclamation to the students in East Hall that nothing should be done to harm the offices or the equipment inside them. The students cooperated with our announcement, and they did indeed behave very well.

After an overnight of occupying East Hall, I consulted with other student leaders on the need to open up a dialogue with the college administration. President Spalding, a fine university educator and administrator of the highest caliber, had made the decision not to involve the local law enforcement agencies in ending the takeover. This made things easier for me since the specter of being deported from the United States because of my involvement was at the back of my mind. We went to President Spalding's residence and started negotiations. We argued that it was important that we keep Prof. Mayer and asked whether, if we were to raise the needed $10,000, the college administration would allow him to teach on campus. President Spalding promised to examine the question and to relay to us the answer as soon as possible but insisted on the need to evacuate East Hall. My view was that, if the answer was positive, then the situation was on its way to an honorable solution.

We returned to the students at East Hall, and I offered my one-hundred-dollar bill to start raising the money needed to hire Prof. Mayer as the "People's Professor" for the 1970–1971 academic year. I had insisted that if the administration would go along with our efforts at keeping Prof. Mayer on campus, then we should immediately evacuate East Hall and go on with our usual student activities and class attendance. Things worked out well, thanks to the wisdom of President Spalding. At one of the meetings that the administration held in the aftermath of the takeover, there was a reference to the efforts of one foreign student at ending the whole episode peacefully and with minimal harm to F&M. I cared for F&M and never contemplated any activity that would harm the college that had offered me a full four-year scholarship and invested in my education and personal development.

Another political incident, which preceded the East Hall takeover, involved a petition that some students had circulated against selling advanced U.S. fighter planes to Israel. I signed the petition, and when I went to East Hall for some business with the Dean of Students, the elderly secretary who usually welcomed me with a warm smile and a hello did not want to speak to me. When I noticed her shunning me, I approached her wanting to know what was wrong. She explained that she was unhappy with my adding my signature to the petition. Apparently whatever I did on campus had become public knowledge. I explained to the good lady that these planes would eventually be involved in military acts that would target also innocent Palestinians and that instead of sending war planes to Israel perhaps the U.S. administration and Congress should be advised on how to promote peace between Israel and its Arab and Palestinian neighbors. I did not know if she was ever convinced by my argument, but the next time around at East Hall, the lady was kind enough to resume her warm greetings.

Graduation

In preparation for the graduation ceremony in June 1970, I went to Robert Hall Clothes in Lancaster to buy a couple of decent outfits for the occasion and discovered that they were having a sale on most items. I chose the least expensive items. When it was time to settle the account, I spoke with the branch manager, beginning the conversation by giving him a briefing on my family background and asking him about his own. It was this personal touch that made it possible for me to bargain further with him on the sale, which, if I recall correctly, amounted to approximately two hundred dollars. As a result of the bargaining skills that I had learned from my Aunt Leonie, this sum was reduced by some 10 percent over and above the discount that the manager told me was reserved for only the most loyal clients of the store. My roommates and friends at the dorm had a good laugh when I told them about the bargaining, and someone remarked that this kind of thing never happened in America.

At the graduation ceremony, which was attended by Mr. Snyder from Knoxville, Tennessee, the father of my friend from the summer camp in Monterrey, Tennessee, I wore my newly purchased outfit and a sign that read something like this: "Would you remain silent if 1984 were to happen?" The graduation ceremony was characterized by a score of the graduates wearing protest signs with statements on the war in Vietnam, on the killings at Kent State University, and on other events of the turbulent sixties. But overall it was a graduation in which the issues and concerns of America were reflected both in the address of the commencement speaker, Benjamin DeMott, Amherst College Professor of English, and in the attire of some of the graduating students. But it was also the culmination of four years at an academically excellent college that made a world of difference for me and for my world-view. I remain thankful to F&M, and a couple of times when I returned to the U.S., I took the opportunity to visit Lancaster and to be with my friend and old roommate Jack, who worked for the local newspaper. The memories of F&M remain, and I often recall the popular song title[2] from 1968: "Those Were the Days!"

2. The song was recorded by Mary Hopkin.

3

Graduate Studies:
The American Interlude, Part Two

The Master's Degree: Research on Palestinian Society

WHEN BRIAN AND I took the trip to Canada at the beginning of August 1970, I missed the application deadline for a PhD program, with full scholarship, at Southern Illinois University. I had applied to this university because it offered a high quality sociology program and with the package it offered I could go through the PhD program without any financial problems. But now that Southern Illinois University was out of the question for my graduate studies, I decided to pursue the last option available to me: the Sociology Department at the University of Virginia (UVA) in Charlottesville. I was made to understand that UVA was a tough place to get into for a person of my background. Being Palestinian in the early seventies was not without its challenges, what with the civil war in Jordan between Palestinians and the Jordanian Arab Army as well as the hijacking of planes and other activities undertaken by Palestinian guerilla groups that were intended to bring to the attention of the world the plight of the Palestinian people. To be accepted into UVA would have meant that several taboos had indeed been broken: the enrollment of a Palestinian with a "hippie-like" appearance, and with liberal views that might not be easily grasped at Jefferson's university, would be a radical departure from the status quo. I was determined, nevertheless, to do everything possible to become part of the UVA tradition. Not that UVA reminded me of the epic movie about the Southern aristocracy *Gone with the Wind*, which I had seen two or three times in Jerusalem; clearly things had changed since the Civil War, and UVA, in spite of the insistence of some Southern families on traditions, had become relatively more open to the realities of a changing world.

One September day I made my way to UVA and started exploring the place. Since I did not have any lodging secured for the night, I began my day by asking students about affordable accommodation. One student, who appeared more like a hippie than a studious graduate student, invited me to stay with him and his girlfriend for the night. I accepted gladly since with my limited means I could not afford the cost of a night's stay at some of the hotels close to the university. My recollection is that my host and his girlfriend were so welcoming that they offered me a puff on a marijuana cigarette apparently laced with some stronger substance. I was anxious lest a police raid might take place and I might find myself in jeopardy not only with regard to the prospects of being accepted by the Sociology Department but most likely of being deported from the country altogether. Luckily my worst fears did not materialize, and I was set for the following day to meet with a variety of people at the University to convince them that my acceptance in the graduate program of the Department of Sociology would be an asset to the program.

I went first to see Prof. Coughlin, head of the department. From the little research I had done on him, I had learned that he was a Quaker, that his affiliation with UVA spanned at least three decades, and that he was about to retire. He asked me why I was intent on coming to UVA, and my answer was that I saw an opportunity at the University that would enable me to earn my Master's degree in a twelve-month period. I made him to understand that I was not interested in politics despite the fact that my appearance at the time suggested that I was an activist or, if not, then certainly anti-establishment. The hour-long discussion yielded some approval from Prof. Coughlin in support of my acceptance to UVA, provided that Mrs. Lucy Hale, International Students Advisor, gave her approval.

I moved from Prof. Coughlin's office to Mrs. Hale's. As soon as I laid my eyes on her, she reminded me of my Aunt Angele, wife of my Uncle Rock, in Amman. She was a slender lady, probably in her early sixties; she sat rigidly upright and exuded an authoritarian air with a stern facial look that, with her Southern accent, made me feel doomed. My approach to Mrs. Hale was simple and straightforward: I am here because I want to earn a Master's degree in as short a time as possible. I promised that I would not be a troublemaker and that I would be out of UVA in twelve months. Something in me convinced Mrs. Hale of my sincerity; my conjecture was that it was my Christian background or that she was in such a mood as to agree to the acceptance of one Palestinian student whose name sounded Italian, who spoke fluent English, and who was eager to make good on his determination to finish his Master's thesis in as short a time as possible, in spite of his appearance. I went out of her office with a good feeling, and when I bade goodbye to Prof. Coughlin, he promised that I would get an answer within a week's time.

As I prepared to move to UVA, my friend Jack from Franklin and Marshall volunteered to transport me and the few belongings I had in his late fifties van. I asked him a couple of times if the van would make it to UVA and back, and he assured me that it was in top mechanical condition. When we arrived in Charlottesville, we started looking for a room in a shared apartment. Eventually we found an apartment within walking distance from the campus, and I signed the lease for a twelve-month period. The rent was too high for my limited means, but the Department of Sociology had offered me a Teaching Assistantship that covered my tuition fees and provided me with a stipend that would barely cover my living expenses. As I settled down, I came to know that my roommate, from a rural area in southern Virginia, was a graduate student in the English Department, and, like me, he had been offered a Teaching Assistantship. He was a very quiet neighbor, and I tried my best to honor his love for quietness and for working silently. He was a smoker as I was, having picked up the habit in my sophomore year at F&M. We did not exchange much conversation as each kept to his own room, and I often spent most of my time in the library and in the coffee shop of the Student Center.

One evening my roommate informed me that he was quitting the university. His reason was that he could not be a judge of other students' work in undergraduate courses. He found himself in a moral dilemma when awarding or refraining from awarding a certain grade to the students. He told me that this kind of academic undertaking was not to his liking because it put him on a collision course with his inner self and because he felt that grading did not give a fair assessment of the student's overall academic work. I was sorry to see him go but was impressed with his honesty to himself and to his values.

One thing that stood out at the University of Virginia was the Student Honor Code. Each student, upon getting accepted to the university, had to sign the Code. Then on every exam or other academic activity the Code was honored repeatedly. We became quite conscientious about signing and committing ourselves to behavior befitting the Honor Code. Whenever there was an assignment in one of the courses, we would ask the professor if it were permissible for the students to work on the assignment together. Plagiarizing of any kind was considered a breach of the Honor Code, and the usual punishment was expulsion from the University.

I had some misgivings about the Honor Code, in part because of its implementation: it encouraged some to report others, often out of personal vendettas, and the Honor Code student peer review was under pressure to stick to the rules by arriving at a judgment of expulsion in cases that did not merit such harsh punishment. Suspension from the University for one or more semesters was a standard verdict for those students fortunate enough not to be expelled. But in general the Honor Code emphasized that the University is a community based on trust and that an individual belonging to the community should commit herself or himself to honoring the rules of the University. While individual students pursued their academic careers and strove to excel, there were also guidelines and values that needed to be respected. The achievement of a university student should be her or his own and not borrowed from others.

The basic dilemma, however, is that all learning is cumulative and one cannot learn without basing her or his knowledge on the work of predecessors. Others would argue against the Honor Code that it restricted the communal efforts of students at solving a problem or dealing with a critical challenge. After all, a university is a place where students learn to work together and to address questions of relevance to society in a collective manner. The Honor Code posed questions on the nature of a university: whether it should cultivate strictly individualistic achievement or an effort of the community of scholars and educators to arrive at an understanding of causes and effects and to contribute to the depository of acquired knowledge.

One of the students with whom I worked on some approved assignments made a sacrifice for his love of his dog. He was of limited financial means, and one day after class he informed me that his dog was in an emergency veterinary clinic because of a car accident. While the injury sustained by the dog was not serious or life-threatening, my friend was advised that he had to take his dog to a Washington, D.C., veterinary hospital for further treatment. My friend was ready to travel with his dog and to spend his savings of five hundred dollars in order to make sure that the dog would get better soon.

This story of a person's love for his dog amazed me, coming as I did from a culture where the level of poverty, caused by our refugee status, prevented us from owning, feeding, and cuddling pets. While I could understand the love and attachment one could feel for a pet, I had a problem then in accepting that a person would spend a small fortune on pet care. I am aware of the moral dilemma, and I am often reminded of media stories in which the whole nation, as well as the wider world, would be following up on a rescue mission of a cat or of some other animal in a dangerous and precarious situation. While a sigh of relief would be a natural outcome for a successful rescue operation, back home people would comment that human beings in some parts of the world were not being treated as decently as some lucky pets in Western societies! I was always reminded of Aunt Leonie's love for animals, but hers was an environment in which persons

and animals cohabited as a normal course of life. As Palestinian society has
evolved economically and socially, some of the middle- and upper-middle-
class families have opted to keep and care for pets. Apparently having pets is
tied to the economic and social advancement of a society. When my sister-
in-law visits us occasionally from Haifa, she comes together with her two
beautiful children; she also brings her pet rabbit and the Siamese cat Julie,
which has become part of the family. When our pet turtle of twenty or so
years recently died, the family felt sad, and our middle son, Zack, gave it a
fitting burial place next to an olive tree in the backyard.

MASTER'S
THESIS

Since I was committed to getting my Master's degree in a twelve-
month period, I decided to enroll in courses for which I could write term
papers related to the various aspects of my Master's thesis. The idea was that
I would collate the term papers for my courses and with some editing would
eventually come up with my Master's thesis. I was to address in my thesis
the question of "The Leading Palestinian Families" during the course of the
British Mandate Period in Palestine between 1920 and 1948. I chose the
topic because of the influence that these families had exerted on Palestinian
society and politics. These were the families that could be compared in some
ways to leading aristocratic families in Virginia and the rest of the South and
also with Japanese families and family hierarchies elsewhere.

While the geography and nature of Palestine were not conducive to the
emergence of a feudal or a martial class of aristocratic families, nevertheless
these families were among the richest and most influential in our society.
Academic study and attention to these families developed first among some
Hebrew scholars, one of whom, Yaakov Shimoni, wrote on the Arabs of
Palestine in 1947, including a chapter on the leading families both in the
cities and in the rural areas of Palestine. His book was in Hebrew, and since
I did not know Hebrew, I started searching for a translation. In my search
I discovered the Human Relations Area Files of Yale University, and when
I looked into the Palestine entry, I discovered to my utmost surprise and
pleasure that Yaakov Shimoni's chapter on the Palestinian families had been
translated into English. This became a principal source for my thesis, but I
also relied on other sources, including some in Arabic, which I researched
at the Library of Congress in Washington and at the New York City Public
Library.

The thesis argued that these families owed their influence to their
religious roots, particularly as many of these families originated with the
Muslim takeover of the country in 637 and with the victory of Saladin in
1187 over the Crusaders in the famous Battle at the Horns of Hittin, near
the Lake of Tiberias (Sea of Galilee). When Caliph Omar, the second Caliph
after the death of the Prophet Mohammed, entered Palestine in the seventh

century, among his army commanders were those who opted to stay in Palestine. Some of these commanders established families that were generously endowed by the Caliph with properties and wealth to enable them to make a place for themselves and for their progeny for generations to come.

In the wake of the Saladin victory some of those who had fought with him, especially those hailing from North Africa, were also endowed by the victorious Saladin. With this religious and military connection, these families assumed the leadership role in Palestinian society. Their role was essentially social; when some of these families, like the Husseinis, were endowed with large tracts of land in rural areas, they assumed the role of protector to the local village community. When the Ottoman Turks, who ruled Palestine between 1516 and 1918, required that the land be registered, many villagers, especially in the northern part of Palestine, registered the land not in their own names but in the names of some of these influential families. This was thought to be a way of protection from excessive taxation by the Ottoman authorities. In reality, though, this added up to the transfer of land from the owners in the villages to the influential families.

Another important function that members of these families carried out was their religious role, as they were known to be the preachers and imams in the great Aqsa Mosque of Jerusalem and its compound. Their additional status as religious judges bestowed further power and privilege on them and their families. Besides, they were learned in religious jurisprudence and interpretation (*ifta*), and Muslims often sought their advice on a variety of topics related to the application of the sacred writings as found in the Qur'an and in the Sunna (the example and sayings of the Prophet).

On the basis of their social and religious influence, with the arrival of the British after World War I, these families became involved in the politics and administration of the country. Some members of these families had gone to Istanbul, Beirut, and other places of learning, where they had earned degrees in a variety of subjects that further consolidated their influence in the society. These members were the first to earn a university degree back in the late nineteenth and early twentieth centuries. This was made possible by the fact that members of these families were the first among Muslims to enroll in Christian private schools such as the Frères School, the Anglican Bishop Gobat School, Al Mutran, among others. These schools were established in the main cities of Palestine—Jerusalem, Jaffa, Haifa, and Nazareth—and offered local Christians an education that gave them an advantage over their other compatriots. There were also some prominent Christian families whose high social standing was gained through the practice of liberal professions; their knowledge of foreign languages gained in the private Christian schools became an added advantage. This

was especially so when the Western consulates in Jerusalem and elsewhere
in the country sought translators or junior clerks to assist them with their
contacts with the local population. The political role of active members of
Palestinian Christian families was to find place in the leading Muslim families' political groups, or "parties," which were really family-based factions
that sprang up during the British Mandate and that reflected polar political
positions between the more accommodationist Nashashibi party and the
less accommodationist Husseini faction.

Writing on the Palestinian families and their social, political, and religious contexts brought me closer to my roots in an attempt to understand
the social dynamics within my own society and how they influenced the
conflict with the Zionist movement. As I wrote the different chapters of the
thesis, I learned to be objective and to take a look from outside at my own
society and to override the inherent limitations of an insider's perspective.
But regardless of how objective one might be, there was an inherent danger
in examining the role of these families in a retrospective manner: the danger
of contributing to a misunderstanding of some of the events and stories
associated with them and their role in politics and society during the British Mandate. Without offering any excuses for failure here and there, the
fact remains that these families were an essential part of Palestinian social
makeup and that no historian can write about the history of Palestine without addressing as well the history of these leading families and some of their
prominent members.

In my thesis I did not dwell on the relationships of these families with
the British administration or with the Zionist political groups that were
waging their own fight to establish their state, promised by the Balfour
Declaration, on the rubble of Palestinian society and its culture. Looking
at these families, nevertheless, made me realize that examining history was
more complex than simply recounting one's own narrative and perspective
on historical events and happenings. Certainly mistakes were committed by
the Palestinian family leadership during the British Mandate. While some
Western sources sympathetic to the fulfillment of the Zionist dream would
have wanted the Palestinians and their leadership to accommodate themselves to that dream, the Palestinians insisted that accommodation was not
possible because this was their country. I once heard an argument between
a Palestinian and a British sympathizer with the Zionist dream, in which the
Palestinian brought up the story of the woman whose child was taken by another woman and of both women presenting themselves to King Solomon
 to be the judge (1 Kings 3:16–28). When King Solomon wanted to ascertain
which mother was the genuine one, he proposed that the child be cut in
two. The true mother rejected the advice and protested to the contrary. The

Palestinian told the British gentleman that this was exactly our story in regard to the land, as we Palestinians have resisted the division of Palestine.

Social life at the University of Virginia was rather dismal for a graduate student like me. Aside from going to classes, working on my various term papers and assignments, and attending lectures and seminars, UVA—in spite of its famous "Corner" where one could find food, books, and eventual yard sales—offered a limited range of challenging opportunities outside of academia for a person with my background. Friends dropped by from Lancaster once in a while, and I traveled by bus or train to Washington, D.C., usually for one day at a time in order to visit the Library of Congress and to consult its vast collection on Middle Eastern history, society, and culture. When visiting the Library I often asked myself whether some members of Congress and their staffs had ever availed themselves of the riches that were contained within the shelves of the Library. This question came to my mind as I felt that much of Congressional policy-making on the Middle East was influenced by one side, Israel, oblivious to the rich historical and political realities on the Palestinian Arab side.

I was reminded of my father's criticism of the British and U.S. administrations when the 1948 Arab-Israeli war made him and many of his generation refugees and thus contributed to the disintegration and fragmentation of Palestinian society. The criticism that Father and many of his generation aimed at American and British politicians of the time was that, when they allowed the tragedy of Palestine to take place, they had not followed the principles and values of justice and compassion, which were felt to be Christian values that many of the Western politicians supposedly subscribed to. A thorough scrutiny of the Library of Congress materials on Palestine and Israel would have stimulated policy-makers to be reflective and perhaps more equitable toward both sides, when considering this or that position. But is this scenario realistic in light of the probability that strategic considerations, together with the guilt that many Western politicians felt in regard to the atrocities inflicted on the Jewish people under Nazi Germany, would take precedence over values of justice and compassion? History teaches us that we should not be judgmental but humble in learning its lessons and drawing the conclusions relevant to our present-day realities. Perhaps if politicians would benefit from history's lessons, we could avoid much of the misery in which our world finds itself today.

The political aspect of life at UVA was invigorated by the presence on campus of no other than Ms. Hanan Mikhail—later Ashrawi upon her marriage to Emile—the prominent Palestinian woman from Ramallah who was to become the spokesperson for the Jordanian-Palestinian delegation to the Madrid Peace Conference in 1991. Hanan was working on her PhD in

English literature, and she was wont to work with pro-Palestinian sympathizers in organizing campus events and lectures to present the Palestinian perspective. I participated in one of these events where Hanan presented her convincing arguments for the Palestinian cause with her characteristically eloquent style. In the question-and-answer period someone asked about the stereotypes that Americans held of Arabs in general and their ignorance of who the Palestinians were. I asked permission to comment, and I remember telling the audience, in a satirical manner, how "A-rabs" still rode their camels and in fact had camel parking lots, similar to car parking lots in America, in our Middle Eastern cities and towns. While some understood the nature of my satire, Ms. Ashrawi asked me to be more serious about the conversation. Later on, when she became more directly involved in Palestinian politics, which took her away from her teaching job at Birzeit University, Ms. Ashrawi developed a good relationship with then-Secretary of State James Baker and Mrs. Baker. As so many others in the West have been, both were impressed with this Palestinian lady and her way of presenting and arguing the case for her people.

Among the professors with whom I was privileged to learn was the business-like Prof. Theodore Caplow, who was credited with establishing the renewed Department of Sociology at UVA between 1970 and 1978 after Prof. Coughlin retired. Prof. Caplow believed in empirical proofs rather than in the kind of sentimentally laden hearsay that is so often the lot of people who are disadvantaged or dispossessed. When you do not have the capability or the opportunity to discover a cause-and-effect relationship, you are more likely to believe in connections or misperceptions that can shape not only your thinking but the way you end up living your life. Even the academic quality of investigation and analysis can be impacted by the kinds of economic, social, and political contexts in which people, including academics, find themselves. This insight can go a long way in explaining why for the same phenomenon there are often so many varied and differing explanations.

I attended one of Prof. Caplow's courses and for a semester worked as a teaching assistant in one of his undergraduate classes. I was fascinated by his *Sociology of Work*, which had been published in 1954 when he was thirty-four years old. Prof. Caplow did not say much whenever we engaged in any conversation about the assistantship obligations, as he gave his orders and I was supposed to execute them attentively. This attitude was perhaps a vestige of his military service during World War II and the head wound that he suffered during his service in the Philippines, which merited the Purple Heart medal, as I learned from his obituary. Prof. Caplow, in spite of my shyness in his presence, saw in me the potential for PhD studies. I was flattered by his assessment, and when, upon earning my MA from UVA, I told him that I was planning to come back, he said that he would facilitate my plan.

Prof. Caplow left an impact on the Department of Sociology at UVA by recruiting top professors from all over, and he transformed the department from one best characterized as an undergraduate department to one that competed with graduate departments of sociology across the U.S. He died on Saturday, the Fourth of July, in 2015 at the age of ninety-five. According to his obituary, he was "a dedicated member of Emmanuel Episcopal Church in Greenwood, Virginia . . ." God bless his soul.

As the summer of 1971 ended and my assistantship expired, I needed to find additional sources of income in order to finish my thesis. I went to the financial aid office and inquired about how best I could secure funding with my willingness to work part-time. One helpful person asked me if I were Armenian; I said no, but that my neighbors in the Dar in the Old City of Jerusalem were. This qualified me to apply for the Galbakian Scholarship, which had been established for Armenian students by an Armenian philanthropist associated with UVA. I was thinking of asking for a maximum of $500 to finish my studies and thesis, but the person in charge of the Galbakian Scholarship made me understand that since there were few Armenian students who qualified to receive the scholarship, I could add to the request the costs of printing my thesis, of secretarial help, and of rent for up to three months as well as other related expenses. I think I asked for a sum of $1200, which in 1971 was a small fortune. I was overwhelmed when my request was approved. Where else but in America would such small miracles have happened? I wonder if they are still happening now, with all the strain in international relations and the changed realities in American society itself.

One of the last places to find a campaign volunteer for the Labor candidate for the local elections was in Charlottesville. But there he was on the Corner (the landmark and gathering-place on the UVA campus) explaining to me the advantages of voting for a candidate who was not associated with the two political parties that ran the country according to their whims and wishes. After listening attentively in order to learn his position and that of the candidate he represented, I conveyed to him that I was in no position to determine the outcome of any election in Charlottesville or elsewhere in the country. Although the model of American democracy is to be lauded, especially as it offers voters the opportunity to choose their representatives and their President on a regular basis, I was always perplexed by the fact that Americans had to choose between two candidates only. What if the two candidates were not up to the challenge? And why would the American people not opt to shun the candidates of the two major parties in favor of one who belonged to a third party or who was independent? Is the American political system geared to accept only presidents who belong to either the Democratic or the Republican party? Maybe I have misunderstood the American system, but why would a great country like the U.S. end up, in some presidential races, with two candidates who do not measure up to the greatness of America and its people? These questions continue to perplex me, even today.

UVA is a charming place. In fact, some consider it to be the most beautiful campus in the entire U.S. Indeed, the UVA grounds are always serene and well maintained and reflect some sort of ideal of perfection that strikes chords in one's being. The grounds, as the campus is known, reminded me of the Bahai quest for perfection as seen in the beautiful and immaculate grounds of the sect in Haifa. Many famous personalities have visited the grounds of UVA. For example, I recall that when I was returning home from class one noontime, I saw a crowd of people that had gathered around the Rotunda; when I approached the crowd, I saw no other than Elizabeth Taylor. Many people opted to have their weddings in the small church across from the Library; on many a Saturday afternoon I had seen the appropriately dressed wedding parties. The place was perfect and, I would say, in sharp contrast with the realities of life in the Old City of Jerusalem and in so many other places in the U.S. itself and around the globe. The bliss of spending a year at UVA could not but be contrasted with the difficult living conditions of my parents back home and the hundreds of thousands of Palestinian refugees who were still waiting for a solution following the 1948 Arab-Israeli war.

In comparison with F&M there were not many foreign students, as UVA apparently was certain that, with its history, traditions, and grounds, it did not need the attraction of large numbers of international students. Nevertheless, some of the foreign students I met at UVA were impressive. I especially remember a couple of Ethiopian army officers who were studying diplomacy and international relations and who, I am sure, assumed important functions in the army and government of their country upon their return home. An American student who had served in Eritrea and had developed severe arthritis in his limbs became a friend, and while sipping a morning or late afternoon coffee or tea, we often shared our opinions and reflections on what was going on in America and the world.

UVA, however, was not a place where a foreign student could readily cultivate a social life. Most students in 1970–1971 were white and Anglo-Saxon, and probably many of them hailed from the South of Gone with the Wind. Some would even place their Confederate flags on their apartment windows while others would wave them at football and basketball games.

UVA in the early seventies was interested in developing its sports programs and teams in order to compete more effectively. Apparently college sports were not only a source of pride for the alumni and an incentive for their contributions to the University, but also a major source of funding that would ease some of the financial burdens of an institution of higher learning. I was fascinated by UVA football games, as they were an outlet for venting one's accumulated tensions and a way to link up with other students who otherwise would go their own way alone. The fanfare accompanying the football and basketball games always appealed to me because of the marching bands and the cheerleaders' zeal and the athletic competition.

A friend of mine from the Middle East once commented on how long it would take for women and men to start watching sports together in our country the way Americans did it. This same friend was so enthusiastically impressed by the marching bands during half-time that he wished we could have the capacities to do something similar in our soccer games back home. These were positive observations that reflected more on the achievements of American society than on the potential of other societies, including Palestinian society, to develop along similar lines. One aspect of the crowds at football games that I personally observed was the participation of young and old not only in watching the football game but also in taking part in the activities and hullaballoo that went on during the game.

I recollect Easter 1971 because the only thing I did was to wake up very early on Easter Sunday in order to assist at a sunrise service in the small outdoor auditorium. There were some hundred students and faculty gathered, and as we went through the service, it became clear to me that Easter Sunday in the U.S. was not much different from other Sundays except for the sunrise service. This made me reflect on the commotion experienced by my folks back home as they spent a whole week, Holy Week, in preparation for Easter Sunday. The excitement of Easter back home was a continuation of the community's centuries-old heritage, with all the traditions, rites, and rituals associated with the commemoration of the Crucifixion and Resurrection of Jesus Christ. At UVA—and I assume across the U.S.—the celebration of Easter was individualistic in the sense that individuals of various backgrounds came together to celebrate, but without the communal links that would have bonded them to each other as happened back in the Palestinian Christian community of Jerusalem. I missed home and its celebrations of Easter, while on an individual, inner level I felt gratified and satisfied with attending the sunrise service and watching as the sun rose on a blessed Easter Sunday in Charlottesville.

My social life and relationships during the twelve-month sojourn at UVA included my friendship with Edith, a fellow graduate student who, if

I remember correctly, hailed from Massachusetts. She was thoroughly preoccupied with her Master's thesis. We attended some classes together and
cooperated on some homework, within the parameters of the Honor Code.
Edith worked on her thesis for three years, and later, when I visited UVA
in 1973, I was surprised to find her still working at finishing her Master's
thesis. I have had no contact with her since that visit, and I wonder if she
went on to get her PhD as she was always hoping to do.

Return to Jerusalem

I returned home in November 1971, on the eve of Thanksgiving Day.
I remember this clearly because when my plane took off from New York
the temperature was quite cold. On arrival at Tel Aviv Airport the pilot informed us that the temperature there was a balmy 23 degrees Centigrade
(73.4 degrees Fahrenheit), which made me feel the warmth of my country
and family immediately. When I arrived at the airport, my mother, Uncle
Rock, and some other family members were waiting for me. It was a sentimental family reunion, and I appreciated the fact that Mother herself was
there to welcome me.

I had high expectations, coming back with a Master's degree from a
prestigious American university. The experiences I had gained in the U.S.
and my exposure to the lifestyle of middle- and upper-middle-class cohorts
of students, particularly at F&M, had implanted in me the desire to imitate that lifestyle. But my family remained a poor family of limited means.
My Master's degree on a topic related to the social structure of Palestinian
society seemed promising as a means to gain influence for my family and
myself on the basis not of religion but of education. After all, wasn't education supposed to be the way forward or upward? And what about my newly
acquired knowledge on the dynamics of Palestinian social life? Wouldn't
this enable me to gain positions and to become part of the elite that would
influence the fate of our people and society? I was naïve and somewhat
idealistic and could not see that influence was acquired with wealth and
economic enterprise as well as with a large extended family that had hundreds of members—not a family like ours with a small number of members.
Another question touched on my religious background: would my being a
Palestinian Catholic enable me to play the wished-for influential social role,
or would it be a hindrance?

Our living quarters in the Dar in the Old City of Jerusalem had not
changed much over the twenty or so years in which we had lived there.
While I wanted to renovate the furniture and to remake the structure of the

two rooms in which we lived, Mom made me understand that this was not possible because of financial constraints. I could not use the Dar to receive friends and to widen my social circle, not because parents and brothers and sisters were not welcoming, but because of the fact that with our limited means, the Dar could not be converted into a social club where influence would be bartered. Possibly my expectations demanded too much from my family with respect to helping me gain influence or prove to the wider community that I was someone special who could make a difference in the affairs of our society. I was reminded both of the Amish and of my Catholic confessor, who associated academic learning with a tendency towards arrogance and away from the natural wisdom that came with only basic socialization and education. Was I conceited about my education, and was this a cause of tensions between Mom and me, as well as with other family members? Mom was a loving person with a natural predisposition to read her children's minds; after all, she was a young person herself. But while she felt sympathy with me and my dilemmas, she could not help much.

What added to my pressures was the fact that I could not find work during the first months of my return home. This made me feel some guilt, as I relied on the support of my parents. I did not want to go back to being a school teacher, even though the principal of my alma mater invited me to do so. I sought something else with the potential for me to use the skills I had acquired by studying sociology. The job market in Jerusalem, however, was not promising. Schools in Jerusalem in the early seventies did not have a curriculum of social science or social thought. The only available jobs were in teaching and in hotel and tourist services in addition to some openings in social work, which was not my area of specialization. Eventually a neighbor of ours in the Dar convinced me to accept a job as a social worker at the National Insurance Institute, which is equivalent to the Social Security system in the States. While I explained to the director of the East Jerusalem branch of the Institute the difference between sociology and social work, he was not altogether impressed with the distinction. He told me that if I had been smart enough to earn a graduate degree in sociology from an American university, I would do well to learn about social work with beneficiaries who were either congenitally disabled or suffered from workplace injuries that had left them disabled.

The experience of working with the disabled in East Jerusalem and throughout the West Bank and Gaza Strip for over four years impacted my life. I was trying to ensure that people who qualified for assistance because of a congenital disability or a work-related accident knew their rights and made the right choices when it came to rehabilitation, compensation, and stipend packages due to them. When a bus accident in 1972 left dozens of

Palestinian workers dead or injured, I traveled to Nablus, north of Jerusalem, where some of their families resided. I advised one widow, who trusted me fully, to get a monthly stipend from the Institute rather than a lump sum, which would easily evaporate in a couple of years or so. Recently her brother saw me in Jerusalem, thanked me for the advice given then, and told me how, even now, his sister still receives a monthly stipend that enables her to go on living decently. Another unforgettable visit was to a refugee camp in the Gaza Strip where a young person had become quadriplegic because of a work-related accident. I was overwhelmed by the living quarters of this young man, which made me nauseous. He was living in a dark room, and, except for his mother, who cared for his elementary needs, he did not have any means of experiencing life except as a bedridden quadriplegic. I did all that I could to help this man best to improve his living conditions. Life, however, got so complicated after the seventies that I do not know whatever happened to this young man later on. ∉

Social work was not the most comfortable of jobs, but it turned out to be the most rewarding. I am not speaking of the feeling one gets when one helps out and stands with people in need. I am referring to the young social worker from Haifa whom I met occasionally in seminars or at conferences on social work. Mary, a slender, beautiful person, appealed to me. I liked her practical attitude to things and her devotion to her work in Nazareth and throughout Galilee. She was more of a social worker than I was, as she had earned her undergraduate degree at Haifa University in Social Work. As we were sitting across a table from each other listening to a lecture or, more precisely, being bored by a presentation that was too technical for my taste, I felt the need while looking at Mary to compose some lines of poetry, which I purposely dispatched to her to see her reaction. She liked what I wrote, and from her facial expressions while reading the few lines of poetry, I knew that I had made it to her heart.

MARY

In Palestinian society, if one intends to make progress towards a serious relationship, it has to become official with the woman's family. So one Sunday morning in September 1973 I traveled together with my brother Tony to Haifa to request formally the honor and privilege of starting a serious relationship with Mary. In Wadi al Nisnas in Haifa, where Mary's family lived, we arrived with a bouquet of flowers and met her parents, Louis and Widad Kandalaft, for the first time. I fell in love with the family not simply because of their warm welcome but also because both parents made me understand that they were hard-working people and that they would expect me to treat their daughter with the dignity owed to diligent parents.

Later on I learned that Mary's father was a tailor of renown in Haifa and throughout Galilee. When weddings and important family events took place, many young people frequented his tailor shop in the Wadi in order to buy handmade suits for such occasions. Louis had gone to the Salesian vocational school in Bethlehem, which was set up in the twenties and thirties of the last century. He was always proud of the certificate, written in Italian and issued sometime in the 1930s, testifying to his tailoring skills and accomplishments. The Salesians are an Italian order of religious men that followed the example of Saint Don Bosco, who in the late eighteenth century ministered to the poorest of the poor in Turin, Italy. Many tailors across Palestine had graduated from the Salesian Bethlehem School; their fame was owed to the Italian style of their suits and to their exacting skills at tailoring. Some of those tailors, like Abu Salim in Jerusalem, were also pioneering with women's dresses. I remember that my mother and other women in our family visited with him in order to take the measurements needed for an appropriate dress for a happy family occasion.

Widad, Mary's mother, was a strong-willed woman. She helped her husband in the tailoring shop and made sure that the amounts Louis charged for various suits, adjustments, and other tailoring jobs were commensurate with the energy and skills invested in the jobs. She always felt that Louis had a soft heart and did not charge the right price. Later on I would discover that Widad, then my mother-in-law, was an excellent cook, perhaps an attribute of her Lebanese background on her mother's side. Another trait that I found laudable in my mother-in-law was her frugality in saving every penny in order to make some valuable investments, like buying jewelry, for her two daughters and her two daughters-in-law.

When it was time for our engagement, we invited Abouna Rafiq, my spiritual counselor, to officiate over the ceremony in Haifa's Latin (Roman Catholic) church. It was a simple ceremony (though not by U.S. standards), where the two families from Jerusalem and Haifa and some from Nazareth were introduced to each other. After all, engagements and weddings in Palestinian society are a family affair, and they are not complete without the necessary introductions between families. For me, having lived in the U.S. for over six years, the whole process seemed to be a necessary task that I had to perform in order to attain the goal.

As I grew to know Mary's family more, I found out that her father had had a big tailor shop, or workshop, prior to the 1948 war and that when the war broke out, he lost everything. But as many others of his generation did, he was determined to start all over again. His tailoring shop in the Wadi was nothing to compare with his previous enterprise, but he was a determined person who never left his town, who wanted to affirm his belonging to his land and people through hard work, and who would never give up. I also discovered that my father-in-law-to-be was an activist: he participated in distributing leaflets calling for an end to the military rule that had been imposed in 1948 by the Israeli government on its Arab citizens with restrictions on movement between villages and towns. The military rule was finally lifted in 1964. The argument used by the Israeli authorities to support it was that the Palestinians who remained in Israel, who numbered around 156,000 back in 1948, were a "fifth column," meaning that they were not to be trusted and that their movements needed to be curtailed and monitored.

The Arab-Jewish Communist Party of Israel, "Rakah," appealed to Arabs who remained in Israel since it was the only venue for them to express their concerns and aspirations with regard to the new realities after the creation of the State of Israel. While I know the sensitivity that most Western readers would have concerning any Communist-affiliated party ("better dead than red," as the saying goes), I got to read the newspaper *Al-Itihad*, which the Communist Party issued daily. The newspaper read like other newspapers with a focus on the issues of the Arab population in Israel and with attention to art and literature, especially that which spoke to the aftermath of the Arab defeat in 1948 and the creation of the State of Israel. Among some of the contributors to the newspaper were names like Emile Habibi, Tawfiq Ziad, Samih al Qasem, Emile Touma, Mahmoud Darwish, Hanna Abou Hanna, Issam Abbasi, Salem Jubran, Tawfiq Toubi, and a host of others who made an imprint on the Arab population of Israel and became known for their literary and other achievements.

These contributors were the literary, cultural, and intellectual elite of the Arab citizens of Israel. A mixture of Christians, Muslims, and Druze, they were spirited people who cared about developments around them and with their poetry, prose, and other forms of literary expression reflected on the realities they experienced and their memories of bygone days and generations. They were a practically-oriented group of exceptional individuals who realized that, in order to create a society open to all and with equality and justice for all its citizens, it was imperative to touch base with Jewish groups and individuals who were like-minded. Emile Habibi became famous for his "pessi-optimist" novel about the experiences of refugees following the 1948 Arab-Israeli war and the accommodation to the new realities under the State of Israel. Mahmoud Darwish went on to become the national poet of Palestinians, and in his honor a museum was established in Ramallah with exhibits of the various phases of his life and the development of his poetic vocation. The museum serves as a venue for cultural, literary, and intellectual meetings in which local literary celebrities as well as those from the Arab world and elsewhere are invited.

One of the activities undertaken by the Israeli Communist Party was the dispatching of promising students by members and friends of the Party to study in the Republics belonging to the Soviet bloc. In this way my two future brothers-in-law earned their degrees in medicine and pharmaceutical science from Poland and Czechoslovakia, respectively. Life then in the Soviet bloc of countries was not expensive, and with their scholarships as well as the little that their parents occasionally sent them, they managed reasonably well. In addition, both ended up with prized Polish and Slovakian brides, and they all lived happily ever after! But, no, my brothers-in-law did not turn out to be communists, just as those among us who studied in the U.S. did not necessarily convert to the capitalist system. In fact, one of my brothers-in-law eventually prospered in Slovakia after the fall of the Soviet Union, and his own son referred to him as my "capitalist father."

Jerusalem in the early seventies saw groups of young Palestinians who wanted to make a difference in their city, now under Israeli occupation. One of the youth initiatives was a group that called itself *Balalin* ("Balloons"). It was a group of spirited youngsters, most of whom were in their early twenties, who wanted to practice theater and to meet to prepare plays. I was never an actor, but I was pulled by the spirit of *Balalin* and its members, who wanted to impress on their society the value of a good theater piece. The members were variably skilled: some played a guitar or *oud* (similar to a lute), others were gifted in photography, and still others had gained experience in short film-making. They all wanted to pool their resources in order to impress and to ensure their identity as Palestinian Jerusalemites. The spirit behind the group was Jack, an Armenian who had gone to school with me and had an artistic take on things. In one of our meetings, we spoke about why we were together, concluding that we were there together in order to celebrate our city and ourselves. We operated as if there were no Israeli occupation, and we tried to fill the cultural void that resulted from Israel's take-over of the Old City of Jerusalem in 1967.

In more than one way we were dreamers who felt that words, music, and acting would create their own world to defy the grim realities of occupation and the absence of opportunities for young Palestinians in the city. Among the members of the group were the Ashrawi brothers from the Old City; one of them, Emile, was an amateur photographer who eventually wedded Hanan Mikhail (and hence her name became Hanan Mikhail Ashrawi). The second brother, Ibrahim, migrated to America, where he made a successful living.

Balalin was active for a number of years but slowly was overtaken by other, more professional groups that sprang up across Palestinian society as it coped with continuing occupation and its disastrous effects. Some of the members of *Balalin*, like Ibrahim, migrated elsewhere. The last time I met my old friend Jack was by chance in one of the streets of Old Jerusalem four or five years ago, when he and his German wife were visiting. Jack had migrated to Germany, where he had made his home; he told me that he was happy in Germany but there was no place like home. He informed me that his father, a shoemaker of renown in the Old City of Jerusalem, had passed on some years back. Apparently the generation that had made up the society of the Old City of Jerusalem was no longer. The Akrouk tailor shop by the Greek Orthodox Patriarchate in the Christian Quarter, which specialized in Turkish fez orders, also closed down, and its owners moved to Amman, Jordan; the Balians continued with their ceramic factory and shop across from the U.S. Consulate in East Jerusalem, but the father had long since passed on; the Kahvedjian photo shop in the Christian Quarter continued through the efforts of Kevork, the son of the famed photographer Elia, to attract tourists and locals with the limited reproductions of the original photographs taken by Elia between 1924 and the 1990s. Kevork immortalized his father with a photo collection entitled "Jerusalem through my Father's Eyes." It was in this collection that I found by chance two photos of my own father from the thirties when he was participating in the Way of the Cross on the famed Via Dolorosa (which retraces the last steps of Jesus as he carried his cross to Golgotha). In one way the demise of *Balalin* reminded me of the demise of the generation of my father: how they lived their lives, each in his profession and with his expertise, and contributed to the makeup of the city. But like members of the older generation who gave up, either because of the natural order of things or because they chose to leave the city, the younger generation also could not withstand the difficulties of transition, and in spite of efforts at staying put, eventually many of the promising youngsters gave up and left the city themselves.

In the early seventies one of my preoccupations was how to make the Church more relevant to the issues and concerns of my people. I was not sure that the Church hierarchies at that time were ready to engage with the local parishioners on a basis of equality and in an encompassing Christian communal spirit. Most Church hierarchies in the Holy Land of the seventies were more concerned with their own internal affairs and with the running of their seminaries, hospitals, schools, convents, and similar institutions. In more than one way it could be argued that these institutions were engaged with the local Christian population and its needs, but Church hierarchies projected more of a management and business-like orientation than the model of spiritual leadership expected of clergy. Possibly I am being too harsh in retrospect, but clearly there was a gap between the hierarchies and the faithful. Some attributed this gap to the fact that expatriate clergy, such as in the Greek Orthodox Church and the Franciscan Custody of the Holy Land, saw their primary duty as the preservation of the Holy Places. The local faithful were mere collateral luggage for whom they, the clergy, needed to preside over rites and rituals, particularly those of life transitions such as baptism, first communion, marriage, and death.

Maybe I am once again being harsh, but the reality then to me was that the local Palestinian Christian community was powerless and in a sense estranged from its own churches and felt like an outsider. Worse, the relationship of dependency on the churches, whether in schools, hospitals, social welfare, or housing, prevented the Palestinian Christians of Jerusalem and elsewhere in the country from gaining self-sufficiency as they relied on the churches to provide them with the essential services. In the eyes of many Palestinian Christians, the churches were wealthy, powerful, and hierarchically self-centered; the link with the local faithful was rather circumstantial and did not empower them to become independent. While the church hierarchies and their leaders possibly viewed the relationship as one of compassion and mercy, as called for by Jesus and his teachings, for many of us, especially the young people in the community, the relationship was, rather, one of power, on the one side, and absence of equality, on the other.

Given the situation of conflict between Israelis and Palestinians, the question I often asked my clergy friends and myself was this: what role is there for the local Palestinian Christians and the Church in advancing prospects for peace and eventual reconciliation? I was at the time a believer in the possibility that through dialogue and exchange among all sides we could arrive at some sort of compromise that would be agreeable to all parties. Perhaps I was too naïve in expecting miracles through talking to each other. By nature I was always a pacifist and did not believe that my Palestinian people could achieve its rights through violence and confrontation. This position was considered by many as defeatist, since many of my generation believed that the way to Palestinian liberation should happen through armed struggle. During my university studies in the U.S., I read both Gandhi and Frantz Fanon, and they were opposite to each other in some aspects of their grasp of colonialism and its power relationships. While I understood through reading Fanon about the effects of colonial rule on the oppressed and their psychology, I learned from Gandhi that love eventually triumphs GANDHI and that the goal was not to hurt people but to overcome their wish to control and oppress others. Was this Gandhian perspective applicable in the Israeli-Palestinian case? I was of the opinion that it was, and that in spite of the wounds that Israeli occupation would inflict on my people, eventually the will to confront the evil of occupation would triumph. If we were to follow this path and to win over Israelis and other international supporters and sympathizers to our side, then surely we would triumph—or so I wished. On the basis of my convictions I was always ready to engage in dialogue, and I did not hesitate to attend seminars or conferences that discussed the relationships between Arabs and Jews in the Holy Land and that studied the various aspects of the complex inter-group relationship between Israelis and Palestinians.

Enthusiasm for dialogue is a laudable trait, but as my son taught me later on: "It needs to have a focus, Dad." I think that dialogue between Israelis and Palestinians, at times, can serve the purpose of providing some sort of legitimacy to an inherently illegal system of occupation and dispossession. In some quarters, dialogue is encouraged in order to change the hearts of Palestinians, as if the hearts of Israelis had already been won. In the mid-seventies the dialogue and peacemaking industry had already started to flourish. The lure of funding and the kind-heartedness of some private donors, as well as international grants, made of the encounter between Palestinians and Israelis some sort of profitable enterprise. Some academics on the Palestinian side, with meager stipends, saw an opportunity for wealth and progress in engaging in the peacemaking industry; others refrained, believing that individual gain did not always add up to communal gain or to the resolution of outstanding problems between Israelis and Palestinians. Others pointed out that the system of occupation and its inherent inequalities and repressive measures needed to change before any dialogue and peacemaking efforts across the two societies would bear fruit.

Losing Mother

Amidst my church, youth, and political engagements, Mother became seriously ill. I was concerned about her health and did everything possible to help whenever I could. I remember early mornings when I went to her Greek doctor, who lived not far away from our Dar, to ask him to call on her because of her worsening condition. We relied on local doctors to take care of Mother's heart problem. Eventually a cardiologist from Ramallah advised that she be admitted to the French hospital in Jerusalem, run by the Palestinian and Arab nuns of Saint Joseph, which is one of the hospitals managed by Christian religious orders and organizations of different persuasions. At a certain point, after she felt better, she asked the doctor to stop her heart medications, and he simply complied. Within a couple of days, on January 7, 1973, she passed away.

It was a very difficult transition for all of us, as she was only fifty-one years of age and as our youngest brother, Daoud, was only in his twelfth year. The passing of my mother created a void in the family and in the Dar ensemble. Because of the proximity of her age to ours, we always felt that she was like us in many ways: her love for music and for following the news, whether on the radio or on the newly acquired television set, in spite of some opposition from Father; her engagement in discussions with us and our friends on political and social issues; her love for her country and her championing of the just cause of her people.

One day, when the Franciscan friar in charge of the Holy Sepulcher was visiting our home, he told her in conversation that the Land belonged to the Jewish people and that there was no place in it for Palestinians of any religion. Mother could not believe her ears, and she retorted, asking why, then, there was the Franciscan Custody of the Holy Land. Was it to preserve the Holy Sites for pilgrims and tourists? And what about the local Christians who have been here since the establishment of the Mother Church of Jerusalem by Jesus himself? "My dear Friar," I remember her telling him, "if there is no place for us Palestinians here, then there is no place for you in our home." The friar left, never to visit our home again.

Mother's prophetic voice was predicting the future; when she was sitting at the window that opens onto the golden Dome of the Rock and the Mount of Olives, she always admonished us not to leave Jerusalem if another war were to take place and we were asked to vacate our premises. She was saying this in the early sixties as if she were sensing that another war would come, and it did in June 1967. Mother and all of us followed her advice when the Israeli forces took over the Old City. In fact, the overwhelming majority of Palestinians followed the same advice as they refused to be moved to Amman, Jordan, in spite of all the encouragements that the new occupants of the land offered.

When Mother was sick, we had a visit from our maternal cousin Nelly from Beirut, Lebanon. It was not easy to come from Beirut to Jerusalem since any visitor needed an Israeli permit and the Lebanese authorities would punish anyone who visited the occupied Palestinian territory as it was under Israeli control and there was fear of espionage and other security problems. Nelly wanted to see Mother and to show solidarity with her and with the family in times of illness and stress. Nelly was beautiful, and I took a natural liking to her. I even hastily proposed to her, later on, by writing her a romantically inspired letter. Nelly did not take my letter seriously even though I sensed that she had taken a liking to me as well. Another cousin, Abe the Barber, in whose shop I had worked as a barber's boy, was in love with her, but there again she was not responding to his advances. Apparently she had decided, most likely upon consultation with her mother, Aunt Angele, that she did not want to wed within the family.

Nelly stayed in Jerusalem for a couple of weeks. Mother's spirits were uplifted, and she kept asking after her sister Angele and other family

members in Beirut. On one of these days, my sister Hilda proposed that
we take Nelly on a tour of Qatamon to show her the home that my father
had built back in 1937. As we approached the site, it was clear that our parents' home was scheduled to be demolished. Hilda was in tears while I was
shocked to see a family history being erased altogether. Because of Hilda's
acquaintance with a Hebrew language teacher at the Ecce Homo, where she
worked and where Hebrew courses were offered to Arabs after 1967, she was
determined to look into the matter further.

With the help of her teacher acquaintance, we gained an appointment
with someone in an Israeli government office that dealt with such matters. When we entered the person's office, he introduced himself as Moshe,
originally from Iraq, and spoke to us in fluent Arabic. Hilda explained the
planned demolition, showed him the legal papers for the Qatamon home
that my parents had kept, and asked him what could be done. His answer
was unequivocal that nothing could be done: the property no longer legally
belonged to our parents since any Arab Palestinian property left after the
1948 war had been taken over by the Custodian of Enemy Property and
hence had come under the control of the State of Israel. Any individual
claims to lost property by Palestinians, like us, were legally impossible in
Israel because of Israeli laws and regulations that denied the consideration
of such claims. The infamous law that considered Palestinians "Present-Ab-
sentee" meant that even though Palestinians were living within the borders
of the State of Israel, they were legally not present in their permanent home
or residence in 1948 and hence could not submit any legal claim to their
lost property. The meeting was futile, and the only thing we learned from
it, as Hilda remarked while we were riding the bus from Qatamon to the
Jaffa Gate of the Old City, was that we were not really on the bus as we were
considered by Israeli law to be legally absent and nonexistent!

One sad note on my cousin Nelly from Lebanon: she worked for the
Embassy of the United States in Beirut. The embassy experienced two disastrous bombings in the second half of the seventies, which left scores of innocent people dead or injured. In the first bombing my cousin Nelly escaped
since it happened at lunchtime when she was out with some colleagues in
one of those beautiful restaurants so numerous in Beirut. Most tragically,
Nelly did not escape the second bombing, and she succumbed immediately
to the serious wounds she suffered. We were grieved and shocked to hear of
her tragic passing. Nelly was a beautiful and promising person; moreover,
all acts of terror take away precious lives, leaving all of us in sorrow and
anguish. We held a special memorial Mass for Nelly in Jerusalem, at which
family and friends gathered to pay the last respects.

Becoming a Husband and Father

The pain of separation from Mother took time to heal, and I doubt that it has ever healed fully. The impact of her death was particularly difficult for the two youngest siblings, Therese and Daoud, while we older ones went on with our preoccupations as we dealt with the pain. Mother never met Mary, my future wife, as the contacts with her family in Haifa did not start in earnest until after Mom passed away.

Before embarking on my engagement and wedding with Mary, I was confused and frustrated about staying in Jerusalem. I felt that the city did not offer any opportunities for advancement; it was a dead end, particularly to those with promising academic and professional credentials. This led me to search for jobs outside the city. Once I saw an advertisement from the American consulate in East Jerusalem inviting interested candidates to apply for translation jobs in Kyrenia, Cyprus, under the auspices of the United States Information Agency's Foreign Broadcasts Information Service (FBIS). The job entailed translating from Arabic into English the editorials of major newspapers across the Arab world and throughout the Middle East. It also included preparing transcriptions of radio statements on topics of interest to the U.S. from a variety of countries in the region. The job paid well, and its location on the Mediterranean Sea in Kyrenia, in the north of Cyprus, promised a different venue for enjoying life.

But in the end I hesitated to accept the job offer. It was Hilda who told me that there was a vacuum in the house with the death of my mother and that we should stick together during this difficult time of transition. This was what I needed to persuade me not to accept the generous American offer. I never regretted declining the job offer since in a year's time Kyrenia would become part of Turkish-occupied Northern Cyprus. Those Palestinians who accepted the employment ended up being transferred to London after the civil war in Cyprus.

It was on March 24, 1974, that Mary and I were officially engaged. We were not sure of the date until I took off my wedding ring and read the date on it. It is customary with Palestinian jewelers to engrave on wedding rings the date of the engagement and not the date of the actual wedding ceremony, which in our case was on October 20, 1974, a week after my maternal cousin Fred and Joujou, a beautiful young Jerusalem woman, were wedded. I remember this because, as Fred's best man, I was fascinated by the way he had chosen his wife-to-be. Fred was working in the Arabian Gulf in some financial company, where he was doing very well and had accumulated some capital. When he wanted to get married, his sister Madeleine sat down with him and compiled a list of potential marriage candidates. It was as simple as that. Then Fred, sometimes accompanied by his sister and sometimes alone, went from school to school, asking for a meeting with the teacher whose name was on the wedding candidates' list. Fred told me about one such interview in which the first question of the teacher candidate was, "How much money do you have, Mr. Fred?" Automatically he was turned off and politely excused himself. He had seen a couple of beautiful young Palestinian women at Bethlehem University, which was in its first year of operation, but when he approached them, it became clear that the difference of religion could not allow him to continue with further marital exploration.

SEARCHING FOR A WIFE

Eventually Fred found Joujou, his match; she was a teacher at a Catholic school inside the Old City of Jerusalem by the Jaffa Gate. Her family had the same social and economic standing as his family, but, most importantly, there was spontaneous chemistry between the two of them. After a couple of years in the Gulf, Fred and Joujou, together with his sisters and brothers and their families, all migrated to Australia, where they believed life would be more stable and predictable. Mary and I keep track of Fred and Joujou, and we had an opportunity to meet up with their daughter in Jerusalem when she made a couple of trips for family occasions. Both she and her sister drifted away from the Catholic Church and ended up in a Protestant church where they felt they would be better able to translate their faith into action, whether in Australia itself or abroad.

After our wedding, Mary continued with her social work and was transferred from Nazareth to Jerusalem. We lived for a while on the slope of the Mount of Olives until we discovered one day that the owner of our rented flat had the key to the flat and visited whenever he wished while we were away at work. One afternoon, when we came home from work, Uncle Rock, who was visiting from Amman, was sitting in our living room. When we asked him how he had gained entrance to our apartment, he told us that the landlord had opened the door for him. We were certainly happy to see Uncle Rock, but we were not pleased with our landlord, who could have called either Mary or me to alert us to Uncle Rock's visit.

In Beit Hanina, north of Jerusalem, where we rented a very small apartment in the Nusseibeh flats—flats that were built with the help of the Jerusalem municipality in order to get Palestinian residents to move out of the Old City—we had the pleasure of becoming parents by welcoming to the world Margo, our firstborn, almost one year to the day after our wedding date. At the maternity ward, where baby Margo saw the first lights of a Jerusalem morning, I was impressed with Margo's big eyes and round face. When I called my in-laws in Haifa to tell them about the birth of Margo, they told me later on that I sounded as if I were apologizing because it was a girl and not a boy. My father-in-law asked me what I meant when I told them that it was a girl but that they should see how beautiful and big her eyes were. Mary and I decided to name her Margo, after my mother. It was customary in Palestinian society, for both Muslims and Christians alike, to name their children after their parents, especially if the latter were deceased.

Margo's first year was not the easiest, as we were new to the art of caring for a baby. One day, when, during a visit, Aunt Leonie was carrying Margo, who was crying hard, she told us that we were depriving the poor girl of food. Mary wanted to breastfeed Margo, but apparently this was not satisfactory to the newborn, who was always crying. We were thinking that the cause was the usual stomach cramps of a newborn until Aunt Leonie made us understand that the poor babe was suffering from hunger and not stomach cramps. Our life during the first couple of years was centered on Margo and on work. Mary wanted to go on working after her maternity leave expired, and we found a neighbor who was ready to take care of Margo during the day for cash.

Although Jerusalem, then as now, did not have much cultural and entertainment life to offer, Mary and I were accustomed to go to movies at night on the western (Israeli) side of the city. As we did not have a car, we used to take the Egged bus. Egged is a major Israeli bus cooperative. The bus, which came down from the military camp across from our apartment, was usually filled up with Israeli soldiers taking the night off. Almost every time we returned on the bus from Jaffa Street on the Israeli side to our Beit Hanina home, the Israeli soldiers who were overcrowding the bus would start singing Arabic songs, particularly those of the famed Egyptian singers Abdel al Halim Hafez and the late Farid al Atrash. Mary and I would look at each other and would murmur something like this: "Was this really an Israeli bus we were on, or a hijacked bus from Damascus or Cairo?" Later on, when I told some Israeli acquaintances about this, they explained to me that in the decade of the seventies, the second generation of Oriental Israelis, hailing from Iraq, Egypt, and Morocco, among other Arab countries, was still attached to the culture of the countries from which their parents had come. But things have changed since then, and nowadays one would not find an Israeli soldier singing Arabic songs!

Bethlehem University

In October 1973, I started teaching at Bethlehem University on a part-time basis. I was one of the few Palestinians with a Master's degree in sociology at the time. Brother Jean-Manuel, a Palestinian member of the Jean Baptiste de la Salle teaching order and the principal of my high school alma

mater at the New Gate in Jerusalem, invited me to see him. He told me that
they were preparing the faculty for the launching of Bethlehem University,
in accord with the wish of His Holiness Pope Paul VI, and that they needed
a part-time instructor in sociology. Elated at the offer, I thought that at last
I was getting the recognition that I had been seeking since my return home
in November 1971. Bethlehem University was started in some classrooms
of the old Frères High School on the hill overlooking Bethlehem. The number of classrooms was very limited, and there were only 112 students in the
first cohort of the University. There was absolutely no academic culture
among the freshman class. They wanted to go on as they had done in high
school: joking, talking, whispering, and being disrespectful to the teacher
and their peers.

At first I was at a loss for how to handle this situation, and added to
it was the Bethlehem-Jerusalem divide as students who hailed from either
town grouped together and started an opposition between the in-group and
the out-group. Slowly but surely I made the students understand that I was
not paying them to come to my lectures and that they were free to leave if
they thought the lecture was boring. If they elected to stay, I would expect
them to respect the class, the teacher, and their peers. Slowly the idea seeped
in, and with this understanding we could start dealing with the artificial
division between Bethlehemite and Jerusalemite students. My colleagues
and I in the first couple of years after the founding of the University needed
to make it clear to our students that there was a university spirit and identity
that superseded the narrow, local identifications that were brought with us
from our towns, villages, and even families. If you were a Bethlehem University student, then you had your identity: as such, you belonged to the
community that made up the University.

Teaching at Bethlehem University was rewarding, but, as with every
new beginning, there were diverse opinions about what the vision of a
Catholic university in a Palestinian context should be. Some argued—and
I was one of them—that Bethlehem University should offer to the students
a new sort of vision whereby teachers and students would share together
in making decisions, with the university administration, for the benefit of
all and the university community in general. This was a vision that would
go counter to the hierarchical one, in which some in the administration of
the University would decide on every little detail of running the institution.
When I discussed with the chief administrator of the University the need
to create a new model of authority relationship in Palestinian society, and
expressed the hope that Bethlehem University could become part of that
new model, he told me in plain language: "Your task, Mr. Sabella, is not to
talk about models; your task is simply to teach."

That was my first disappointment in teaching; perhaps I was disappointed because I was too naïve, thinking that administrators of a university could contemplate an alternate vision. Why should they share their power and position in order to please someone who did not know anything about the realities of running an institution? But a dreamer and a visionary I was during the early years of my teaching at Bethlehem University, and we needed visionaries and dreamers then as urgently as we continue to need them today in Palestinian society. The divergence of my views from those of the Bethlehem University administration led me eventually to leave the University, which pained me tremendously.

Yet my departure from BU was facilitated by my having an alternate plan: Mary, who wanted to go on with her studies, and I had resolved, in spite of the relatively good incomes we had from stable jobs, to pursue our higher studies in the U.S. All the time that I was teaching at BU, I would ask the administrators for scholarships to pursue PhD studies, but to no avail. The invitation of Prof. Ted Caplow, chairperson of the Department of Sociology at University of Virginia, was always present in my mind. I communicated with him and told him of my plan to come back to UVA, which, to my delight and that of Mary, he welcomed. The problem, however, was that we did not have enough money to cover our move, besides the fact that parents, especially Mary's parents, blamed us for leaving secure jobs to seek additional paper degrees. But we persevered, as the Department of Sociology at UVA offered me an assistantship and as the money we saved from our work enabled us to buy the flight tickets and to have some nine hundred U.S. dollars in our pockets in preparation for the big transition!

Further Studies in Virginia

As we were preparing to move back to the U.S., we received a strange letter from a Libby Cohen from Charlottesville. She explained that she would like, together with her husband, Prof. Ralph Cohen of the English Department at UVA, to welcome us into her host family of international students. I answered that we welcomed her invitation if she and Prof. Ralph did not mind the fact that we were a Palestinian family. Her response was truly uplifting as she wrote, ". . . and you would have thought that I would ever think that with a name like Epiphan," which is my official name, "you would end up Jewish!?" Her response convinced us that we should accept the Cohens' invitation to become part of their activity of hosting foreign students.

When we arrived at the Charlottesville bus station on one of those hot and humid August days in 1976, no other than Prof. Cohen himself was there to welcome and assist us. He drove us to his home in his Volvo, and after a day or so of respite and relaxation, Libby found us a temporary place to stay at the University dorms. But she promised that she would insist on our living in Copley Hills, where married students had their residence. Both Ralph and Libby cared for our comfort and ensured that we found an appropriate place where we could start our university life without hindrance. We came to love and appreciate the Cohens, and Margo, our eldest, has always communicated with them, even after she was married and settled down in Edinburgh. There has always been a special place in our family for the Cohens, and we have loved them dearly.

In March 1978 an Israeli military operation in Lebanon, "Operation Litani," resulted in the deaths of around two thousand Palestinians and Lebanese and the forced displacement of close to a quarter of a million residents of South Lebanon to an area above the Litani River. The military operation also cost the lives of twenty Israeli soldiers. I was personally devastated emotionally by the costs of this Israeli incursion into South Lebanon. When Chaim Herzog, the Israeli envoy to the UN, was invited to UVA to speak about the rationale for and the results of "Operation Litani," Mary and I were in the audience. I was calm and reflective, listening to his eloquent defense of the military actions of Israel, but when he said something to the effect that the operation was also intended to bring peace to South Lebanon and Northern Israel, I found myself yelling at him from the back of the hall: "And about those killed and displaced, do you think that the operation would bring them peace, too?" The security guards of UVA asked me kindly to leave the hall, and I complied but was burning inside at the way Mr. Herzog presented a whitewashed image of the devastation that South Lebanon and its people suffered because of the Israeli military operation.

There were two repercussions from my spontaneous emotional response to Mr. Herzog's speech. The first, which concerned me most, was the reaction of Ralph and Libby Cohen to what happened. The small Jewish community in Charlottesville always insinuated that the host relationship that the Cohens extended to us was wrong from the very beginning, and to prove it they pointed to my outburst. But because we cared about the Cohens, I went to Ralph's office in the English Department and explained to him the reasons for my outburst. I shared with him a letter to the editor of the *Cavalier Daily*, the student newspaper at UVA, in which I made clear why I disagreed with some of the points raised by Mr. Herzog in his speech. We liked Ralph and Libby because they were willing to open up to us when we first arrived at Charlottesville—especially Libby. She acted towards us, particularly towards Mary and Margo, as a surrogate mother and grandmother. She was loving and caring. We felt sorry that they were hurt by the incident, particularly in front of the Jewish community in Charlottesville. We assured them that our friendship was a lasting one and that we continued to appreciate their caring and their decency, which transcended fleeting incidents.

The second repercussion of my outburst and the letter to the editor of the *Cavalier Daily* came one night when a big rock was hurled through the window of the room where our two-year-old Margo was sleeping. The rock missed her head by inches, and to us it was a true miracle that she was not hurt. Some student activists on campus wanted an investigation by the University to discover who had thrown the rock and to bring that person or persons to answer for their act. In exchanges of letters between those student activists and the University administration, there was an expression of regret by the administration over what had happened and a promise that there would be a follow-up on the rock-throwing incident. Nothing of the sort happened, but I could see that the University police patrol cars were more frequent in our neighborhood, especially at night.

I was not apologetic about my outburst. The incident, however, taught me that what we Palestinians needed were eloquent spokespersons who could present our case in a rational, calculated manner apart from emotions. Whatever eloquent spokespersons would achieve could help to redress the imbalance and pro-Israel bias in the presentation of the Palestinian-Israeli conflict in the main media outlets in the U.S. When I was at UVA, I believed that I should advocate for my people and describe the injustice that had befallen us with anyone who cared to listen. Of late, although this is not to be discounted, I am more doubtful of the role of advocacy and eloquent talk simply because the structural, strategic, international, and internal U.S. factors and considerations are stacked against Palestinians.

Aside from the outburst and its repercussions, life at UVA continued calm and unperturbed. Jefferson's university was a haven of peace and striking beauty. Because of our limited means, my wife Mary engaged in some babysitting, baked Arabic bread for sale, and made intelligently planned, penny-saving shopping trips for essential food items. Eventually Mary started exploring how she could go on with her studies in Counseling Psychology. There were few opportunities, as UVA did not offer the degree sought by Mary. She tried at a college in Richmond, an hour's drive from Charlottesville, but she had to give up when the car that a friend of hers was driving almost had a serious collision because of winter weather conditions. So Mary contented herself with doing household projects and getting to know a circle of Charlottesville women associated with the University who hosted international students themselves. Besides, we had the opportunity to entertain some family and friends visiting from the U.S., including even Mary's mother from Haifa.

My mother-in-law, then in her mid-sixties, decided to come and visit us. She sent us details of her flight itinerary: she was supposed to change planes at John F. Kennedy (JFK) Airport and then to arrive at a certain hour on a particular flight to National Airport in Washington, D.C. For some reason she did not make the transfer flight at JFK and took another flight. This may sound feasible for most experienced travelers, but Mary's mother did not know a word of English, and therefore when the change of planes took place, she was lost. We were lost, too, as we searched for my mother-in-law in the airport and could not find her. When we inquired with the airline, they said that they could not ascertain whether she was on the alternate flight from JFK. So we waited and toured the airport once or twice. When I finally told Mary that we should head back to Charlottesville and come back the next day to look for her mother, her instinctive reaction, based on the fact that National Airport was closed at night, was that we should continue looking. So we embarked on an exploration of another terminal, and—lo and behold!—an elderly lady was sitting there with her back to us. As we approached her, we saw that she was crying but was deeply relieved to see us. At the end of her visit, when I accompanied my mother-in-law back to JFK by train and we passed some of the ghettoes along the way, she remarked that some of the scenes she saw from the train were worse than the poorest neighborhoods that she had seen in her life growing up in Haifa.

Among the visitors who came to Charlottesville were a couple of American friends whom we had known in Jerusalem. Dr. James Chrisman, or Jim as we were accustomed to calling him, came for one weekend with his wife Ruth in their trailer home. Jim was a dentist in Normal, Illinois, who had acquired an impressive reputation for his practice in the local community. When Mary and I took the longer-than-twelve-hour ride from Charlottesville to Normal, Illinois, in 1978, Jim invited me to meet with the Lions Club of the town. We were well received, and I could see that Jim was highly regarded in his community.

I first encountered Jim back in 1972 when he was visiting Jerusalem on his own. As he disliked traveling in organized tours, he was visiting the Ecce Homo on the Way of the Cross by himself when he met my sister Hilda, who was working there. Friendship grew between the two of them, and Hilda invited him during his stay to come and meet the family and to break bread occasionally. What impressed me about Jim was his insistence that when he traveled away from Normal, Illinois, his purpose, aside from seeing the sights, was to connect with the local people and to share their lives. This was an intelligent and beautiful attitude in an American tourist, in contrast to the "ugly American" stereotype. Jim related how during his visits to India he got to meet with local families and to mingle with them, experiencing their way of life. On one of his visits to Jerusalem Jim showed us photos he had taken of an Indian family with whom he had visited prior to his arrival in Jerusalem. We were intrigued with the photos, as they showed how involved Jim was with the life and traditions of this family, including the decoratively venerated cow of the family. We liked Jim because of this attitude. In 1979 we received the sad news of Jim's sudden passing as a result of an aneurism in the stomach. I wrote a piece mourning his passing, which was published in the local Normal newspaper.

Another person who visited with us was no other than LeRoy, who was working in Jerusalem with the Mennonite Central Committee with his wife, a nurse by profession, and their three children. I got to know him in the early seventies because of his strong belief in the possibility of peace and reconciliation in the Holy Land between Arabs and Jews. LeRoy wanted to make a difference, but at the same time he and his wife were burdened with the fact that their middle son, if I remember correctly, suffered from advanced multiple sclerosis without any possibility of halting the advance of this debilitating illness. LeRoy had to carry his son, who had a heavy build, to enable him to perform the simplest of tasks. While I do not want to dwell on LeRoy's family's internal affairs, suffice it to say that when we saw him at UVA in 1977, he was being shunned by his community—a painful experience that left its imprint on him. Nevertheless, he continued with his Mennonite faith and caring tirelessly for his son.

The friendship of LeRoy made me aware of the role of the Mennonites and similar religious minorities such as the Quakers, known to us as the Friends, and their attempts since the 1948 Arab-Israeli war to work on issues of justice and peace in the troubled Holy Land. The Friends had started two schools in Ramallah: one, a girls' school, probably the first ever established in Palestine, was founded in 1869, and the other, a boys' school, in 1901. In addition, on the main street of Ramallah sits a beautifully preserved Friends House that continues to serve the small number of indigenous Palestinians who decided to join the Friends.

The Mennonite Central Committee had had a presence in Palestine from the early forties, whether in schools or development and aid activities for a number of Palestinian rural communities, particularly in the West Bank following Israeli occupation in 1967. The American Friends Service Committee likewise had had a long presence in the country, and in the early seventies I recall making the acquaintance of American legal experts who came to Israel in order to offer legal aid to Palestinians through an office in East Jerusalem, set up by the Friends, on matters pertaining to residency rights, housing, and social security concerns. In my mind I could not separate the Mennonites from the Quakers since at the time they worked together, cooperating in their efforts to promote peace and justice through nonviolence and in line with the dignity with which individuals of all backgrounds and religions should be treated. It was this friendship with LeRoy and other likeminded Mennonites and Friends that led me to explore in greater depth the principles and beliefs of the Quakers and the Mennonites and to put these in the context of religious freedom experienced in the "good ole USA," which opened its arms to all persecuted religious groups in Europe.

Frostburg, Maryland

In 1978 I was fortunate to be offered a lectureship for one year at Frostburg State College (to become Frostburg State University in 1987) in the Sociology and Social Work Department. Frostburg is a small Maryland town in the Appalachian Mountains. In spite of its different terrain, its social relations reminded me of some closely knit quarters, such as the Christian Quarter, in the Old City of Jerusalem. We rented an apartment close to campus as we did not have a car, and we were warned that Frostburg fell in the same climate category as northern Michigan with its heavy snows and freezing winters. During the first few weeks we took the bus down the road to Cumberland, where on weekends we could enjoy the various activities around the pedestrian shopping streets and our three-year-old Margo could have fun. I recollect that one Saturday, when we took the bus back to Frostburg, there was just a handful of passengers on it, including an elderly lady. As we approached our apartment, this lady rang the "stop" signal and then turned to us, sitting at the back of the bus (because this was Margo's preferred seat), and informed us that this was our stop. Amazed at this, I told my colleague at the College about what had happened. Having been a local resident for over twenty years, he commented, "Don't be surprised, Bernie, if most of the town people know what you cook and where you go for shopping and other details of daily life."

Frostburg was unique in that people were close to people. One day I saw the President of the College with his wife at a fast-food restaurant; he invited us to sit with them and to have a bite together. Another friendship was developed with the Edwards, both of whom taught at the College. They invited us frequently to go out together, and a real friendship arose. Another couple with whom we formed a close relationship was the Olsons; Michael taught with me, and he was keen on developing the friendship, as this was his first year at Frostburg. When he was set to give a lecture, he would prepare it thoroughly to the last word, whereas by contrast I would go in with some ideas in my head and prepare to pose questions to my class that would elicit discussions and hopefully would contribute to an understanding of the assigned material.

In Frostburg Mary discovered that she could work on her Master's in Counseling Psychology. A professor in the Department, Tony LoGuidice, guided Mary in her choice of courses and was ready to supervise her work. Maureen, his friend, was a faculty member in the Sociology Department, and we got together once in a while as Mary's studies progressed. Frostburg was very different from the University of Virginia, as the students came mostly from the greater Washington, D.C., area and many of the parents were federal government employees. A three-hour drive from the District through scenic roads and beautiful mountainous vistas, Frostburg was affordable for middle- and lower-middle-class parents.

One day, as I was teaching a class and snow was starting to fall, I saw one of the employees with his snowmobile cleaning the paths across from the classroom. As we were in the "Social Stratification" course, I asked the class what a person like him would like to see his children achieve. And was it possible in the structure of economic, social, and political power in the local environment and across the U.S. for working people like him, who devotedly display the American flag in front of their modest homes, to attain their hopes and expectations? Possibly I was not fair to the man, and this became clear to me when one of the students approached me after class and told me that the man out there was his father. I apologized for my reference to him, but my student told me that I said nothing demeaning as I was explaining what I perceived to be the situation of this working person.

In September 1978, when we arrived in Frostburg, there was excitement about an event that was taking place at Camp David, about an hour's drive from the college. Prime Minister Menachem Begin of Israel, President Anwar Sadat of Egypt, and President Jimmy Carter of the United States were meeting at Camp David to explore possibilities for peace-making and an end to the conflict between Israel and Egypt. We listened to the news with excitement, and we were incredulous as we followed on television the signing of the Camp David Accords during a Sunday afternoon football game. When the broadcasting station interrupted the football game in order to cover the signing of the Camp David Accords, hundreds of football fans called the station to protest this interruption. When some of the viewers were asked live if they knew about the Camp David Accords and about Begin and Sadat, we were shocked to hear an interviewee say, "What are these things?" I am sure, however, that for a majority of Americans who cared about the Middle East and the issues that divided people from people, the work and good intentions of President Carter were something that made them feel proud of the success of their President.

We fell in love with Frostburg with its down-to-earth and caring people. Frostburg was a trusting town: doors remained open when we all went out for a picnic or for other activities. Across from us in the apartment building was an eightyish senior citizen, father of a professor at the College and a medical doctor in the local hospital. Our friendship with him and his "girlfriend," also eightyish, who was residing in an "assisted living" facility, led to mutual visits. He was always speaking about a restaurant, at some one-and-a-half-hour's driving distance, that he regarded as the best in the area. On one of these special occasions he insisted on driving us to that restaurant. What was interesting was the drive itself, as the elderly man passed by small towns and their cemeteries and stopped at each one of them, remembering his late wife, his friends, and various relatives. This was touching indeed and reminded me how back home we prayed regularly for deceased parents, friends, and acquaintances. For me, this was the continuity of the generations at its best: the living preserving the memory of the departed.

Whereas the idea of death in Western cultures is often ignored, in Middle Eastern, including Palestinian, culture we are always reminded of the inevitability of passing on. This differing attitude may explain why certain cultures are future-oriented and economically and socially enterprising, whereas others are more or less unchanging and cling to the traditions and legacies of past generations. A "death-centered" culture could be one that stresses the collectivity, the family in particular, in contrast to a "future-oriented" culture that puts the stress on the individual and her or his potential for achievement. But the questions that I often asked myself were whether a culture like my own in Palestinian society could enable individuals to excel and why it was that Palestinian students who were deemed average in their school and other areas of performance back home suddenly began to excel in an American university, an environment that did not put constraints on their individual performance. Or was it the influence of religion that kept reminding people in my culture and society of the inevitability of death and the life hereafter, and thus fostered a mindset of futility when it came to engaging in new and challenging tasks?

The Appalachian scenery of Frostburg included vestiges of the coal-mining and brick-making industries. In fact, when Frostburg State College was founded back in 1898, many of those who contributed money for buying the land for the College were coal miners. What Frostburg meant to us was a place where we could meet friendly people; their warmth indeed compensated for the cold and snowy winter months. During those months, we could not use the backyard of our apartment as snow piled up to half a meter (about nineteen inches). Walking to school for my classes, which were only a few meters away, proved impossible because the snow had hardened into thick, frozen surfaces. One time I tried to walk over a frozen plain but had to sit down and slide to the parking lot of one of the classroom buildings. This was fun for me, coming from a climate that was usually warm and with only occasional snowy days in some years. And, yes, it did snow in Jerusalem, contrary to what most Westerners thought!

Mary used her weekends in Frostburg to volunteer for the Fire and Rescue Squad in town. On some Saturday mornings and sometimes on Friday evenings she monitored emergency calls and alerted volunteers from Frostburg and surrounding areas to various emergencies. The townspeople and the squad volunteers appreciated Mary's volunteer work, which she found fulfilling. When we returned home in 1981, Mary suggested to me that in our neighborhood in Jerusalem we should start the system of volunteers and emergency squads like the one in Frostburg. Unfortunately, for various reasons, we could not implement what we thought was a valuable idea.

In the summer, when fruits and produce abounded, I was accustomed to frequent a farmers' market on Main Street in Frostburg every other day and to replenish our variety of fruits at home. One day a young lady at the cashier's counter asked me if I had a large family, and when I asked why she was posing such a question, she responded, "Because you are a regular here, and the quantities of fruit you buy are sufficient for a large family." I helped her to understand that back home in Jerusalem, when we purchased fruits of all kinds, we were accustomed to buy them in kilos, that is, in large quantities, and that we never adjusted to the way Americans bought their fruits and vegetables in such limited quantities. Whenever I went shopping for food or fruits, I was amazed at some shoppers who would buy only one lemon or a couple of oranges and a couple of onions. My shopping style, especially for fruits, was inherited from the old ways back home. The question of the young cashier at the farmers' market did not inhibit my inherited approach to shopping, to the financial advantage of the farmers' market.

In Frostburg and its environs we could see that some people were indeed very poor. Once I bought a used car with a loan from the local bank, which readily provided it when I told the bank manager that I was a teacher at Frostburg State. With the car we explored and discovered the extent of the poverty in the Allegheny Mountains of the Appalachian range. We could not believe it when we saw some shacks with television antennas on top and our American companion told us that most likely there was a family of eight living in the shack. The "Assisted Housing" program, just steps from our apartment, also made us aware that not all Americans were affluent and that some of the elderly in particular were in dire circumstances and in need of support to go on living with dignity. Frostburg was an overall lesson to us that the United States was not only the University of Virginia with its beautiful landscape and the relative wealth that walked and lived on its grounds. This insight made us love the U.S. even more, and we grew attached to Frostburg as we came to identify with its people and appreciate their will to live in a dignified manner.

Our Dodge Monaco was always driven by Mary because I did not have a driver's license. Mary, a courageous and daring person, would drive wherever needed. Nevertheless, when we went at Christmastime to Uncle Jack's home on Long Island, she was terrified crossing the Verrazano Bridge from New Jersey and then entering the Lincoln Tunnel. She had many nightmares about the drive for some nights to come. We bought our car from a clergyman, an alumnus of Franklin and Marshall, and I thought that F&M alumni, especially the Reverends among them, would never ever lie about a car's mechanical condition. When, however, we settled down with Uncle Jack's family on Long Island and we wanted to use the car the next day, we found out that the car would not start and that its motor needed an overhaul. We ended up spending some hefty sum, five hundred or so dollars back in 1978, to fix the problem—a sum that was fifty percent of what the car had cost in the first place. Not that I would distrust Reverends for car purchases from now on—but I would be careful with them the next time around!

Completing Our Studies

Returning to UVA, Mary and I were ready for the final stage of our graduate studies. Prof. Milner had agreed to serve as my dissertation advisor on the topic of "Jordanian Cabinet Turnover: 1948 to 1980." I had chosen this topic because the composition of the Jordanian cabinet almost always reflected the different components of the population and the geographical areas of Jordan. The king was the maker of the prime ministers, who traditionally served as ambassadors in either the UK or the U.S. before being nominated to the post of prime minister. The system in Jordan, according to my advisor, resembled a relatively large organization with the king acting as chief execu- tive and with the prime minister and the cabinet implementing his policies and plans. What was intriguing about Jordan and its cabinet of ministers was the rapid turnover from one cabinet to another. This was the gist of the dissertation: to account for the frequency of the turnovers and to explore the environmental reasons, both internal and external, that had affected the king's decision to sack a government and to replace it with another. While this topic may sound too academic to most readers, it is important to know that the cabinet turnover in Jordan was a way to ensure the stability of the country, so vital to regional and international interests. Since I had excelled in History in high school, I was predisposed to assume that writing about the cabinet turnover in Jordan would involve more historical analysis than critical reflection on the phenomenon. My advisor argued to the contrary and pointed out again and again that my problem was with conceptualization and not with historical narrative.

In the summer of 1979 we went back to Frostburg for Mary to complete the requirements for her Master's degree in Counseling Psychology. Prof. Tony, who was Mary's academic advisor, graciously devoted his time in the summer to seeing her through. The Edwards, whom we had befriended the year before and who were both professors at the College, very kindly invited us to stay with them in their spacious home, close to the College, in order to make things easy for us.

Margo, our eldest, found good friends in Mary and Matthew, children of the Edwards. They shared childhood pursuits, and I still remember many afternoons in which I served as a babysitter for the three of them as Mary, my wife, and the Edwards were applying themselves to lofty academic tasks. Margo loved the Edwards' cat, but one afternoon as she was playing with it, the cat scratched her to the extent that she needed medical attention. The cat was quarantined, and a clean bill of health was given both to the cat and to Margo, to the relief of all. We had a fortuitous opportunity to meet once again with the Edwards in 2009 when we were in Indiana to attend the graduation of Mona, our youngest daughter, from Earlham College. Since the Edwards were also visiting nearby in Indiana, we were able to enjoy a festive lunch together. We still maintain contact, especially with Mary Edwards on social media, communicating with her on developments in both of our families.

As Mary, my wife, went on with her work, I decided to take a course in black-and-white photography. Our instructor had asked us to practice what we learned about photo composition by going out and shooting photos in and around Frostburg. I found myself taking photos of old houses, windows, doors, church buildings, and the like. As Margo wanted to be entertained, she always accompanied me on my photographic expeditions. Eventually I hatched the idea of taking photos of Margo, including some with Mary, and I developed these photos in the College's photo lab myself. I remain proud of the fact that today in the Edinburgh home of Margo and her husband, Paul Marshall, two of these photos—one of Margo holding balloons and the other of Margo and Mary chatting with each other—adorn the entrance hall.

During that summer at Frostburg I worked hard to develop what I thought was a key chapter for my PhD dissertation. Using an old-fashioned, primitive computer that read punch-cards of information on the biographical backgrounds of individual prime ministers and cabinet ministers of Jordan, some 250 of them, I had to go every morning to the computer lab to feed card after card into the machine, which was as wide as a mid-sized room. No advanced computer systems had been developed yet, and I had to put up with repetition upon repetition whenever a period or an apostrophe had been punched incorrectly.

When we returned to UVA at the end of that summer, one of the first things I did was to submit the chapter written in Frostburg to my advisor. I went back after a number of days to receive feedback from him, and he told me that I did not get it right; once again my problem was lack of conceptualization. There were lots of facts and figures in my chapter but not conceptualization. I grew despondent about my advisor's assessment, and I went back to Mary to tell her that I thought it would be best for us to pack and go back home without my finishing the PhD. When I consulted our host friend, Prof. Cohen, he told me that even though a PhD was not the ultimate goal of my existence, I should try to check with my advisor on how best we could together advance the prospects of finishing my dissertation. With this valuable advice I went back to my advisor and asked him what he could do to improve my skill in the area of conceptualization. He liked the challenge and promised that he would ask at least a couple of the faculty members to join him one afternoon to explore with me the meaning and process of conceptualization. This was accomplished, and I found myself listening and posing questions to three prominent professors of Sociology who spent three to four hours in dialogue with me to help me to understand the essentials of the conceptualization process. I benefited greatly from this exercise, and once again I was humbled: where else than in the U.S. could you have three professors sitting with one graduate student to help him to progress in his work on his dissertation?

Eventually I finished my dissertation, and so did Mary her Master's. We were set in July of 1981 to return home. We sent our CVs to three universities back home: Najah University in Nablus; Birzeit University in Birzeit, north of Ramallah; and Bethlehem University. I also had sent out my CV (*curriculum vitae*) to a couple of Virginia colleges and universities, just in case. Both Najah and Bethlehem University offered both Mary and me teaching jobs in the relevant departments. Since Bethlehem was only eight miles south of Jerusalem, we felt more comfortable with accepting its offer than in joining Najah, which was some twenty-five miles to the north on a hilly and difficult ride from Jerusalem. Besides, we were already familiar with the setting of Bethlehem University, and we felt that it would be expedient to teach there, closer to home, and to offer our newly acquired knowledge and experience to Palestinian students from the greater Jerusalem and Bethlehem areas.

As we were packing our last items in Charlottesville, I received a call from the head of the Sociology Department at a college in Blacksburg, Virginia, offering me a teaching position for a year. He told me that the college was ready to secure permission for me to work in the U.S. if I would accept the offer. After pondering this option, Mary and I were of the opinion that, since we had an offer from back home and since our life vocation was in teaching, then it may be more appropriate to teach Palestinian students as the impact hopefully would be much greater.

Bethlehem University was generous enough to advance us some money for the transition. I recall that someone in the family had asked me about my savings in the U.S. When I told him that I had none and that I calculated on the flight back home from the U.S. the estimated costs of our education, Mary's and mine, to be in the thousands of dollars and that we considered these costs as our savings because education is an investment for the future, he was not altogether understanding.

4

Experiencing Bethlehem University and the Palestinian Rebirth

Education for Palestinians

FOR PALESTINIANS EDUCATION WAS always an inviting proposition. When the British Mandate on Palestine (1920–1948) was imposed by the League of Nations, education received the attention of the new rulers of the country. As part of their policy of encouraging Arab Palestinian communities to build schools, the British were willing to contribute 50 percent of the costs on condition that the local population would contribute the other 50 percent. Many of the over nine hundred villages that dotted the Palestinian landscape accepted the offer; often a number of villages in close proximity to each other would pool their resources and invite the British officials to act on their promise of building a school. Education was not simply a personal matter for the student, as his or her family was involved and in fact the whole village community saw in it a reflection of their social standing and commitment. Often when a village family boasted that one of its sons had achieved an advanced degree in education, other families felt jealous, and their envy led them to consecrate part of their resources, often meager, to the task of sending one of their children to school or even to a higher institution of learning in Jerusalem or abroad. The love of education among Palestinians was thus rooted within family and village social structure. This has had a lasting effect on the society at large, if one recalls that close to 65 percent of the population of Palestine during the British Mandate was of rural village background. The 1931 census of population by the British Mandate administration showed that out of a population of almost one million, 650,000 were rural Palestinians.[1]

The love of education accompanied us as we were growing up in the Old City of Jerusalem. Most families of the city, Christian and Muslim alike,

1. Census of Palestine 1931.

would send their children to school; often Christians sent their children to the privately operated Christian schools that abounded in the city. My own family, in spite of limited resources, sent us boys to the Frères School at New Gate, one of the seven Gates of the Wall of Jerusalem, while my sisters were educated at the Sisters of Zion School on the Via Dolorosa or the Way of the Cross. Education for us was not simply a value but a way to ensure that we had something—some sort of qualifications or skills—that nobody could take away from us. For us, as a refugee and dispossessed population, education came to be the symbol of perseverance and survival against all kinds of odds. Once out of high school some of us, in fact a growing number, wanted to go on to higher education, preferably to the "good ole USA."

The Establishment of Bethlehem University

Until the early seventies of the last century, there was no institution of higher education in the Palestinian territory of East Jerusalem and the West Bank. Birzeit University, then a junior college some miles north of Ramallah, offered a diploma for two years of post-secondary schooling. The Palestinian Christian community and its leaders were anxious lest the graduates of high schools in Jerusalem, Bethlehem, and Ramallah, and elsewhere in the country, might opt to go abroad to continue their higher education. With dwindling numbers of Palestinian Christians, which had become a main worry, the leaders of the community used the visit of Pope Paul VI to the Holy Land in 1964 (the first-ever trip for a Pope outside the bounds of Vatican City) to explain to him the precarious position of young Palestinians, especially Christians, as they were wooed by prospects of higher education in foreign and distant lands. They proposed to His Holiness that one way for stemming the tide of youth emigration was for the Holy See to help establish a university in the Holy Land that would cater to young Palestinians and thus contribute to their staying put in their own country. This was how Bethlehem University was started. The idea, planted in the 1964 meeting with Pope Paul VI, saw the light in October of 1973, when Bethlehem University began its first semester by sharing the buildings of the Collège des Frères, an old school of the Lasallian Brothers that had been initiated in Bethlehem in 1897.

In more than one way, Bethlehem University, the first university established in the Palestinian Territory, was a reflection of the insistence of the Christian community on staying put and continuing the traditions and heritage of the forefathers. It also highlighted the symbiotic relationship between local Christians and the larger Church community. As an institution of higher learning it encouraged some of the highly qualified Palestinians, who had finished their PhDs and Master's degrees primarily in the U.S., to come back home and contribute to the education of young generations of Palestinians. Those who returned were a dedicated and committed group of individuals who saw their vocation as passing on their knowledge to younger Palestinians. The University symbolized the love of education and its high value to Palestinians. When Bethlehem University was established in 1973, Israel had been in control of the town of Bethlehem and the Palestinian Territory for six years since 1967. A functioning university that catered to Palestinian youngsters was seen as a way to highlight the will of Palestinians to go on, irrespective of the restrictive measures of a volatile political situation.

Mary's Career in Counseling at Bethlehem University

Mary and I returned to Bethlehem University in September 1981, and we never regretted the calling that Bethlehem and its university presented to us. Mary, whose educational background was in Counseling Psychology, was intent on offering the listening and caring skills that she had acquired to Palestinian youngsters as they faced the challenges of higher education. Mary served as the sole student counselor to a campus then of two thousand students and over two hundred faculty and staff. When she retired in 2014, she had served for thirty-three years.

It was not one's length of service as a counselor or teacher that mattered in the end; it was the quality of work in one's area of expertise. Mary was always a caring and compassionate counselor. I cannot count the number of times when she almost had tears in her eyes as she related to me, without mentioning names, students' stories that needed individual, professional, psychological help and intervention on the family level. Often the stories touched on the lives and experiences of young Palestinian women who enrolled at Bethlehem University with some restrictions and requirements imposed by their families. At times the stories touched on social relationships across the social and religious divides in our society, as, for example, the city girl who was attracted to a refugee boy and whose family, refusing to accept the relationship, threatened to pull her out of the university. The family of the girl would have believed that the disparity between its status and that of a refugee boy would preclude the possibility of a good social match. Another example was the Bethlehem Christian girl who fell in love with a Muslim boy; they decided to elope and get married. The family of the girl would have nothing to do with this shocking development and cut all relations with their errant daughter.

The traumas and intensities that surrounded these stories required professional counseling interventions, which Mary worked hard to provide. In addition, there were the normal psychological pressures of being in a college environment with academic expectations to fulfill as well as new relationships to explore, particularly across gender lines, and the challenges of self-development and self-discovery in a society more prone to collective and family orientations. In fact, Mary was so determined to offer this kind of professional help that she insisted all along on the need for a counseling office open to all students and staff of the University. This was not particularly the concern of administrators and long-term planners for the University, as, constrained by limited financial resources, they sought to retain only the most essential staff and faculty in order to save on salaries and related running costs. Our concern, Mary's and mine—and, I am sure, that of the scores of dedicated Palestinian and expatriate colleagues—was to touch base with our students and their concerns, whether in academia or in the wider society. A colleague of mine, a sociologist at Birzeit University, once remarked that university enrollment for many of our Palestinian students tended to function as a social experiment or experience, especially across the divisions due to gender, geographic locality, religious background, and other particular traits, as most of our university students came from schools that were gender-segregated and that did not allow for interactions across gender or religious or social lines.

Mary once told me of a Muslim coed from a village in the Hebron region, south of Bethlehem, who was the first of the children in her family to come to any university. Some members of her family warned her that Bethlehem University was a Christian school and she should be on the lookout as a Muslim for any activity that may tend to influence her own religious beliefs. Another coed was warned by her father and brothers that she should not mingle with boys and that any news of such a thing happening would mean her immediate withdrawal from the University. "Never let us catch you smiling at boys, or you will never go back to Bethlehem University," as one of my coed students characterized her brothers' attitude on her joining the University.

These, however, were exceptional stories. When my doctoral dissertation advisor, a fine gentleman from Texas, visited us at Bethlehem University sometime in the early 1980s, I invited him to lecture to two of my classes. He stayed at the university for a couple of days and mingled with Palestinian faculty and students. When it was time for him to leave, I asked him about his impressions of his visit. His conclusive remark was that

Bethlehem University was similar to any college its size in the U.S. and that the students were not very different from students in any American college, except perhaps for the headscarf worn by some coeds.

Questions and Challenges Faced by Bethlehem University

Some of the questions and challenges raised by the founding of Bethlehem University back in 1973 remained relevant in the early eighties: How would an institution of higher learning for Palestinians make a difference in their social and cultural environment? Could Bethlehem University, with its emphasis on vocational occupations such as nursing, physiotherapy, and hotel management, make the hoped-for impact across the society? Should Bethlehem University focus exclusively on teaching as opposed to research? And could we combine both, given the small size of the university? Could we pay attention to the individual needs of students and promote their sense of civic responsibilities as citizens? How should a university like Bethlehem deal with the challenges of a continuing Israeli military occupation and the confrontations that often occurred between young students and the Israeli military and that caused the University to be cordoned off particularly on national occasions and important Palestinian days, such as May fifteenth, the date of the partition of Palestine back in 1948? How should we, as a young university, make use of the experience and expertise of universities worldwide, particularly in the U.S. and Europe but also in the southern hemisphere, to promote the quality of education and to follow up on developments in academic disciplines? Could we, as a young Palestinian university, benefit from the Israeli universities with their vast and acknowledged academic excellence? Or is the political situation a hindrance to relations with these universities? These and other questions remained at the heart of the educational process at the University. It was exciting to be part of this environment of growth as we were seeking answers to these pressing questions.

A university cannot develop the quality of its education except when the administration, staff, and faculty have the motivation to excel in the division of labor that makes a university effective. A couple of my colleagues provided the model. Hard at work to develop their physics, biology, and chemistry labs, both of them would arrive early in the morning and leave late in the evening. When a colleague, a physics professor who had earned his PhD in an American university, had been invited to attend a conference in a university in one of the rich Arabian Gulf countries, upon his return he remarked that the equipment, labs, and infrastructure in the Gulf university were on a par with those of the best universities in the U.S. and elsewhere. But in terms of producing research, Bethlehem University with its meager resources could come up with similar, if not higher-quality, research in comparison to what was produced in the Arabian Gulf university.

Teaching Introductory Sociology to Nursing Students

The Nursing Faculty, the pride of Bethlehem University, slowly gained a reputation as one of the best nursing schools in the Palestinian Territory. Graduates of the Nursing Faculty found employment in Palestinian and Israeli hospitals and specialized clinics. A couple of times when I visited the wards of Israeli hospitals, the nurses who were ministering to the patients reminded me that I had taught them at Bethlehem University. What gave me special pleasure was the fact that they still recognized me and acknowledged my contribution. But just as important was the fact that the hospitals would not have employed Bethlehem University nursing graduates if these were not fully qualified to assume the delicate medical tasks entrusted to them.

"Introduction to Sociology" was a required course for the nursing students, and I had the privilege to teach it once in a while. Every time I taught it, I was impressed with the studiousness of the students and at a loss as to how to explain their intense competitiveness for higher grades. Clearly the students who were admitted to the Nursing Faculty at Bethlehem University were the top students in their high schools. This was heartwarming and encouraging, and it reinforced for me, as well as for Mary, our decision to come back home to work at Bethlehem University. I was asked one time by an American colleague, who had managed to secure a teaching position for me at a college in the mountains of Virginia, why I decided to decline the position and to return home. My answer was that Mary and I thought it over, and we decided that since we would be involved in teaching and counseling, we may as well do it in Palestine and thus contribute to the development of our own society and its young people. Mary reminded me that a facet of our discussion of whether to stay in the U.S. or to go back home was the fact that in the U.S., if we opted to stay, we would be only two among many others, while back home we could make a difference.

One nursing student of whom I felt particularly proud, Hussein, a Muslim man from a town close to Hebron, eventually went on to earn his PhD in hospital management at Glasgow University in Scotland. After many years I met Hussein by chance, and during our conversation I asked him what had impressed him most in my introductory course in sociology. His answer was unexpected: he said that he was most impressed with how

I tried to open up students' minds by pointing out that what they thought
were unchanging truths and ways of living could be quite dissimilar in other
contexts and societies. Hussein pointed out to me that the example I gave
was about a Palestinian village whose inhabitants most likely got up at the
same time every morning, had a similar breakfast and partook of similar
meals during the day, felt and believed more or less similarly, and saw the
world from their own collective vantage point. My challenge to the class, as
Hussein recalled, revolved around whether this would be similar to the way
in which Jerusalem inhabitants, not to speak of the inhabitants of Cairo,
New York, Bombay, and other large cities, would experience daily life and
accordingly develop their different vantage points. The conclusion of Hussein was that what we often thought of as unchanging and binding may not
be so in different contexts and environments.

The Social Science Department

The Social Science Department at Bethlehem University, to which I devoted
over twenty-five years of my life, was known as attracting those students
who would not do well in other disciplines. In fact, I still remember what
one community leader told me about my sociology degree: you make a "science" out of daily occurrences that need no science to explain, but rather
simple common sense. Apparently some of the students who enrolled in the
Social Science Department felt the same way about sociology. Nevertheless,
the students in the department were the most active politically, and some of
them, years later, became high-ranking officials in the various positions of
the Palestinian government.

The faculty in Social Science attempted to engage the students with
the methodological approach to understanding the "common sense" conditions under which we lived. Those colleagues who taught the course on
methodology, among them an Arab lawyer from West Jerusalem who went
on to become a senior judge in the Israeli legal system, were hard at work
to explain why causal relationships between different social phenomena
could shed light not only on the phenomena themselves but more broadly
on developments in the society that had caused them in the first place. One
example that I often cited when we addressed methodological questions was
that of emigration out of Palestine. I argued that, while we could simply
give numbers of people leaving, it would be more relevant to know why
they were leaving and the breakdown of the migrating population by age,
religion, and socio-economic characteristics. The causes for the departure
of Palestinians from their country would thus give us ideas about what was

wrong with the living conditions that pushed them to leave and how we could work to rectify these conditions in order to keep them from leaving. The way we addressed problems and issues was related to how the society, through home and school and other institutions, nurtured us into understanding the developments around us. The scientific approach, while not necessarily opposed to religious and traditionalist precepts, offered a different interpretation of the changes in both the social and the physical worlds.

Introducing a methodological approach to explain phenomena was necessarily challenging to the minds of the students at Bethlehem University. I still remember the difficulty of one of my students—who went on to become herself a professor at the School of Education at the University—in comprehending the term "consumer society." She asked me in class to give explicit examples of a consumer society in order for her to understand the concept. Years later, when I saw her in an academic meeting, she approached me, saying that now she fully understood the concept as a good number of Palestinians had indeed joined the consumer society by buying unnecessarily: specifically, by eating out frequently and being lured by innovative and not-so-innovative home and other appliances and commodities. This was before the technological revolution with its mobile phones, iPads, social media, and other tools now common for even crawling babies!

The Film *Gandhi* and its Potential Lessons

One of my favorite activities for "Introduction to Sociology" classes was to show the film *Gandhi* (starring Ben Kingsley, 1982). The idea behind showing the film was to expose the students to a model of nonviolent struggle for the independence of India. The film also highlighted the discussions that went on in the Indian leadership and that eventually led to the division of India into India and Pakistan. The whole process of getting nonviolence to work, inspired by Gandhi, was not an easy process, as it demanded sacrifices from the people who followed Gandhi's example. Some paid the ultimate cost, losing their lives as they protested and stood up to the forces that wanted to deny them their basic human and national rights. Nonviolence is not an easy enterprise, I used to tell my students. In fact, violence is much easier than nonviolence.

During the discussions that usually followed the screening of the film, students would argue that Gandhi's context was unique and that it was difficult to duplicate his model in the Arab-Israeli conflict. But many lauded the nonviolent struggle waged by Gandhi as well as his personal traits and characteristics, which presented a model of leadership to be emulated by modern-day Palestinian and other politicians. Some of my students were writing term papers on Gandhi and how nonviolence related to our own struggle to end Israeli occupation. Not all students who attended my courses were of the same political view or party: some were on the left; others were sympathizers of the Islamic resistance movement, Hamas, which was founded in 1988 and embraced armed struggle as the only way out; still others were members of the Fatah group, militant yet amenable to talks with Israel in search of a way out of the political impasse between Palestinians and Israelis.

I was often accused by leftist students of holding the stick in the middle and failing to express political or social views that would identify me with a certain group or political party. I think that their criticism was correct, yet I always believed that the purpose of the classroom was not for the teacher to express her or his social and political beliefs and opinions, but that it was a place where students would learn new things and would come to appreciate opposite views and respect different positions. I often asked myself if I succeeded in relaying this message to the thousands of students whom I taught during my years at Bethlehem University.

The First Intifada, 1988–1993

In December 1988 the first Palestinian Intifada began. It came at a time when Palestinians were frustrated with the continuing Israeli occupation and the lack of prospects for a political solution. It took an unfortunate traffic accident at the Erez Checkpoint, an entry point between Israel and Occupied Gaza, to spark the Intifada. Four Palestinian workers returning from their jobs in Israel lost their lives as their car was slammed by an Israeli military truck on December 9, 1987. As funerals for those killed were being held in the Jabalia Refugee Camp, which is one of the eight refugee camps that dot the Gaza Strip landscape, mass demonstrations started spontaneously in the camp and in other Gaza Strip localities—demonstrations in which Israeli soldiers were pelted with stones and burning tires.

The Israeli military thought that it would be merely a matter of days before the demonstrators would get tired and their protests would be halted, but the demonstrations spread to other cities and towns in the Gaza Strip. Two weeks passed, and by then cities, towns, and villages in the West Bank joined the protests. These were an expression of people's frustration and anger at being treated as nobodies and of their desire to see an end to the Israeli occupation. Palestinian protesters used no firearms but opted for stones and burning tires to confront the Israeli military, in addition to boycotting Israeli products, refraining from working in Israel or its illegal settlements, refusing to pay taxes, or burning Israeli-issued identity cards as signs of civil disobedience.

One prominent example of civil disobedience was that of the Palestinian Christian town of Beit Sahour, which sits one kilometer from Bethlehem. It is known as the "Shepherds' Field" town because local lore has identified it as the place where shepherds heard the angelic announcement of the birth of Jesus. Citizens of Beit Sahour declared that they would do no business with the Israeli authorities, and hence they burned their identity cards or turned them in and refused to pay their taxes for an extended number of months. Certainly the Israeli authorities had to exert a heavy hand in dealing with this kind of nonviolent protest as they took care to prevent it from spreading to other localities. The use of the stone in the First Intifada turned out to be a mighty tool, and the Israeli authorities were at a loss as to how to confront and stop the protests. Eventually, breaking the bones of young Palestinian stone-throwers became an Israeli tactic that was not well received by audiences and followers of international media. Thanks to some eloquent Palestinian spokespersons, like Dr. Hanan Ashrawi (who had earned her PhD from the English Department of the University of Virginia), the Palestinians appeared to have won the hearts of those Americans who came to recognize the need for a political solution between Palestinians and Israelis.

Involvement of People from All Walks of Life

The First Intifada saw the involvement of people from all walks of life. Mothers would go out with their youngsters at midnight to make sure that their painting of slogans opposing occupation went smoothly as they stood guard to warn their youngsters of approaching Israeli soldiers. The same occurred with the distribution of the monthly leaflet by the Unified Palestinian Leadership, a group of local leaders from various political and civil society groups who directed the course of the Intifada. The monthly leaflet was distributed in the middle of the night, the most appropriate time to avoid being caught in the act by the soldiers. The leaflet was illegal since it provided guidelines for the nonviolent activities and suggested dates for general strikes, which were usually held on the ninth of each month because the Intifada was ignited by the fatal car accident on the ninth of December in 1987. Anyone caught distributing the leaflet would be arrested on the spot.

Whenever the Israeli military imposed a long curfew on a locality because of protests there, Palestinians elsewhere contacted those under curfew,

such as the residents of the Jalazoun Refugee Camp north of Ramallah, and
asked them about their basic needs. Most often the answer would be that
they were in need of babies' milk and children's essentials. A campaign by
word of mouth would then be mounted to collect all the necessary items for
babies and children and to pass them on through back-door channels to the
affected refugee camp or locality. In various localities of the West Bank and
because of travel restrictions, people started planting their own vegetables
in any small plots that were accessible in their back yards.

Palestinians relied on themselves and started working together as a
collectivity without waiting for any instructions from the Palestine Liberation Organization (PLO) leadership, which was headquartered outside
the Occupied Territory. In fact, there was some tension between the PLO
leadership outside the Occupied Territory and the local Unified Palestinian Leadership, as the "outsiders" became nervous about losing their grip
on the local population within the Occupied Territory. There was also the
generational factor that seemed to pit the younger generation of activists
against the non-action of the older generation vis-à-vis the Israeli occupation. In a discussion I had with one of my students on his perception of the
Intifada, he said, "Your generation, dear Professor, has failed us, and now it
is our turn to come up with a solution through the actions we mount in the
course of the Intifada."

The first Intifada lasted for over five years between 1988 and 1993, and
it was credited with the political developments that made possible, with an
American and international patronage, the convening of the Madrid Peace
Conference in 1991 and the eventual signing of the Oslo Accords on the
White House lawn on September 13, 1993. The Oslo Accords enabled the
return of the Palestinian leader Yasser Arafat and many of the members of
the Palestine Liberation Organization to the West Bank and the Gaza Strip.
This was the political development that enabled the "outsiders" to return
home and to establish the Palestinian National Authority (PNA), the virtual
government of Palestinians. The PNA continues to function to this day.

Closure of Bethlehem and Other Palestinian Universities

As one of its measures to stop the Intifada, the Israeli military in October
1987 ordered the closure of Bethlehem University, which lasted until October 1990. All other Palestinian universities, including Birzeit University,
as well as the Palestinian schools, were also closed for an indefinite time. In
dealing with the closure we taught at churches, hotels, private homes, and
any place that could host our classes. The educational process nevertheless

suffered, as there was no academic community but only individual courses offered by instructors in makeshift classrooms.

During the time of the universities' closure, I was asked to teach a course in sociology for a Birzeit University class at my home. It turned out to be a memorable experience, as the students from Birzeit endured long travel times and other hurdles to attend my class conscientiously. One student in one of the sessions informed me that she had spotted some Israeli security personnel outside my home. I told her not to worry, as I was simply hosting the students as friends over a cup of coffee, come what may. I found some of those students well equipped intellectually at handling the class material, particularly that of a conceptual and theoretical nature. As I did at Bethlehem University, I opted for an approach that would emphasize distancing ourselves from what is taking place in order to assess objectively the social reality and its different aspects. This approach, with my own preference for nonviolence to achieve Palestinian national goals, impressed some of the students, but not all.

I was nevertheless surprised when one of my students related in class an experience she had had with a Jewish settler family in El-Bireh, the twin town of Ramallah. At the top of Al Tawil Mountain in El-Bireh sat an illegal Israeli settlement that was without protective walls or wired electronic fences of the kind that would encircle the settlement years later. One late afternoon, the student related, a two-year-old toddler found her way down the mountain to the front yard of the student's home. Her intuition immediately told her that the toddler must have belonged to one of the Jewish families up the mountain. She held the toddler to her chest and walked up the mountain to find the toddler's mother. And indeed she did find her when she knocked on the first door in the settlement. Lo and behold, a woman appeared who, when she saw the toddler safe and sound, was overjoyed and confirmed that she was her baby. She thanked my student profusely with appreciation for bringing the toddler back home.

When my student recounted the story, she told me that she hoped that I was pleased with what she had done because, she added, "You are for nonviolence, Professor." I reminded the class, nonetheless, that in the early decades of the twentieth century, when Jews, Muslims, and Christians lived side-by-side in harmony, it was customary for mothers who had just delivered their babies in maternity wards to breastfeed those newborns, irrespective of religious background, whose own mothers could not breastfeed them. Thus those babies became "blood brothers and sisters" across the religious divide.

One shining example of the Palestinian love for education was the volunteering of university professors and other teachers to teach classes of elementary and secondary high schools at their homes, since schools were also closed during the Intifada years. I remember colleagues, including my wife Mary, who took turns to coach students with the various assignments that were dispatched to them by word of mouth.

All these popular actions, in which thousands of people participated voluntarily, indicated clearly that a society is made up of its people and not simply of its rulers or the virtual government in power. When people are challenged to emerge from their daily routines, their reaction could really spell: "Power to the People!" The restrictions by the Israeli authorities were such that even flying a Palestinian flag out of one's window was cause for arrest. Our middle son, Zack, defied this ban by flying a Palestinian flag he himself had designed out of his room's window.

A Fulbright Visitor at Princeton University

During the Intifada, which lasted for five years, I had the opportunity to be a Fulbright Scholar at Princeton University for one academic year, 1988–1989. I was hoping that the Princetonian setting, an ideal academic environment, would motivate me to do some serious research. But I was in for some disappointments at this prestigious university. My first disappointment at Princeton was that I was not offered space in the faculty rooms to feel at ease and thus to develop a sense of belonging. It is customary for a university receiving Fulbright Scholars to offer space in order to facilitate the implementation of plans for academic work. Nevertheless, I was warned beforehand that space might not be available. The pretentiousness (or what I felt was pretentiousness) of some of the faculty members and the condescending attitude toward me as a middle-aged and unpublished Palestinian academic made me feel out of place.

One time there was a department-wide event to which all members and scholars were invited, with the exception of the two Palestinian Fulbright Scholars. Infuriated, I communicated my strong displeasure to the head of the department, who apologized and rectified the situation by starting to invite us to departmental events. Apparently we Palestinians do not always take it lying down.

A faculty member whose name I do not recall invited me a couple of times to talk to his class on the modern Middle East. I elaborated some of my own reflections on the Intifada and proposed some options for the way out of the political impasse between Palestinians and Israelis. I did not feel, as I recall, that my listeners were altogether impressed with my thoughts. Perhaps I was not well polished intellectually for a place like Princeton. Or possibly Princeton was not the appropriate academic environment for a person with my Palestinian background to promote my mid-level university career.

Reaching Out at Princeton

A couple of events that happened while I was in Princeton were to remain with me: I had the opportunity to meet on two occasions with the late Prof. Yehoshufat Harkabi, an Israeli general and author, who had become a peace activist after having been a hawk on Palestinian issues, specifically on the Palestine Liberation Organization. After his long military career, he had come to realize that the only way out was through a political process rather than through military means. He advocated this position in writings, interviews, and other channels in Israel and summarized his work in a couple of lectures he gave at Princeton. At one of them I asked him if a peaceful solution between our two peoples was possible without justice for the Palestinian people. His answer was illuminating and realistic: "There could be no full justice for the Palestinians, as you know what this would mean for Israel and its continuity as a state of the Jewish people." If full justice were to be meted out to the Palestinians, then hundreds of thousands of them would return to their homes in what is now Israel. This would clearly spell the end to the Jewish state, from his perspective. I held Harkabi in high regard at a time when a host of Israeli politicians and commentators played down his ideas and his pacifist position.

The other event was the visit that I paid to the young Jewish rabbi on campus who, I thought, would be a key to the Jewish community, not simply at the university but in town as well. I ventured into his office hoping for an eventual meeting with some Jewish students and townspeople. My motivation was to discuss issues of mutual interest and concern, particularly those touching on the sensitive Arab-Israeli conflict and ways to expedite a political process forward that would see an end to the century-old conflict between Palestinians and Zionists. The rabbi promised to contact those concerned in the community and on campus and to get back to me within a couple of weeks. As weeks were extended to a couple of months, I paid another visit to the rabbi, who informed me that the desired meetings were not possible since I was considered as a propagandist for the PLO position. I did not believe my ears at first, and then, realizing that this was the end of a dialogue that did not bear fruit, I thanked the rabbi for his effort and wished him well.

Apparently the whole problem was with me and not with Princeton and its prestigious reputation, with its multitudes of graduates and world-renowned professors who have made an impact not merely on American society but worldwide. I remember fondly seeing the famous parade or walk of Princeton alumni during their weekend on campus, when they would march *en groupe*. I spotted Ralph Nader among the other well-known personalities who had graduated from Princeton. Here was the pinnacle of the best of what America offered in education, research, and influence. As a Palestinian academic, I never doubted the contributions that the higher system of education in the "good ole USA" provided, not only for Americans but for all those fortunate enough to make it to the shores of this great country. Despite my somewhat disappointing experience at Princeton, I felt it was important to me as a Palestinian to stand firm on my own grounds and to continue to advocate freedom for my people. I often contemplated what was meant by the statement of an American acquaintance at Princeton who said on one occasion that the Princeton University Department of Near Eastern Studies was known in the forties and fifties to be the extension of the American University of Beirut (AUB) because many of the visiting professors and scholars then hailed from AUB. At the time of my sabbatical year, however, the department had become known, according to my American acquaintance, as the northern extension of the Hebrew University of Jerusalem.

In spite of this debatable perception, Princeton University hosted an evening in the fall of 1989 with Prof. Edward Said, the well-known Palestinian-American professor at Columbia University who had received his Bachelor of Arts degree from Princeton, and with Prof. Hanan Ashrawi, the Palestinian activist and spokesperson. They were tasked with addressing the question of the Intifada and the prospects and conditions for going forward in the political process between Israelis and Palestinians. More than five hundred people attended. One of the professors in the Department of Near Eastern Studies was not altogether happy with the evening, as he protested that both speakers were only highlighting the Palestinian position without reference to the Israeli one. I gently reminded him that whenever there were Israeli speakers on any U.S. campus, Palestinians were never invited to present their position. In fact, throughout the experiences of my stay in the United States, it was often the case that when an institution of learning or a think tank or even a church group invited a Palestinian speaker, they made it a policy to pair the Palestinian speaker with an Israeli one. Apparently equal opportunity was advanced when it was seen as advantageous to the Israeli position or because of a fear on the part of the event-planners of being accused of harboring anti-Israeli sentiments or worse.

Talks at Universities and Colleges

While at Princeton I was invited to give talks at universities and colleges across the United States. Among those talks that I remember were the ones I gave at a junior college in Rochester, Minnesota. On the highway to the college, my hostess pointed out at a distance the Mayo Clinic. Rochester, as I recall, is a small town, but what impressed me about my audience was the fact that some of those in attendance were quite knowledgeable about the situation back home and expressed their support for the Palestinian people. In fact, I thought that I had been invited to address the audience at this Rochester junior college because of the interest and inclination of those present. Whenever some Palestinians accuse Americans of being naïve on the Palestinian-Israeli conflict and its history, they must be reminded that this is not always so. Generalizations tend to lump people together without distinction and thus make one overlook important facts about varieties and possibilities in any one situation.

A visit to Earlham College in Richmond, Indiana, left me impressed with how the students were organizing the graduation ceremony themselves and were deciding on whom to honor as their most favored teacher. They were also entrusted with the task of choosing the valedictorian of their class as well as the key guest speaker for the graduation. I was not altogether brilliant when I addressed a couple of classes at Earlham who were taking courses on the Middle East or international politics. I arrived in Earlham when there was a tornado watch, which made me nervous and ill at ease. My communication skills were affected as well as the content of what I had to say. But my awe at what I saw at Earlham could be summarized by my admiration for the way in which the individual student was nurtured into becoming responsible both for him- or herself and for the community. The college experience was not meant to put materials into the student's head but rather to equip her or him to digest this material and to draw her or his own conclusions. Based on this approach the student then has to make the effort to chart a course of life that would fulfill her or his potential in whatever field was chosen and that would combine with the efforts of others in dealing with academic, artistic, societal, and communal challenges. The student thus becomes the center of the whole educational process without any pretension from faculty or staff members. I was so impressed with this model that years later I managed to persuade my youngest daughter, Mona, to enroll at Earlham College, and I am quite pleased with how Mona has developed in terms of her work with human rights and being a defender of those who work for the human rights of others in different countries.

A Harvard Visit

While at Princeton, both my colleague from Birzeit University, who was also on sabbatical at Princeton, and I were invited to an event conducted by Prof. Herbert Kelman, the conflict resolution specialist and prominent social psychologist at Harvard University who was determined to get Israelis and Palestinians together. Our invitation had a special purpose: to sit in an enclosed cubicle and to talk for one day, in front of an audience of students, about our perspective on developments in Palestine and how we saw a way out of the conflict. The second day the enclosed cubicle would be lifted, and we would have a free exchange with the students on what they had heard on the first day and on whatever issues they deemed fit for an exchange. I saw nothing wrong in this approach, which involved a laboratory-like setting and would have allowed us to speak our minds unhindered in response to some key questions posed by the professor. My colleague from Birzeit took exception to this approach and withdrew, explaining that he did not agree to be an experimental "guinea-pig." He went to his hotel, packed, and took the train back to Princeton.

Later I learned that Prof. Kelman was a fervent, unofficial, third-party mediator between Israelis and Palestinians. He sought in his work to change attitudes and to make people listen to both sides of the divide. He was realistic in that he expressly emphasized that these encounters would not lead to a formal peace agreement but would at least increase the number of people, on both sides, who would understand the position of the other side. Personally, I believed then that encounters of this kind could promote the possibility of peacemaking or at least could lead to a better understanding of each other as well as helping to sensitize outsiders to the conflict and its realities from the two opposed positions. I continued to hold to this belief for some time to come.

Benefits to My Family in Princeton

When I left Princeton, I had no academic work to account for my year there. I felt that I had spent my sabbatical year as a loafer, and, perhaps because of my Catholic background with its propensities toward a sense of guilt, I was ready when I came back home to engage in some serious research and academic work to liberate me from the guilt-ridden emotional impact of my Princeton experience. What salvaged the year in Princeton was the fact that Mary, my wife, took some psychology courses at Rider University, which was less than half an hour's drive from Princeton.

Another benefit was the placement of Margo, our eldest daughter, at the public school in Princeton, which was considered one of the top public schools in the U.S. Margo liked her experience and the individual attention she received so much that when it was time to leave, she asked us if she could stay by herself and finish school in Princeton, which was not possible. What made her feel attached to the school setting at Princeton was the fact that back home in Jerusalem her school was run by a local Catholic nuns' order that opted for a strict disciplinary approach to schooling. Individual students and their potential did not figure much in addressing educational and pedagogical matters. Often the Jerusalem school gave preferential treatment to some students and failed to respect the feelings of others. Besides, classes had such a disproportionately large number of students that it was impossible for teachers to pay attention to their individual development. Margo's experience of the liberating environment of the Princeton public school made it difficult for her to return to the constraining environment of her Jerusalem school. But she did, and eventually she became a brilliant communications expert, thanks also to her Princeton public school experience.

One other "plus" of our Princeton experience was the enrollment of Zack, then our youngest, at age five in a costly kindergarten. The first day we took him to the kindergarten in the fall, he kept insisting that we should not forget him there. The trauma of entry into the kindergarten was possibly heightened by the fact that he did not know any word of English. When, prior to the Christmas vacation, we had a consultation with his teacher on his progress, she told us that if she had not known it herself, she would not have believed that he did not know a word of English when he first enrolled in September. She remarked that not only did he speak English fluently, but he also spoke it with a New Jersey accent.

We never regretted the year at Princeton, as we learned new things that contrasted with our old ways of learning. To each member of our family our experiences in Princeton provided the benefits of culture contact in changing minds and promoting openness to others. Thus culture contact proved to be effective in spite of my own misgivings.

Back in Bethlehem

Back in Bethlehem, the University continued to be closed. Faculty members returned to the old routine of teaching classes in dispersed, hospitable locations, taking care that the Israelis would not interfere and stop us. We managed rather well, but the vigor of an academic community was not there, as each of us had to maneuver individually in order to impart knowledge to students. Meanwhile my research developed a definite focus.

For a long time I had been hearing about the emigration of Palestinian Christians, but there were no figures showing the extent, nor were there any studies specifying the causes that led them to leave. I knew from my readings that there was a relatively large Palestinian Christian migration, especially from the Bethlehem area, south of Jerusalem, to Chile and other South American countries at the beginning of the twentieth century. The arduous trip from Buenos Aires, the port of arrival, to Santiago de Chile, sometimes by donkey ride over the Andes mountain range between Argentina and Chile, was a hallmark of early Palestinian immigration to Chile. Those who opted to leave, including three Sabella families from Jerusalem who left in 1905, went first to the port of Beirut and from there took a ship to Marseille in France, where they waited for some weeks until a ship arrived that was set to leave for America. Most often its final destination would be Buenos Aires. Palestinians who made it to Chile struggled hard, and in their sobriety, frugality, and hard work they were reminiscent of early Protestants as portrayed by Max Weber in his book *The Protestant Ethic and the Spirit of Capitalism.*

I knew also that the emigration of Palestinian Christians from Ramallah, north of Jerusalem, was destined for North America, particularly the U.S., and that there were small communities of Ramallah Christians in Chicago, Detroit, and San Francisco. In the sixties, the Australian authorities opened the possibility of migration to people from the Middle East, and it was then that scores of Palestinian Christian families, including a sizable number from Jerusalem, opted to make Australia their new home. Although the migratory trend of Palestinian Christians was known, there were no indicators locally within Palestine for the numbers and makeup of those wanting to leave, the cause for their wanting to leave, or their preferred destination.

It was because of this lack of documentation as to what was happening locally with regard to emigration that I started on my first survey of Palestinian Christian emigration. Many more were to follow with the collaboration of international scholars. Al Liqa' Center (the Arabic name can be translated into "The Encounter Center"), headed by one of my Bethlehem University colleagues, the late Dr. Geries Khoury from Fassouta village in the north of the country, focused its activities on the prevailing conditions among Palestinian Christians and worked for better interfaith relations, particularly between Christians and Muslims. The Center commissioned me to do a comparative survey of emigration trends in the Bethlehem, Jerusalem, and Ramallah areas.

The results of the survey, which appeared in 1991, showed willingness ⟨٩٩١⟩ to emigrate among a great number of Palestinian Christians, approaching 25 percent in some localities. The reasons often cited for wanting to leave were economic, such as the lack of job opportunities, and political, such as the constraints and restrictions that the continuing Israeli occupation placed on the population and its future prospects. Often family heads showed concern for the future of their children as they argued that there was "no future in this land of conflict." What I discovered from this initial survey and later surveys was that those who were most likely to leave were young families with both parents in their late thirties or early forties who were in general financially successful, having managed to accumulate some savings, and most often had close family members abroad. When questioned why they would do so, the simple answer was often the desire to find opportunities for their children that most likely would not be available under the present political realities of occupation and conflict.

"Voting with Their Own Two Feet"

The emigration of Palestinian Christians from their ancestral home has been described as "voting with their own two feet." Leaving one's country is a difficult thing because it involves not only a risky transition process but also letting go of a long family history and the memory of the places and people usually associated with growing up. Even today, many of the Palestinian Christian emigrants to Australia still recall the narrow alleys of the Old City of Jerusalem that led them to their schools and the teachers—nuns and other teachers—who taught them in high school. The heart remains where the original home is! The process of emigration, nevertheless, which also touched thousands of Muslim Palestinians, pointed to the grim realities caused by the absence of peace and of normal relations between Israelis and Palestinians, which had affected Palestinians in general and the Christian community in particular. As a result of the migratory tendency, the composition of the Palestinian Christian population had become older because of the loss of members of the younger generation, who could have contributed to the community's welfare and future development.

As I studied the migratory trends within the Christian community, I inadvertently became an expert on the Palestinian Christian community for those with interest in it. To my satisfaction, academic interest in the topic developed and grew, as witnessed by the many students and scholars who visited and sought interviews, some of whom let me know that they were working on either a Master's or a PhD degree or simply writing a story or a class paper. In spite of all this growing interest I do not believe that the Palestinian Christian situation gained greater attention among Westerners in general. There was always the sentiment among local Palestinian and Arab Christians that Western Christians ought to pay more attention to their brothers and sisters in Christ who had remained faithful to the Holy Places where Christianity originated. The Holy Places themselves are important to keep, but just as important are the local Christians with their long heritage and perseverance on the land. The local churches had tried their best to offer the needed encouragement for their parishioners to stay put, through the schools, health facilities, housing opportunities, universities, and other extraordinary services provided by these churches; in the end, however, it is the overarching political and social environment that pushes people to leave their country.

Plight of Christian and Other Minorities

At present the plight of Christian and other religious and ethnic communities in the Arab and Muslim world, particularly those in Syria and Iraq, has gained international attention. While governments, including those of Western countries, voice support for these communities under duress, the essential task is how to keep these communities viable in their original locations. While the preference of some policy-makers on migration in Western countries is to open up to Christian immigrants from the countries experiencing civil war, like Syria, this policy poses a clear danger to the survival of these communities in their original countries. During his recent visit to Jerusalem I met the Archbishop of Canterbury briefly at a reception held by the British Consul General. In answer to my worry that Europe is more generous toward accepting Christian immigrants than toward Muslim ones from the Middle East, the Archbishop assured me that this was not so. Those in charge of processing refugees' and asylum seekers' applications confine the processing to those persons living in refugee camps in Turkey, Jordan, or Lebanon. Most Arab Christian refugees do not live in refugee camps, and hence they are not likely to be included in the process of selection, according to the Archbishop's sources.

This assurance was comforting to me, but the challenge that remains for Arab Christians, and likewise for Muslims in their countries of origin, is how to construct, on the basis of a consensus, a society open to all its citizens, irrespective of religious, national, or ethnic background. I was always concerned about this topic of finding a consensus for a society for all of its citizens; in fact, I wrote a couple of academic papers on the topic. In particular I recall writing a paper on "The Status of Non-Muslims in a Palestinian State," in which I compared and contrasted what the status would be in a secular Palestinian state, in a religious Palestinian state, and in a state in which Israel and Palestine have merged as one. In the West, some politicians speak of the need to build democratic societies in the Arab and Muslim countries. But these politicians often project their own understanding of the long process of the democratization of their own societies onto the societies of the Middle East and elsewhere. Specific religious, ethnic, tribal, and other socio-economic factors that necessarily intervene in the democratization process, particularly in the Middle East, are often overlooked by these Western politicians.

Once I argued with a Dutch Muslim parliamentarian on the need to consider the specificities of societies when we discuss democracy and its values; her answer was that you either adopt democracy in its entirety, embracing its values, or you don't. Her answer poses a particular challenge to all of us in the Middle East: how can we evolve into democratic societies where all citizens feel equal in obligations and rights, without reference to gender or to religious, ethnic, geographic, or tribal background? Or is this impossible? Will the average citizen in Middle Eastern societies continue to suffer from the lack of measures to ensure her or his dignity and security in the context of democracy for all?

Nonetheless, one criticism of Western politicians who like to insist on the need for democracy in Middle Eastern societies is that they often have double standards, as when they look the other way and, on a *de facto* basis, exempt "friendly" countries from affording rights of religious belief and practice, not to speak of political rights, to those different from the dominant group, that is, to all of their citizens and residents. This double standard stems from economic, military, or strategic considerations that take priority over issues of human rights, including the basic right to exercise one's belief and traditions.

Conferences

Because of my work on the Palestinian Christian community I was invited to international conferences, both those on interfaith relations and those focusing on the situation of Palestinian Christians. One such conference was held in Windsor in the UK in 1990; more than twenty Palestinian Christians were invited by Al Tajer Foundation, a Muslim charitable organization run by a British intellectual, to discuss from various vantage points the dimensions and challenges of the Palestinian Christian presence in the Holy Land.

There were some prominent religious and secular Palestinian Christian community leaders: one was the head of Birzeit University, the late Gaby Baramki, a prominent Greek Orthodox Palestinian; another was Dr. Sami Geraisy, also Greek Orthodox, the first Arab Israeli Christian to earn a PhD degree from Cornell University, and the chairperson of the Department of Service to Palestinian Refugees of the Middle East Council of Churches. The Roman Catholic, Greek Orthodox, and Protestant bishops and church leaders of Jerusalem were also there. Also present were three academics from Bethlehem University, including the late Jacqueline Sfeir, who was known in the society at large for her pioneering work on childhood education. It was an opportunity to let the Palestinian Christians know that there were those who cared for them and wanted to listen to them in order to help them to help themselves to stay put on their land.

The first Windsor conference led to another a year or so later at Cumberland Lodge in Windsor Great Park; this one was an interreligious and interfaith encounter that hosted Jews, Christians, Muslims, and Buddhists, among others. It was truly an eye-opener for me, as some of the speakers insisted on the common bonds that united us and the need to work together to resolve outstanding issues. Since we did not have any politicians in our midst, we were hoping that the conference recommendations would be shared with politicians.

The surprise of the second Windsor conference came on Sunday when the organizer of the conference asked the participants if they would like to attend church at the Royal Chapel. I gave an emphatically positive reply and asked the organizer if the Queen would be there. He told me that no one knew if the Queen would attend. Someone else familiar with the Royal Chapel informed me that usually when the Queen was in attendance, the curtain of the Royal Balcony would be drawn. At the end of the church service, the organizer approached the conference participants and informed us that the Queen would be outside the church, greeting each one of us individually. He asked us not to extend our hand unless the Queen first extended her hand. When it was my turn, the Queen extended her hand and I reciprocated. The organizer told Her Majesty that I was a Palestinian from Bethlehem University. She responded by saying something to the effect that peace would be good for the people of the Holy Land. For me this was the highlight of the conference since I had been made to understand that it was almost impossible to meet the Queen and to exchange words with her and to shake her hand.

Interest in the Palestinian Christian community at the academic level was on the agenda of some European think tanks. An Italian friend of mine, who later became a priest, invited a Palestinian Islamist and me to participate at a Turin conference on Christian-Muslim relations, including relations of Muslim citizens with their host societies in Europe, in particular Italy. Another conference, this one on the topic of the Holy Places, was held in Milan and was sponsored by, among others, the Italian Foreign Ministry. A specialized conference took place in Bari, a city in the south of Italy, with focus on the Crusades and the resulting culture contact between medieval Europe and the Muslim East. Bari was an important transit port for some of the Crusades, and it also served as a vital commercial link between Italian and Middle Eastern cities in the Middle Ages.

All these conferences were personally enriching to me, as I came to meet a variety of scholars, historians, and other specialists. Once you are in the conference circuit, you are most likely to be invited to other conferences addressing the same topics. In each of these conferences I presented papers that touched on Palestinian Christians and the Christian community in the Holy Land. The nineties of the last century were indeed a busy time for me as well as a time for growth and learning.

The Tragic End of Albert Glock

As the First Intifada went into its fifth year, we were shocked when on January 19, 1992, we received the sad news that Albert Glock, our next-door neighbor and director of the Institute of Palestinian Archaeology at Birzeit University, was shot down in Birzeit by a masked assailant. Because of his professional stature and his efforts to link the Palestinians to their land through archaeology, the assassination of Al, as we were wont to call him, raised questions as to who had perpetrated it. These questions were never resolved. His wife Lois, a good family friend, was persistent in inquiring who had plotted and carried out the killing of her husband. She communicated with American, Palestinian, and Israeli officials for a number of years, seeking answers. She never stopped striving to find out what had happened on that fateful day when Al was murdered. The community mourned the loss of an American friend to the Palestinian people who devoted his scholarship to advancing the prospects for a peaceful resolution of the conflict and for the fulfillment of Palestinian rights to independence and a free state.[2]

We had many evenings with the Glocks as we broke bread together and exchanged views on the political realities of and prospects for our troubled land. We could see Al during the Intifada days driving his Volkswagen van to his office at Birzeit University. Once when I asked him if it were safe to drive from Jerusalem to Birzeit, given the tense atmosphere of the Intifada

2. Fox, "The Mysterious Death."

and possible road closures, he shrugged away any potential hazard or impediment to reaching his office.

Whenever Lois returned to Jerusalem for further clues and answers, she visited with us. We enjoyed her company, and our children cherished the grandmotherly love she showed them. Lois never let go, and I remember that on one of her visits, she was accompanied by her daughter and son and their children. Lois's attachment to the Land and its people was reflected in her various educational and social activities among Palestinians. She saw herself as a peacemaker, and she always sought ways to implement her convictions in practical ways. In 2011 Lois passed away at the age of ninety-one in Madison, New Jersey.

Bethlehem University and Hebrew University: Student Exchange

One of the exchange and dialogue experiences that I had in the early nineties involved some of my students at Bethlehem University together with some students from Hebrew University in Jerusalem. The late Prof. Rafael Moses, a prominent psychoanalyst, wanted to arrange meetings between Palestinian and Israeli students. He approached me with the idea, and I welcomed it without hesitation. We had to find some sort of neutral place where we could hold our monthly meetings, and we ended up agreeing that the ideal place would be Tantur Ecumenical Institute, which had been set up by His Holiness Pope Paul VI. The meetings took place in 1991 as the First Intifada was still going on. Moses believed, as I did, that understanding the other may have the effect of mitigating the impact of events and of our confrontations with each other. We started the meetings with parallel groups of five or six students each. Most of the discussions centered on who we were: our backgrounds, our religious and social identifications, and our political perspectives.

I am not quite sure, now, about what impact these meetings had on both groups: that is, about what kinds of change occurred in attitudes and whether these encounters promoted more understanding of the other and of the fears and expectations that the group had. A memorable aspect of this encounter group was the way one of my coed students, Muslim and wearing a scarf, responded to the question of whether the students had ever met an Israeli or a Palestinian and what their impressions were. My student responded that it was strange to her to be sitting across from Israelis who were there without guns since she had never met an Israeli who did not have a gun on his or her shoulder. The Israeli students, on the other hand, seemed self-centered as they presented themselves as proud Israelis and Zionists with their own vantage point and declared that they wanted to live in peace with the Palestinians. When the difficult issues of land, refugees, Jerusalem, and the ending of Israeli occupation arose, there was no consensus in the Israeli-Palestinian discussion. Some of the Israeli students related how their parents and grandparents hailed from Arab countries and that they, too, considered Arab culture as that of their forefathers. They appealed to this common cultural heritage to say that we needed to make peace.

But the relationship between the two groups, in spite of being friendly, also showed the asymmetry in the power relationship. Perhaps Prof. Moses, as did Prof. Kelman at Harvard, was hoping to create the nucleus of an environment in which attitudes would start to change in the two sides. I do not recall exactly how long we had been meeting, but we did hold more than five or six sessions before the group dissolved. Later on I learned from Mary, my wife, that Prof. Moses was taken ill. She was studying for a Master's degree at a Freudian institute in West Jerusalem where Prof. Moses was teaching. We kept in touch with Mrs. Moses as Mary went to meet her a couple of times at the Institute. Sadly we heard that Prof. Moses had passed on, and we visited Mrs. Moses to pay our respects.

One other activity to which I became devotedly dedicated was a think tank, IPCRI (Israel/Palestine Center for Research and Information), which had an Israeli and a Palestinian director and which sought to find ways to enable both groups to live side-by-side, or at best to achieve workable political solutions on issues such as Jerusalem. In particular, IPCRI worked with academics from a Belgian university, with support from the Belgian government, to undertake research on how Palestinian and Israeli communities could share the city of Jerusalem, similarly to the Brussels model. Brussels is the capital of Belgium, but at the same time it had three different population groups that each considered it as their particular capital as well. We even contemplated the Vatican example as a cloistered city-state and whether this example could be appropriate for future scenarios of the city of Jerusalem when peace and a political agreement would have been worked out. Aside from producing some scholarly articles and attending a couple of conferences, both in Jerusalem and in Brussels, I am not sure now that our work had any impact with politicians and decision-makers. In retrospect I feel that we were acting like Don Quixote when he fought the windmills and felt that he was victorious.

In today's "anti-normalization" argument, IPCRI is characterized as an organization that seeks to accommodate the political realities of Israeli occupation and its policies. I am not sure of this myself, as I still consider sensitization to each other's perspectives and outlooks to be a positive thing, even if it does not lead to changing the political realities. Certainly when I engaged with IPCRI back in the nineties, I was hoping that we could establish some bases for a comprehensive vision for Jerusalem that will include all.

The Oslo Accords and the "Peace Industry"

1983   When the Oslo Accords were signed in 1993, interest in the future of relations between Israelis and Palestinians spiraled. Many academics, journalists, politicians, analysts, and those with personal commitment to promote progress between the two peoples descended on the country from mostly Western countries, hoping to score points in the quest for peace. Some were more scholarly than most and hence undertook to examine the new realities of the establishment of the Palestinian National Authority and the preparations being made by Palestinians to have their first democratic elections both for the president and the parliament. The American Colony in Jerusalem, within walking distance from the Damascus Gate of the Old City, became a hub for all kinds of enthusiasts, peaceniks, negotiators and would-be negotiators, diplomats, international experts in all sorts of human relations processes, financiers and bankers, government and private sector experts, civil society activists, intelligence officers, and many others, for some of whom the political process between Israelis and Palestinians provided not only a breakthrough but, as important if not more so, personal gain and advancement. Hence the term "Peace Industry" became prevalent.

But, to be fair, some among us saw in Oslo the beginning of the end to the long and difficult conflict between Israelis and Palestinians. We were excited about the prospect that, at last, we could agree on common bases for establishing a peace that would end all wars. Perhaps we were naïve when we celebrated Oslo by popping open a champagne bottle, as a couple of dear Palestinian friends did at the time of the signing of the Oslo Accords on the White House lawn in September of 1993.

I continued my academic preoccupations without being overexcited by what was going on not far from my parents' home in the Old City. In fact, I often questioned why all these people were overwhelmed with the process and what impact they were hoping for. I felt that their euphoria was premature but that it was of the kind in which individuals got engaged in the process, hoping for its success but at the same time counting on the prospects of personal and profitable gains. The Oslo process and the coming of the Palestinian National Authority to the West Bank and Gaza saw the mushrooming of local Palestinian civil society organizations eager to participate in the different aspects of developing the society. For some of these civil society organizations, there was also a political objective to bring together Palestinians and Israelis in efforts of exchange, dialogue, and the quest for common ground on which the two sides could agree. Some of the civil society organizations were not restricted to Palestine, as they were founded in the U.S. and elsewhere in the Western countries. It seemed to me as if opportunities abounded for making progress between Israelis and Palestinians; for some it was genuine commitment, but for others it was another opportunity to make some money in the process.

The Jerusalem University College Experience

Amidst the expectations and hopes of the early nineties, a friend of mine introduced me to a small American college on Mount Zion that operates on a property owned by the local Anglican Church. Jerusalem University College (JUC) was previously known as the Institute of Holy Land Studies, which was established in 1957 "to study the Christian Scriptures in the context of the land where the events occurred as well as the languages, social and political culture, religions and historical relationships of the Middle East."[3] In the fall of 1994 I was asked by Sidney DeWaal, the President of JUC, to teach a course on "Palestinian Society and Politics." The students came, for a semester or a year, to attend JUC as an extension of their own universities, seminaries, or colleges back home. Students from the Midwestern states predominated. The current President of JUC, Prof. Paul Wright, describes the college as "an institution that is decidedly Christian. We support a consortium of associated schools (Christian liberal arts colleges, Bible colleges, seminaries and graduate schools) that represent the spectrum of evangelicalism."[4]

The opportunity to teach a course on Palestinian society at this evangelical college was one that I could not miss. My course, which was a noncompulsory elective, was offered once a year in the fall. The students who enrolled in my course were eager to learn about Palestinians in general and the makeup of their society. Also they wanted to learn how Palestinians view the Palestinian-Israeli conflict and the prospects for its resolution. My course outline included a historical and geographical introduction as well as an overview of the population, the political factions, refugees, Jerusalem, Israeli and Palestinian positions on contested issues, and Palestinian Christians.

3. Jerusalem University College website, "Return Home."
4. Jerusalem University College website, "Alumni & Donors."

Some of the students, particularly those who were preparing for a graduate degree, already had some knowledge of Palestinian society and its components. But most undergraduate students did not know much about the topic. In 2012 (if I recall the year correctly) one evangelical student informed me that she actually did not know that there were Palestinian or Arab Christians since to her mind all Palestinians and Arabs are Muslims. When she discovered the presence of Palestinian Christians, she set out to write a term paper reflecting on how she, an American Evangelical Christian, a "preacher's kid" as I remember her telling me, saw Palestinian Christians and their spiritual and political experience. Reading her paper made me realize how important it was for American students to spend a semester or two in Jerusalem in order to learn about the complexities and realities of life in this Holy Land.

Another experience that stood out in my association with JUC was the horror of 9/11. On Tuesday, September 11, 2001, I was set to teach an evening class for my "Palestinian Society and Politics" course. When I arrived at the college, I was overwhelmed by the trauma and shock that the students of JUC were experiencing as all of them were sitting around a giant television set watching the news reports from the scene of the twin towers. Parents were calling their sons and daughters to return home immediately since the overall environment was one of panic and uncertainty. Prof. Wright asked me if I could address the students and provide them with some words of advice. I told the students that they should take it easy for the next couple of days and advise their parents to do likewise until things became clearer. I also told them that from my own take on things here in the Holy Land, there was no immediate reason for them to consider leaving Jerusalem and going back home. So the overall advice I offered was one of "wait-and-see" how things developed. Although a couple of students had to leave because of the insistence of their parents, most students remained, and we managed to complete the semester as planned.

I continue to teach the "Palestinian Society and Politics" course every fall. I truly enjoy it since it provides an opportunity to touch base with young American students who most likely have only foggy ideas about Palestinians, not to speak of Palestinian Christians. But another factor that makes my experience at JUC endearing is the wise management and amicable relationships, as well as the home environment, that the Wrights, both Prof. Paul and Mrs. Diane, create with their perseverance and caring for the college and its community. I have been blessed with the teaching at Jerusalem University College as it has provided me with an experience of academic life in Jerusalem that is different from the experience at Bethlehem University—both rich, but in varying ways.

Are Palestinians Democratic?

Among the serious attempts to examine and understand the situation was a proposition that I received from a distinguished German specialist on the Middle East, Prof. Theodor Hanf of the Arnold Bergstraesser Institute in Freiburg, Germany. As Palestinians were preparing for the first elections in 1996, he proposed that we undertake a sample survey of Palestinians in the West Bank and the Gaza Strip to discover their attitudes to democracy. We sought to find out from the survey how democratic the Palestinians were and whether political institutions and economic development would be seen by Palestinians as promoting democracy. We entitled our book of 203 pages, *A Date with Democracy: Palestinians on Society and Politics—An Empirical Survey.* It was published in 1996 by the Arnold Bergstraesser Institute in Freiburg, Germany, after the first Palestinian elections were held in the West Bank and Gaza Strip. In those elections, Hamas, the Islamic Resistance Movement, decided not to take part, and so the results of the parliamentary elections saw the victory of the Fatah group, which is a secularist group, together with the left and with independent personalities who believed in nonviolence in pursuit of a solution to the conflict with Israel. Our conclusions were optimistic that Palestinians would seek to develop democratic institutions and that they would subscribe to economic development with the support of the international community.

Democracy is a difficult process of political and social engagement. I often argued that democracy is not a ready-made package that a people opting for it would only need to unpack before assembling its pieces. On the contrary, the pieces need to be out there in social, economic, and educational achievements that would involve a majority of the population and that would encourage a sort of collective contract to promote democratic processes and actions. In the mid-1990s, like so many other peoples and in spite of a continuing Israeli military occupation, Palestinians felt enthusiastic about the practice of democracy. We were hoping then that with democratic political institutions we could develop all our institutions and promote economic development for the benefit of all. This would contribute to the efforts of peacemaking and would at the same time, if democratization bears fruit, show that resolving long-standing conflicts with the Israelis could be achieved in a sort of democratic decision-making.

But the practice of democracy, as was shown by many countries, could lead to a loss of interest among growing numbers of people, particularly if those democratically elected into office did not perform as was expected from them in the first place. This fear and the fear that there would be undemocratic practices within the new Palestinian government led many to

warn that democracy under continuing Israeli occupation carried a contra-
diction: how could we claim to be democratic and at the same time operate
under a military occupation? And would the Palestinian leaders, including
those elected, opt for practical and functional measures for sorting things
out with the Israelis in order to keep power? Would this situation facilitate
corruption, and accordingly would the objectives of a democratic electoral
process be missed? These were questions on the minds of many Palestinians, and they reflected the serious manner with which issues that touched
on our lives and future prospects were approached by the average citizen.

Christian-Muslim Dialogue

As I continued my work at Bethlehem University, I became attracted to interfaith exchanges and meetings. As a Palestinian Christian who had grown
up with Muslim Palestinians, I always felt that I did not know enough about
the religion of my compatriots. I could read the Qur'an, the holy book of Islam, because my mother tongue is Arabic, but the principles and the forces
that made of a person a devout Muslim I did not have the opportunity to
appreciate. Accordingly, whenever there were meetings, seminars, and conferences that touched on Christian-Muslim relations, I was always ready to
contribute my remarks and to offer my analysis with a critical mind. Al Liqa'
Center, to which I alluded above, organized yearly Christian-Muslim conferences at which the speakers were Christian and Muslim religious leaders
but also academics like myself, who provided a more academic approach
to common concerns and to understanding the complex relations between
Muslims and Christians.

     In high school, although we met each other, there was never an oppor-
tunity to know in depth the religion of those others. Our school curriculum
forbade teaching about other religions, as this was considered by some as
a means for proselytization. Accordingly our knowledge of each other as
Muslims and Christians was shallow, and this deficiency left ground for stereotypes and myths to be the basis of our mutual perceptions. When I was at
Franklin and Marshall College, I chose to write a term paper on "Max Weber and Islam" for the purpose not only of learning more about what Weber,
a prominent father of sociology, knew about the religion, but also to add to
my own knowledge of Islam. It is easy to brush away a religion of millions
of people as hearsay or humbug, but the fact that a complex and appealing
belief system draws millions of people into its fold can also be debased by
stereotyping. Ignorance is a cardinal sin when it comes to understanding, if
not to appreciating, the belief systems of others. This ignorance often leads
to adopting positions that are not based on facts but on what we imagine

of the other and her or his religion without really taking time to examine in depth the facts that could lead us to a more informed appreciation of the other and the belief system to which she or he adheres.

In the Palestinian culture, as in the entire Middle East, religion continues to play an important role in defining both personal and communal relations, unlike in the U.S. and other Western societies, where freedom of religion means a more individualistic religious attachment rather than one that is tied to the family and to the community with its history and its social relations. Accordingly, if in the Middle East someone decides to convert from one religion to another, the conversion is often kept secret and not advertised. The story of Muhammad at a certain Bethlehem institution, who told me back in the eighties that he had converted to Christianity, could not become public because his safety could be compromised. But he confided in me that only his mother knew about his conversion. And there is the story of the newlyweds, he a Christian and she a Muslim, who decided to wed in a church and that the bride would be baptized—a story that could not be made public. In the United States and in the modern secular societies, one can go to sleep with one faith and wake up with another. This would never happen in Palestine or elsewhere in the Middle East. Once born into a religion, one is destined to live out her or his life in that religion.

This is why an American Jesuit friend of mine, Father Peter Dubrul, who had taught for over forty years at Bethlehem University and had lectured in Arabic since his graduation in the sixties from the University of Damascus (in Syria) in Philosophy, argued with me one time that our faith, the faith of Palestinian Christians, is a traditional and not a personal one. He seemed to be suggesting that for the faith to move mountains it needed to be a personal one developed out of conviction. As for me, I argued that traditional faith could also have its advantages, as it celebrated the community and linked up to its historic roots and its ties with the land and its holy places. The drama is not in the belief system itself but in the way it is interpreted by some to allow for various injustices as well as hostile and sometimes violent behavior towards others who are not of the same religious persuasion. The Islam we were brought up with in the Old City of Jerusalem was one that was tolerant and open to others. Our forefathers and parents always spoke of the cultural, linguistic, and national links that brought us Palestinian Christians close to our Palestinian Muslim neighbors. Our lives together extended through school, workplace, and other public spaces, and through happy and sad times. We saw in each other's faces the face of the Almighty, and we respected our different beliefs without questioning or pronouncing any derogatory remarks. We all felt then that we were made in the image of God and that as such we were all indeed the children of God.

5

Church and Civil Society: Striving for Progress

Education for Understanding the Other

GROWING UP IN THE Old City of Jerusalem and going to the Frères School at the New Gate provided me with the experience of mingling with students who were different from me. Whether these students were Armenians, Greek Orthodox, Melkites, Syriacs, Ethiopians, or Muslims did not matter much because the joint experience of studying together worked eventually to dispel differences of religion or race. Our school never taught us about other religions, as this was officially forbidden by the Jordan Ministry of Education at the time. The fear was that such teaching on other religions could function as proselytization and cause negative public discourse. On the other hand, the Lasallian Christian Brothers, who taught us catechism and obliged us to attend the daily Mass, heaped praise on the Christian religion and emphasized its advantages over and above other religions. There were also those Muslim students who participated on occasion by attending Mass and sitting in on catechism lessons. At the same time, discussions on religious matters among us, so rare if I recall correctly, dwelt more on what unites us rather than on what divides us from each other. Our relations with Jews and our understanding of Judaism were even more obscure. Sitting in our classrooms, we could spot once in a while a religious Jewish person and other Israeli figures passing in the street overlooked by our classroom across the Jerusalem city wall that in the sixties divided Israeli West Jerusalem from Jordanian East Jerusalem. But none of us, neither Muslim nor Christian students, ever formally learned about each other's religions, notwithstanding our complete ignorance about Judaism and the Jewish people—aside from the conflict and war of 1948, which made most of us students and our parents refugees.

This lack of formal education about the religions of others irked me as I grew up and went on to the U.S. for my undergraduate and graduate studies. This dissatisfaction was most likely the reason why I decided to enroll in courses on religion while at Franklin and Marshall College and to write a couple of course papers on Islam while I was pursuing my Master's and PhD degrees at the University of Virginia. There is a saying in Arabic, *Al Insan Aduwa Ma Yajhalo* ("Man is an Enemy of What He Does Not Know"), which appropriately conveys the observation that ignorance of something or someone may lead to opposition and enmity. Hence knowledge is essential, and it is even more so at the present time in order to dispel all sorts of myths, misconceptions, and stereotypes of each other that we fabricate.

When Mary and I settled down at Bethlehem University, I again had the opportunity to work with Muslims and sporadically with Jewish colleagues. The experience was revealing as these compatriot and expatriate colleagues had the interest of the students at heart. Some of them worked harder than I did at providing excellent quality education and interaction with their students. I marveled at the dedication and commitment of these people, whose performance was not influenced by religion and background. The situation was similar with my students, some of whom were devout Muslims as well as models of discipline and compliance with the requirements of the courses being taught. I liked especially the respect they showed to the teacher and their sensitivity in avoiding offense to other students. My overall experience at Bethlehem University in the eighties and the nineties of the twentieth century was one of conviviality, mutual acceptance, and cooperation among faculty colleagues in promoting the educational opportunities of our young people.

The Arab world towards the end of the twentieth century was both searching for identity and examining the roots of the golden age of the spread of Islam and the rule of Arabs in Andalusia. Often the questions that were discussed at Bethlehem University faculty meetings were those of trying to do research relevant to our local context and to the larger Arab world. The topic that we often addressed was how we could make a difference and affirm the best in Arab and Muslim culture and civilization. It is unfortunate that some of those expatriates, who devoted their entire lives to teaching and nurturing young Palestinians and Arabs, often thought of the Arab world as a *tabula rasa* on which they would inscribe the best in Western civilization and culture.

The history of Arab culture and civilization is a complex one, beginning even before the arrival of Islam and spanning centuries. Writings and discussions on interreligious matters, the contributions of Arab Christians to the development of Arab and Muslim culture and civilization through translation of Greek philosophical masterpieces, the architectural grandeur of some of the mosques and public buildings with the contributions of different nationalities and backgrounds, the openness and pluralism of Andalusia, which enabled Christian, Muslim, and Jew to interact freely and produce some of the more theologically and philosophically relevant works, the welcoming of Armenian refugees from the massacres to which they were exposed in the Ottoman Empire towards the turn of the twentieth century—all were indications of an Arab and Muslim Middle East accepting of the other and welcoming him or her at the hour of need.

Some may discount this narrative as selective or as referring to certain eras and not applicable across history. The counter-argument, nevertheless, is to say that there are antecedent examples of settings in which Muslims, Christians, Jews, and others lived and worked side-by-side in harmony and mutual acceptance. A Jordanian friend of mine, Monsignor Khaled Akasheh, the head of the Vatican's Office for Relations with Islam, reminded me recently of the complexity of relationships in the Middle East. Visiting with him in Rome during a conference of one of the UN agencies stationed in the city, Mary and I were invited to a meal he prepared himself at his apartment near the Vatican. I explained to him during the evening that when it was time for me to inform my father, who was then seventy-four years of age, of my intention to enter into marital engagement, his visceral reaction was: "Is she a Muslim?" When I told him that she was Melkite, or Greek Catholic, and that she hailed from Haifa, he was indeed relieved. During my childhood and youth in the Old City of Jerusalem, it was quite normal to have social, artistic, cultural, and academic activities that brought boys and girls, Muslims and Christians, locals and expatriates together. That was the special beauty of Jerusalem and the reason why my father feared that I would choose my future wife across the religious divide. The warmth that emanated from the different transcultural relationships emphasized the human bond rather than the background characteristics of the young Jerusalemites. This is the Jerusalem that I remember and that compelled me, together with my wife, to insist on coming back home after six years of graduate studies in the "good ole USA."

It was this environment that encouraged me to explore further the relationship across religions. My U.S. education also encouraged me to look at others from their perspective and outlook rather than my own. I would never forget the seminar on religion and literature given by the late Professor Dewey at Franklin and Marshall College. In one of the discussions I wondered why some people, my father for example, had grown to be deeply religious. The answer given by Professor Dewey was illuminating when he said in sort of a jest that extreme religiosity could be a sign of addiction.

As a pious youth I saw the world from the perspective of a devout Catholic abiding by the rules and assisting in the religious and ceremonial rites and rituals that further strengthened my religiosity. One chemistry teacher, who owned a pharmacy next to the Holy Sepulcher where we often bought our medications, accused me and people at school who were like me of being hypocritical; he expressly stated one day in class that my pronounced religiosity, including my regular church attendance, hindered the development of relations with others and acceptance of their differences. Yet being a devout Catholic never stopped me from respecting the religious beliefs of others. His accusation made me uneasy, but I thought that his comments reflected also his own insecurity in regard to relations with others. I wondered whether he wished that he could be religious like me! The perceptions and perspectives both of my Franklin and Marshall professor of religion and of my Frères School chemistry teacher are relevant in that the complexity and challenges of dialogue across religions, cultures, and nationalities have to do with whether as practitioners we tend to see ourselves and our belief system as inclusive versus exclusive, and whether in our practices we are sensitive to others and their belief systems and practices.

It is possible that my acceptance of others was due to the inclusive Arab Nationalist sentiments of the time, which saw Christian, Muslim, and Jew as part of the Arab Nation, the one condition for such inclusivity being the Arabic language and the sharing of similar cultural traits. In this context I will never forget an Israeli academic who gave a presentation on what it meant to be an Arab Jew. I was perplexed by the presentation, and when he finished the lecture, I asked him how he could reconcile being a Jew with being an Arab at the same time. His answer was revealing. He told me that his parents hailed from Iraq; that as he grew up, the one language spoken by his parents continued to be the Iraqi dialect of Arabic; and that their songs, foods, clothes, and preferences all belonged to the Iraqi Arab culture. He convinced me with this argument, especially when he added that I described myself as Palestinian Christian, which for many is a confusing combination. He pointed out that I had grown up in a Palestinian context and experienced what other Palestinians experienced and yet at the same time held Christian beliefs that I had inherited from countless generations of my family.

With regard to the effects of terrorism perpetrated by DAESH (or ISIS, the "Islamic State of Iraq and Syria," also called the "Islamic State of Iraq and al-Shams") and by similar groups, I do not offer any advice. One topic, however, that is often discussed in some circles of Arab and Palestinian educators and intellectuals is the pressing need to change our pedagogical approach in the public schools, where textbooks and teachers are prone to present the world solely from a strictly one-sided religious perspective. While learning about one's religion at school is an accepted norm in the Middle East, what bothers me and countless others in Palestinian and Arab society is the message sent to children that those who do not subscribe to one's own religion are infidels deserving of the worst fate in this world and the next. Some argue that the exclusivist attitude nurtured in our public schools does not leave space for appreciating others or for at least attempting to understand them. Hence an exclusivist religious education, in our case, spells failure to sensitize students to the presence of others different in religion or ethnicity, or both. This failure necessarily prepares the ground for the emergence of extremist and fanatical ideas, perceptions, and stereotypes that eventually shape our relations with others who do not share our own religion or ethnic or national background. The challenge, then, is how to move from a narrow religious pedagogy to a religious education that is open to seeing others on their own grounds rather than from the perspective of our own religious training.

Dialogue

As one who was attempting to come to grips with a multi-religious society in Palestine and elsewhere in the Middle East, I engaged in dialogue conferences both at home and abroad. Although the existential exercise of accepting others and their own definitions of themselves without being judgmental is relaxing—inducing interior harmony and providing energy for all sorts of relationships and encounters—often I had difficulty with well-meaning enthusiasts for dialogue and exchange who were full of self-justification. Such enthusiasts often gave the impression that they were similar to "missionaries" striving to save poor souls from eternal damnation. From my perspective, coming to dialogue encounters meant that I did not need to be apologetic for my beliefs and practices and that likewise those others did not need to be apologetic about theirs. Dialogue and exchange are meant to explore, to examine differences, to discover similarities, and to chart courses of action in which our similarities and differences could become assets in advancing better environments, societies, and habitats in which all of us have a stake. As my son Zack often reminds me when I inform him of yet another attempt at dialogue or encounter: "What is the purpose, Dad?" and "Could you have dialogue without being precise about your purpose for this dialogue?"

The challenge of dialogue across religions is not simply that of overcoming our ignorance and stereotypes of each other but also to learn the points of convergence. The banal categorization of any religion as evil and as a source of hatred and conflict does not do justice to the universal traditions, values, and legacies intrinsic to every religion. The approach I personally favor when dealing with other religions, cultures, ethnicities, and national groups is to try to view them in their own context or environment. Often the image of a flower, a tulip, or a natural wild sprout in its own environment comes to my mind: when I appreciate people and their backgrounds in this way, I feel at peace with myself and also with these others that I am trying to understand. There are certainly issues like the question of separation between religion and state; the freedom of religion and of making individual choices of a religious nature; the application of civil law to all citizens irrespective of their religious or other backgrounds; and the problematic of having religious law as a standard for judging and organizing society, among other issues. The purpose of dialogue is not to convert others but to find out whether on certain theological and practical issues there could be common ground as a basis for agreement. A Muslim student of mine, who went on to become an imam and a religious jurist and who was a participant himself in interreligious dialogue, told me that the best kind of dialogue was the one that avoided theological matters and that dwelt on the practical concerns facing the believers of different religions. I am not totally in agreement with his view since theological matters do influence relationships, practices, and mutual perceptions.

I was often asked to present papers on specific topics at conferences such as the one I attended in Bari, Italy, where the Crusades were the topic of discussion. In that conference I learned that Bari, at the southern tip of Italy, was an important venue not only for the voyages of the Crusaders but also for commerce and trade with the Arab and Muslim world across the Mediterranean. I also listened to experts exploring the various aspects of the Crusades and how they shaped relationships between Europe and the Muslim and Arab world. Another conference, held by the Agnelli Foundation in Turin, focused on the relationships of Muslims in their European contexts. Other conferences were held in Italy to explore the legal status of the Holy Places in Jerusalem and the Holy Land and how to regulate these in the eventuality of peace between Palestinians and Israelis. Both of the conferences in the UK on Christian communities in Palestine and on interreligious relations, held at Windsor and sponsored by the Muslim Al Tajer Foundation, were also important learning stations for me. Because of my interest and involvement in these various conferences, I was invited to attend the more privileged and closed dialogue sessions between the Holy See and Al Azhar Institute of Cairo, the leading Muslim theological institution.

My involvement with Catholic-Muslim dialogue in the Vatican goes back to the mid-1990s when I was first invited by my previously mentioned friend Monsignor Khaled Akasheh, who was in charge of the Office for Relations with Islam of the Pontifical Council for Interreligious Dialogue, to attend a meeting with European Muslims, most likely representatives of the recently founded (in 1989) Federation of Islamic Organizations in Europe. Having attended previous conferences in Italy on the complex relations between religions in Europe and across the Mediterranean, I had an idea of what to expect from the Vatican-sponsored meeting: to explore common values and to promote mutual understanding and respect. What surprised me, though, was the frankness with which both sides addressed each other: I recall that when a priest started mentioning how some Muslim textbooks, teachings, and mosque sermons portrayed Christians and Christianity in a very negative manner, the Muslim participants retorted that Christian textbooks, teachings, and sermons often portrayed Islam and the Prophet in very unflattering language, to say the least.

This somewhat heated exchange was a reflection of the great gulf that existed between Christianity on the one hand and Islam on the other. Often Muslims accused Christians of not appreciating the life and teachings (*Al-Sirah*) of the Prophet Mohammed; in addition, some Christians did not refrain from using derogatory language to refer to Islam and its rich spiritual heritage. The Prophet Mohammed passed on the message of the Holy Qur'an to over 1.6 billion believers the world over, making Islam the second largest religion after Christianity with its 2.3 billion believers. Christians often pointed out that Muslims did not revere the principle of Trinity and accused Christians of being idolaters because they installed statues, paintings, and other pieces of visual art in their churches. One of the main points of dissension between the two religions has always been the crucifixion of Jesus Christ and his resurrection; Muslims believe neither that Jesus was crucified nor that he was the Son of God, and they consider Jesus as a prophet of the same category as their own Prophet. The Truth according to Muslims is in the Qur'an whereas from the Christian perspective it lies primarily in the life, crucifixion, and resurrection of Jesus Christ and in the New and Old Testaments. Even when the Qur'an refers to Jesus or to Mary, his mother, with reverence and total respect, it does so in the context of Muslim beliefs and not in the context with which Christians understand and venerate them. Certainly, the fact that the holy book of Islam pays respect to Jesus and Mary can be a common ground on which to build further ties of mutual understanding between the two religions. Nevertheless, the divergence between Christianity and Islam from a theological perspective is real, and accordingly those involved in dialogue between the two sides often distance themselves from theological exchanges. Instead, they focus on the challenges and practical problems facing the believers of the two religions, particularly those living side-by-side in the societies of the Middle East and elsewhere.

Three times between 1990 and 2010 I attended the Catholic-Muslim dialogue initiated by both the Holy See and Al Azhar Institute of Cairo. The first meeting, alluded to above, was an open one in which many representatives from Islamic organizations across Europe were present. Mutual recriminations took place about the judgmental perceptions of the other's religion. While public recriminations could be therapeutic, in the sense that participants could express their feelings openly, such statements in dialogue encounters should lead to some common understanding on where the future relations should be.

One of the purposes of dialogue is to dispel the doubts and possibly the fears we have of others' religions and their forms of expression. At Bethlehem University some of my Muslim students asked me about the statues and wall paintings in the Chapel of the Infant Babe at the University and whether we Christians worship these. My answer was that we venerate them but do not worship them. Not knowing exactly what these religious symbols stand for, many of the Muslim students were hesitant to visit the chapel; others, however, were more open to recognition and respect for another religion.

Someone remarked in the first meeting I attended that the history of Christian-Muslim encounter was one of enmity and war. He alluded to the way in which Islam was spread across the Mediterranean and how the Byzantine and Christian character of lands such as Palestine and Syria was transformed into a Muslim one. The Crusades, he reminded the audience, were another instance of interreligious encounter when the "Christian West" chose to confront the "Saracens," a term used in the Middle Ages to refer to Muslims, in order to liberate the Holy Sepulcher from the grasp of "infidels." In the process of military confrontation, thousands of people perished and scores of cities and towns were obliterated. Most significant is that this military confrontation left deeply rooted suspicions of the other on questions of trust, forgiveness, and mutual acknowledgment and acceptance. Another participant, nonetheless, argued that in spite of the historical narrative that pits the believers of the two religions against each other, there were many instances and periods throughout history in which openness and outreach occurred. The example of Andalusia kept coming back, together with the contributions of Arab Christians, as well as Arab Jews, to Islamic and Arab civilization, whether as translators or as initiators of linguistic, cultural, artistic, and other activities, especially during the *Nahda*, that is, the Arab Renaissance of the eighteenth and nineteenth centuries.

2016

In December 2016 I presented a paper at the Villanova University conference on "Christians in the Contemporary Middle East" (to which I alluded above in chapter 2), in which I addressed specifically the topic "Christian Contributions to Art, Culture and Literature in the Arab-Islamic World."[1] A striking example of Christian participation in the Arab Renaissance, which I mentioned in my paper, is the introduction of the printing press by the Lebanese Christian religious orders on Mount Lebanon; moreover, they contributed significantly to the knowledge and rejuvenation of the Arabic language and its literary and cultural riches. In fact, both Christian Arabs and Jews were instrumental in promoting the various cultural and artistic developments in the Arab world as part of its Renaissance.

Islam also contributed to the enrichment of Western civilization through its legacy as witnessed in contacts, not excepting those that occurred during the Crusades; in geography and commerce; in the minor arts and crafts of artisans in textile and jewelry design; in painting and architecture as well as in literature, mysticism, philosophy, and theology. Islam's legacy in the West also influenced matters of law and society, science and medicine, music, astronomy, and mathematics.[2] Some apologists would go as far as claiming that the Renaissance in Western society would not have been possible without the contributions of Muslim scholarship and the translations by indigenous Christians, mostly Syriacs, from Greek and other ancient tongues into Arabic and then onward into the modernizing European languages.

The early contributions of Islamic and Arab civilization to the European Renaissance cannot be overestimated. An oft-repeated expression, irrelevant in my view, says that London was a mere village when Baghdad was at its zenith in the tenth and eleventh centuries. According to some, there was no possibility in Islam, subsequent to this zenith, for further philosophical or contextual theological developments—not to speak of economic versatility that would promote the kind of "capitalistic" economies that eventually developed in Europe. Thus whereas Europe, according to this argument, advanced rapidly and became a colonial and domineering power, at the same time Islam and Arabs, particularly those in North Africa and the Middle East, experienced a period of regression in almost all spheres of life. This disparity between the colonizers and the colonized could be, as one Frenchman explained to me, at the base of some of the present-day

---

1. Sabella, "Christian Contributions," 2016.

2. See Arnold and Guillaume, eds., *Legacy of Islam*.

conflictual relationships between Europe and some of its Muslim citizens. Terror groups that strike in Europe and elsewhere in the name of Islam may invoke this troublesome relationship of the colonizer and the colonized as justification. The fact that most Arab countries, with their overwhelming Muslim majorities, have not succeeded in emancipating themselves from the long-standing problems inherited from European colonial rule and the inability of their local elites to chart a course of genuine development and advancement for their post-colonial, independent societies has also contributed to the gulf that continues to exist between the masses of Arabs and Muslims, on the one side, and the Western world, on the other.

For me as a Palestinian Christian, these questions of Western-Muslim relations are not academic because they relate to issues and concerns faced daily as one follows the news. The opinions held by Western politicians on Islam and Muslims and their pronouncements, particularly on those Muslims living in Europe and the U.S. or those seeking to enter as immigrants—including the most recent waves—have pointed to disparities and inconsistencies in understanding both Islam and its believers. It is with this problematic nature of the Western-Muslim relationship that one approaches the question of dialogue between Christianity and Islam.

An example of the importance of careful, nuanced perception is an evening gathering in Jerusalem to which four Palestinian academics were invited by the Consul General of Italy Fabio Sokolowicz to brief Italian President Sergio Mattarella during his visit to the Holy Land in November 2016. Realizing that the Italian President was a native of Palermo on the island of Sicily, and having done some research on the origin of my own Sabella family, which concluded that all the Sabellas originated in Sicily, I started my briefing to the President by saying, "You may be asking what a person with an Italian-sounding family name like Sabella is doing here in this holy city." I answered my own question by pointing out to him and to the distinguished group accompanying him that my ancestors some one thousand years previously had come from Sicily as Crusaders. I continued by remarking that they had not succeeded in "saving" the Holy Land and that generations of my family have become Arabized while others here and elsewhere in the world are still dreaming about "saving" the Holy Land. My introduction broke the ice as the President laughed, but it also pointed out the complexities of the backgrounds of the inhabitants of this blessed land.

The horrendous church bombings in Egypt, on Christmas Eve of 2016 and Palm Sunday of 2017, beg the question of assessing the value—if there is any at all—of religious dialogue among intellectual and religious elites if the insights gained thereby have no results among the masses. I do believe that every religious dialogue or encounter group must be followed up by a plan of action on how to convey the points of agreement to as broad an audience as possible. Certainly this is only one approach for checking fanaticism and rejection of the other. The social, educational, and economic conditions, including illiteracy (which is suffered by at least 30 percent of the population of the Middle East), all contribute to an environment where fanaticism and rejection of others can develop. Accordingly, the challenge is not simply to see the points of convergence among Christianity, Islam, and Judaism, but how to use this convergence to develop programs of action that aim at changing minds and winning hearts to address common challenges, whether socio-economic, such as poverty eradication and offering employment opportunities to unemployed youth, or political, such as ensuring that conflicts are resolved by nonviolent means and in keeping with the aspirations of the underdog and weak in any society.

The target groups for such an exercise are not confined to Muslims since fanaticism and non-acceptance are found across religious and national groups. But my concern as a Palestinian Christian certainly focuses on the historical example, inherited from our forebears, of those living together in my region. Certainly there are phenomena of xenophobia and Islamophobia in Western societies that need to be addressed by the concerned members of these societies. But we do have a global challenge for making dialogue meetings and encounters serve as catalysts for what needs to be accomplished locally, regionally, and worldwide, depending on the nature of the dialogue group and its objective. We cannot, as people engaged in dialogue and encounter groups, assume that our meetings are important in and of themselves only. If no concrete action plans come out of these meetings, then they do indeed remain an intellectual exercise of interest only to a few.

The 2004 Christian-Muslim Dialogue at the Vatican

2004

In January 2004 I was invited by a Jordanian friend, Father Khaled Akasheh, head of the Vatican's Office for Relations with Islam, as I mentioned previously, to attend the meeting of the Islamic-Catholic Liaison Committee in the Vatican. The theme of the get-together was "Human Dignity and Human Rights in Times of Conflict." Two presentations impressed me: one by a Muslim scholar exploring how Islam treats human rights during war and natural disasters, and the other by a member of the Pontifical Council for Justice and Peace on "The Church and Human Law." Both presentations made clear that there was extensive common ground between the Catholic and Muslim positions on human rights during times of conflict. The discussion dwelt on how the confluence or convergence on the same points pertaining to human rights could be translated into mutual acknowledgment and acceptance of each other and into mechanisms and practices in the various societies where Christians and Muslims are found. The exercise of finding areas of agreement on how religions treat particular themes, such as peace, poverty, or human rights, should provide a tool for dialogue partners to work toward reshaping the distorted views of the other, whether within one's own religion or in the larger society.

Even at the pontifical level, our dialogue revealed our awareness of the fact that followers of both Christianity and Islam shared the same concerns and challenges of daily life in their respective societies. The anxieties raised by an exclusively Islamic religious identity within Arab and Muslim societies concerning the identity and status of Christian and other minorities were also addressed, especially since exclusivity on one side could lead to exclusivity on the other. The recognition of the joint challenges facing society at large and the concerted efforts needed to confront them could be weakened, causing negative repercussions across society. It was clear that without addressing the question of citizenship (*Al Mawataneh*), the feeling of Arab Christians and other non-Muslims could be uncertain in regard to the bonds that brought them together with others in society as citizens. Another interesting point raised was that in the West there was almost universal disregard of the long history of shared Christian-Muslim habitation in the Middle East and elsewhere.

In fact, I am always surprised and shocked to hear from American and other Western Christian pilgrims in the Holy Land their amazed reaction to discovering the presence of indigenous Palestinian and Arab Christians in our part of the world. Moreover, in the Muslim and Arab world there was an equal disregard or ignorance of Christianity and what it stood for. In some parts of the Arab world, including some countries in the Arabian Gulf and North Africa, there is ignorance about the existence of indigenous Arab Christian communities, as if being Christian is always associated with being Western. A colleague of mine who works at the Palestinian Legislative Council (Parliament) and who was brought up in Algeria before moving to Ramallah told me about his "culture shock" when he discovered that there are indigenous Palestinian Christians whose mother tongue is Arabic and who are part and parcel of Palestinian society and its fabric. He confided in me that it took him some time for the concept of Palestinian Christians to take hold. Another anecdote is that of a Saudi Arabian colleague at the University of Virginia. On one occasion he questioned me on how I could be an Arab with a name like Bernard. I explained to him that Palestinian society was multi-religious, but the idea apparently did not seep in. When we met by chance at the local grocery store, where I was pushing the shopping cart with Margo, our eldest, in it, he inquired about her name. When I told him that her name was Margo, he emphatically spelled out the verdict: You are definitely not Arab with names like these. He never spoke to me again as I was clearly a hopeless case for him to grasp.

Thus the dialogue meeting of 2004, while highlighting points of convergence, also developed awareness of the obstacles that hindered a genuine understanding of each other. The late Pope Saint John Paul II summarized the challenges of dialogue when he met with the conferees at the end of the two-day conference: His Holiness reminded us that the high expectations we had held for a world of peace and harmony had not materialized. The catastrophes that our world was continuing to experience, according to the Pope, made it even more important to convince people of the possibility of establishing peace and that we should all work for this purpose. His Holiness encouraged us to persevere with a culture of dialogue that would promote mutual respect and acknowledgment.

As we shook the Pope's hand at the end of the audience, I noticed a Muslim woman with a headscarf taking a longer time speaking to the Pontiff. When we left the hall, I asked her what she had said to him; she replied that she had thanked His Holiness for the positions he had taken on the war on Iraq and its disastrous consequences and on Palestine and the unresolved conflict there and for his insistence on the need to continue with Muslim-Christian dialogue. This was a nice touch on the part of this participant, who reflected the eagerness to acknowledge and respect the positions taken by the Holy See on the Middle East and its hot, murky issues.

In my presentation at the 2004 conference convened by the Islamic-Catholic Liaison Committee, I focused on Christian-Muslim relations in Palestinian society. On the eve of the first Arab-Israeli wars in 1948, there were 145,000 Palestinian Christians living under British administration in what was then Mandatory Palestine. With the establishment of Israel, following the war, 60,000 of these Palestinian Christians became refugees, including my own family, as I have mentioned previously. The indigenous Palestinian Christians who remained in Israel upon its establishment numbered 35,000 in 1948. Another 50,000 Christians were living in the West Bank and Gaza. Many of the Christian Palestinian refugees chose to emigrate to more distant lands such as the U.S. and Canada, Latin America, and Australia. The demographics of Palestinian Christians are as much shaped by the politics of the Arab-Israeli conflict as are the demographics of Palestinians in general. This is confirmed by the fact that in 2004 almost 30 percent of the actual Christian Palestinian population in the West Bank and Gaza Strip was of refugee status. This may not be apparent to many simply because Christians are an urban population and they have chosen, almost all of them, not to live in the twenty-eight refugee camps dotting the Palestinian landscape. The only Palestinian Christian refugee camp was established in Dbayieh, north of Beirut in Lebanon, where until today some 5,000 to 6,000 Palestinian Christian refugees and their descendants continue to live.

In general, the relations between Christians and Muslims in Palestine were harmonious; Muslims and Christians were living side-by-side in the cities of Jerusalem, Bethlehem, Ramallah, Nablus, Jericho, and, in what is now Israel, Nazareth, Jaffa, and Haifa. The conviviality of living together developed our identities both as Palestinians and as dwellers in specific cities. In the rural areas, Palestinian Christians were found in a number of villages. Zababdeh, a predominantly Christian town in the most northern part of the West Bank, had always enjoyed excellent relations with neighboring Muslim villages. Birzeit, of a mixed Christian-Muslim population, saw the founding of Birzeit University, which is considered the national university of Palestine, by the Palestinian Anglican Nasser family. Taybeh village, which is almost exclusively inhabited by Christian Palestinians, saw the establishment of the first Palestinian brewery by the Greek Orthodox Khoury family. Jifnah, a village next to Jalazoun refugee camp, north of Ramallah, exported its Christian teachers, entrepreneurs, and other professionals to Ramallah and Jerusalem. Ein Arik and Aboud, two villages with mixed Muslim-Christian populations in the proximity of Ramallah, cemented Muslim-Christian relations as they developed shared communal events on religious occasions and took part in each other's family occasions, both happy and sad. While Artas village, south of Bethlehem, did not have any Christian population, it boasted nevertheless the beautiful Hortus Conclusus convent, which derived its name from the enclosed garden of King Solomon in the Song of Songs. The convent is home to orphaned girls from throughout the country.

I did not want to paint an ideal picture of the relationship between Muslims and Christians in Palestinian society. My intention was to describe the mutual acknowledgment existing between the believers of the two religions. Certainly one factor in this acknowledgment was the respectful attitude of Muslims toward the sites associated with the life and resurrection of Jesus Christ, in recognition that Palestine is a holy land for both faiths. The example of the Muslim Caliph Omar, who came personally to Jerusalem in 638 CE in order to accept its surrender from the Christian Patriarch Sophronius and who refused to pray the Muslim noon prayer in the Church of the Holy Sepulcher, had become a model to Muslims on the need to respect the integrity of Christian holy places. I also reminded the participants in the dialogue meeting that the churches in Palestine and Christian Palestinians have always been active in catering to the educational, health, caritative, and other needs of the population, irrespective of religious background. Thus the roots and causes of a harmonious relationship between Muslims and Christians are mutual: one side cannot do it alone!

In regard to this tradition of healthy interreligious relations, I noted that with the rise of "political Islam" and the calls by some Muslims to make the Shari'a Law (the Muslim religious law based on the Qur'an and the life of the Prophet) the basis for governance in all Muslim societies, Christians and other non-Muslims felt that they had become marginalized. The imposition of a religiously inspired law would mean that the exercise of *Muwataneh*, or equal citizenship, would be rendered impossible. The fear of exclusivity under a strictly religious governance system had become worrisome to many Christians and non-Christians alike, including the secular-leaning Muslims.

I pointed out in my presentation the challenges facing Palestinians in particular as we strive to end the Israeli occupation. But ending the occupation was not the only goal: we needed concerted Christian-Muslim efforts to attend to the socio-economic, educational, and other needs of Arab Palestinian and Muslim societies, particularly those of the weak segments of the population: women, children and youth, the elderly, and the disabled. I argued for more respect across faith groups, for more understanding in light of the challenges confronting the Arab world, whether those of economic reforms, of increasing the employment opportunities for youth, of tending to the wounds of long, drawn-out civil conflicts, or of forging partnerships with others. The shared traditions of living together and a long history of communal togetherness should aid in the prospects of building together a brighter and more peaceful future.

Some in the Arab and Muslim world do not understand the attachment and love that Arab Christians have for their homeland. This lack of understanding emanates, in my opinion, from too much preoccupation with self and from failing to note the contributions of Arab Christians to the awakening of the Arab and Muslim world since the beginning of the nineteenth century. When people are in a numerical majority, they usually do not feel a need to understand what others, particularly religious and ethnic minorities, are doing and how they are feeling about issues and concerns that touch on the quality of life for everyone. The world is seen from the majority vantage point. This is true in different places and with regard to different religions, national groups, and contexts. The minorities, again in terms of numbers, are usually more defensive, and they tend to see every move by the majority or some of its members as being directed specifically against them. Hence majorities do not notice, and minorities are too easily offended. But the need to be accepted the way we are, shaped by the beliefs and traditions that our parents and forebears have passed on to us, is an elementary one in promoting mutual acceptance and sharing of the present and the future.

I addressed specifically the challenges of peacemaking and eventual reconciliation between Palestinians and Israelis and how dialogue and contact between the two sides could facilitate the prospect of a just peace. I stated that we all, Palestinians and Israelis alike, are in the midst of a very painful conflict in which all of us are paying a heavy price. Palestinians and Israelis have never been so polarized in their long conflict with its ups and downs over the years. In fact, as of this writing, separation and polarization have become the norm rather than an exception between Israelis and Palestinians. This situation clearly accentuates the need for coming together on the human and religious levels, as well as on the political level. Accordingly, exchanges among religious leaders and others are important to pursue.

Talking to the other does not mean that we agree with the policies of the other's government, but it is simply a way to affirm that there are wider concerns that touch all of us and that have to do with the human face of people created in God's image. Hence exchange and dialogue are intended to affirm the dignity of people and their rights, amidst even the most difficult circumstances that result from continued conflict. Sometimes there is skepticism about the potential of exchange and dialogue for the mitigation of ongoing suffering caused by disrespect for human rights and dignity. But the message of exchange and dialogue is simply that we are all together in the same predicament and that we need to find ways to promote the common tenets of human dignity and human rights.

Some would argue that exchange and dialogue between Palestinians and Israelis must come after the occupation is over and after the other side acknowledges its sins, so to speak. This position, however, because it often arises from the pain of injustice, hides the fact that the other also has a human face—that, in spite of all masks and positions adopted by the other, others are like us, with human faces and caring hearts, even though they may not care about us but only about their own. It is this caring that brings them to the exchange, just as it is our caring that propels us.

Holy Land Christians

As I stated in the 2004 meeting, our security—that of both Israelis and Palestinians—cannot be assured by constructing an ever-increasing number of walls, whether they are physical or psychological. The Israeli government, backed by a significant number of its constituents, believes that the so-called "security wall" (Palestinians refer to it as the "separation wall") is the solution to security issues. When the separation wall was being constructed between the town of Abu Dis and the city of Jerusalem, I was visiting the Sisters of Our Lady of Sorrows, whose order originated in France and who run a home for elderly people of all faiths just a few meters from where the wall was being built. I witnessed how some Palestinian women who worked for the Sisters had tears in their eyes when they observed the construction of the wall. Apparently these women were crying because the wall was about to shut them off, with their children and families, from the surrounding environment. It would exclude them from the conviviality of being with their friends, relatives, and parents and from their right to spend time in their city of Jerusalem.

In fact, the consequences were even graver than the women seemed to perceive: the wall would imprison them by depriving them of freedom of movement. The denial of this basic right is intended by the Israeli builders of the wall to bring a sense of security to Israelis. But what would people imprisoned in this manner think of? What would walled-in people think when they look at the separation wall? Some would argue that because of this wall, all exercises of dialogue and exchange are futile. But I would agree with what an Israeli educator, an acquaintance of mine, said: that all this is temporary and that therefore the need is even more urgent for exchange, dialogue, and meetings to emphasize the right of all people to be free of all separation walls. I agreed fully with her because, like her, I believed, as I do now, that the wall would eventually fall and that was why it was important to recognize the other, to talk to the other, and to work with the other to secure respect for human dignity and rights through working for a just and lasting peace.

As Christian Palestinians, in spite of our small numbers—a small "flock," in church parlance—we have an important role to play in the Holy Land of Palestine and Israel. I reminded the esteemed participants in the 2004 meeting that the Holy Land is not simply a place of roots for us; it is also the place where Christian Palestinians live as citizens, whether in Palestine or in Israel. This had been beautifully pointed out in the statement issued by Heads of Churches on Jerusalem as "the place of roots" in November 1994.[3] Accordingly, and in spite of their small numbers, Christians of the Holy Land have as much right as any other group to contribute input to the process of peace-making and eventual reconciliation. In fact, the Christian dimension in the present conflict is important as a reminder, especially to those who simplistically reduce the conflict to Jewish-Muslim religious

3. "The Significance of Jerusalem," 1994. Quoted words are in paragraph 9.

differences, that the conflict and its solution are not a strictly religious question but a political and nationalist question.

The Church, therefore, is called upon to emphasize the Christian dimension and to remind all that our presence here is not simply a question of numbers, as it has a rich heritage of history and of belonging to the land where Christianity first arose. This position does not contradict the claims and narratives of others, be they Muslims or Jews, as the churches' statement of November 1994 explained. The Church is also called upon to encourage all kinds of contacts and exchanges among the different nationalities and faiths that make up this blessed part of our world. This is important because the more frequently Israelis, Palestinians, Muslims, Jews, and Christians come together, the greater is the likelihood of developing a common vision for the future of all.

In my concluding remarks at the 2004 conference, I highlighted the importance and significance of a comprehensive peace between Israel and the Arab world. The current reality is that Israel poses a more serious hindrance to such a comprehensive peace than the Arabs do. There was a time when the Arab states refused to recognize Israel. Today, however, the issues of war and peace between Israel and its neighbors are quite different from those of five years ago or even of one year ago. More of the Arab countries have come to recognize Israel, whether officially, as in the establishment of formal diplomatic relations between Egypt and Israel and between Jordan and Israel, or through unofficial contacts, as is the case with some North African and Arabian Gulf countries. The role of the United States is crucial in peacemaking between Israel and its neighbors—not simply because it is a superpower in today's world but especially because of its unfortunate direct involvement in Iraq and with Israel (in regard to the latter, ever since Israel's birth). The Israelis will not make peace on their own accord. Some of them feel that their military power is sufficient to contain any and all security threats—a viewpoint that is viable only for the short or medium term. In the long term, Israel is as much in need of peace as we are. Sacrifices need to be made on all sides, and Israel has to face up to these sacrifices. Without the proper pressure, or, to put it more diplomatically, assertive encouragement, from the U.S. administration, it is unlikely that Israel will move forward on a peace agenda. The Church can provide an input to policy-makers in the different countries by stressing the need for painful sacrifices on all sides. But in the end peace is made between people, real people, and hence there is need for continued dialogue, exchange, and mutual learning about each other. The process is hard, difficult, and painful. At times it leads to pessimism and a sense of defeat, but there can be no justification for yielding to these sentiments, understandable though they are. If we do not work together for peace, we will perish together in continued war and conflict.

As I write, the tragic and horrific attacks on two churches in Egypt have killed or injured scores of the Christian faithful on Palm Sunday, April 9, 2017. The atrocity has shocked all here in Jerusalem. My wife commented that this act was particularly barbarous because Palm Sunday for the Christians of the Middle East is an occasion to bring children with their decorated palm branches to the processions that take place in the churches across the region. It is a joyful occasion where children meet children, and families exchange warm wishes for a blessed Palm Sunday and Holy Week. It is the community coming together. The bombings in the two churches, which sent shock waves across indigenous Christian communities, were condemned by politicians of the international community. What saddened us here in Jerusalem was the certainty that the bombings, like the previous one, also in Egypt, which took place on Christmas Eve, will eventually arouse a desire among local Christians to leave their countries.

We all know, Muslims and Christians alike, that DAESH (or ISIS) is a terrorist organization that allows no place in the region for Christians and other non-Muslims, or even for Muslims of differing sects. It is an exclusivist terrorist organization that abuses religion to reach its objectives. It also aims at sowing the seeds of sectarian strife in the societies of the Arab world in order to weaken the political regimes that it perceives as too moderate or secular. The most poignant remark I heard from a fellow Palestinian Christian as we were watching the traditional Palm Sunday procession in Jerusalem was that these terrorist attacks would continue and that it was our destiny in the Middle East to live with threats and instability. My worry as a student of Christian emigration from the Middle East is that these attacks and other manifestations of religious exclusivity in our societies will surely be an impetus for more and more Christians to leave their countries of origin. This will be indeed sad, especially since the Middle East is the cradle of Christianity, and countless generations of hermits in the Egyptian and Syrian deserts—as well as active priests, nuns, friars, and religious sisters in various Middle Eastern lands—have given their lives to serve and mold Christian witness throughout the region. Christian families in Egypt, Iraq, Syria, Lebanon, Jordan, Palestine, and Israel nurture their children on the faith of the forefathers, who were always attached to the motherland as the place of roots. Most unfortunate are the voices, often heard in the West, asserting that if Western countries were to receive refugees and immigrants from the Middle East, it would be preferable if these were Christians and not Muslims. This discriminatory attitude of some in the West could eventually lead to the emptying of the Middle East of its indigenous Christians,

and this pains us as it pains our long history in this holy and troubled region. Middle Eastern Christians in particular countries, such as Iraq and
Syria, feel that they can no longer live in an environment lacking in mutual
acceptance and respect for religious difference; hence any opportunity that
comes their way to settle in a Western country is welcome. On the other
end, European governments and societies are wary that more Muslim immigrants who refuse to integrate and accept the values of the host society
could pose a potential danger of intercommunal conflict. Middle Eastern
Christians, according to this view, do not have a problem in integrating and
in accepting the values of the host European society.

At the 1997 Synod for Asia in the Vatican, I was given the unique opportunity and privilege to have dinner, together with eleven other participants,
with His Holiness Pope Saint John Paul II. The questions the Pope asked of
me, as well as of Bishop Maroun Al Lahham, the Latin (Roman Catholic)
Bishop from Jordan, revolved around Jordanian and Palestinian Christians
and their relations with Muslims. The Pope was interested in knowing more
about the indigenous Christians who are citizens of Jordan and those in
Palestine. When he inquired specifically about priestly vocations, he was
told that particularly in Jordan we were blessed with many vocations among
the youth. He also wanted to know about Bethlehem University and its
contributions to Christian-Muslim relations. I told His Holiness about the
fact that Bethlehem University serves Muslims and Christians alike, with a
student population that is 70 percent Muslim and 30 percent Christian. I
invited His Holiness to visit Bethlehem University when his planned visit to
the Holy Land would take place.

Another Vatican Dialogue, 2009

In February 2009 I was invited again to the meeting of the Islamic-Catholic
Liaison Committee in the Vatican. Monsignor Khaled Akasheh, who heads
the Office for Relations with Islam of the Pontifical Council for Interreligious
Dialogue, was instrumental in procuring an invitation for me to take part
in this meeting. To those acquainted with Arabic names, the Monsignor's
name sounds not only Arabic but also Islamic. The reality, though, is that
Monsignor Khaled hails from a Christian tribal family in the Hashemite
Kingdom of Jordan, just across the river Jordan from Palestine.

The Akasheh family is one of the oldest tribal families in Jordan
that espoused Christianity long before Columbus discovered America! In
fact, the Akasheh belong to the Ghassanids, a tribal group from the Arabian Desert, now in Saudi Arabia, that has embraced Christianity since its

early centuries. Some also link the Akasheh and other Christian Jordanian
families to the Nabateans, the inhabitants and founders of the famous "Rose
City," Petra. When Islam arrived in Jordan and in the Arabian Desert in the
seventh century, many Christian tribes and tribal families, including the
Akasheh, adhered to their faith. The Christianity of the Akasheh and other
Jordanian and Palestinian Christians is so ancient that it reveals the history of Western Christianity in the West to be relatively recent. Those who
are surprised that there are indigenous Christians in the Arab and Muslim
world should be reminded that the Bible (Acts 2:8–11) mentions Arabs as
among the earliest of those who were evangelized and believed in Jesus and
his words. Arabs, as the Bible says, were telling in their own tongue "the
mighty works of God" (verse 11, RSV).

The pride that the Akasheh and other Jordanian families have in their
sustaining faith is reflected in the fact that they encourage their children
to join the priesthood or religious life. When a Jordanian family has a son
ordained or a daughter taking the vows of a nun, it is a source of much happiness and pride. The Akasheh, like other Christian families in Jordan and
Palestine, have given much for their society, whether as priests and nuns
or as professionals in private and public institutions, including government
ministries and the parliament, and they have maintained excellent relations
with their neighbors, irrespective of religion or other characteristics. In their
ongoing witness they exemplify what is referred to as the "Dialogue of Life."

The theme of the 2009 meeting, "The Role of Religion in the Promotion of a Pedagogy and Culture of Peace," conveyed the challenge offered
to the participants, namely, to discover the common grounds that bring us
together. After identifying the common grounds, we could then examine
how in practice we could transform them into bases for mutual relations
of understanding and openness to one another in daily life. The theme also
highlights the fact that our region has witnessed continuing wars, of which
the Arab-Israeli conflict is but one example, and it is a region where the
three monotheistic religions, Judaism, Christianity, and Islam, had their
beginnings. It is also a region where misunderstandings, misperceptions,
and stereotypes abound, and these are spread across our world, affecting
many people's perceptions of other religions and traditions. The Middle East
region, as well as other regions in our world, urgently needs a process for
nurturing new generations, across all religious groups, in the values indis-
pensable for peace. A stable and prosperous society cannot be had without a
basis of harmonious relations across religious, ethnic, and national groups.
It is the task of creating the system that could ensure such harmonious relations that poses the most poignant challenge to all of us as we strive to work
ourselves out of hatred, violence, and non-acceptance of others.

For this Islamic-Catholic meeting I was asked to prepare a paper on the theme of the meeting. I was awed when the paper, originally composed in Arabic and translated later into French, was accepted as the Catholic position. In the paper presented, I emphasized that the continued warfare and ethnic, religious, and tribal animosities and confrontations are a clear indication that the world order has failed us. I reminded the participants of the Barcelona Declaration of December 1994, the "Declaration on the Role of Religion in the Promotion of a Culture of Peace," issued as a result of a conference organized by UNESCO that gathered distinguished religious leaders from the world's different religions.[4] The Declaration affirmed that the intermingling of cultures and the mobility of peoples in our world make us all interdependent and hence we have a joint challenge. Religion, according to the Declaration, cannot be the only remedy, but it has a most important role to play in a world with cultural and religious diversity. Each culture, according to the Declaration, is a universe in its own right, but no culture is hermetically sealed. Hence a call to recognize pluralism, as cultures make contact with each other, and to respect diversity, as not all people are alike in their religious and cultural preferences. The Declaration pointed out that religions did indeed contribute to peace in the world but that they had also led to division, hatred, and war. The Barcelona Declaration described peace as the full preservation of love, compassion, human dignity, and justice.

Dr. Mahmoud Zakzouk, who had been a participant in the 1994 Barcelona Conference on behalf of Al Azhar, the leading Islamic institution of jurisprudence in the Arab and Muslim world, stressed in his Barcelona presentation that peace originates within us. Thus we are called to nurture the inner selves of our children to the values of peace, love, and openness to others. Accordingly one of the primary challenges to all of us is how to build a culture of peace from within ourselves and across our families, communities, and national and ethnic groups in order to promote mutual understanding, tolerance, dialogue, and justice.

I highlighted the point that education for peace is a complex process since it involves the different actors that imprint their influence on the child and the adult alike. The family, the religious community, the school, the culture, the system of governance, and even the habitat or environment where we live—all these cause us to develop certain tendencies and attitudes. How can we harmonize these attitudes, which at times reject outsiders, with the values inherent in the acceptance of others and their unique cultural and religious experiences? The formula for a culture of peace needs, then, to take

---

4. "Declaration on the Role of Religion," 1994. UNESCO is the United Nations Educational, Cultural and Scientific Organization.

into consideration the roles of the different actors in education for peace. And how do we educate children exposed to the ills of war and ongoing conflict to a culture of peace? Is peace possible without working for justice, as many assume?

Some warn that peace within us and full acceptance of others can lead some to think that the world is in an optimal state. This attitude can turn into a passive one that posits that if I am at peace with myself and others, then all is fine and I do not need to undertake any effort to examine realities and to seek opportunities to change them. We cannot, however, have genuine peace within us without activating this feeling to change the difficult realities of political conflict, social and economic inequalities, religious intolerance, and the marginalization of illiterate people, women, youth, and the disabled. Thus peace within us is a nucleus for a plan of action that seeks to redress injustices and to work together to promote reconciliation and harmony among people. A difficult agenda indeed, but we need to entertain it because otherwise we lose our grip not only on our own lives but, as importantly, on the life and health of our planet and its various cultures, religions, and nationalities.

The Second Vatican Council in its document *Nostra Aetate* of October 1965 referred specifically to relations with Islam. I reminded the distinguished participants in the 2009 Islamic-Catholic dialogue meeting of the importance of *Nostra Aetate*. The Church in that document expressed high regard for Muslims, who worship the one God, submit themselves to God as Abraham did, venerate Jesus as a prophet, and honor the Virgin Mary. But *Nostra Aetate* also pointed out that throughout the centuries there have been many instances of discord between Christians and Muslims. Thus the Council pleaded with all to transcend the past and to work sincerely to achieve mutual understanding in order to preserve and promote together the values of peace, liberty, and social justice. Citing 1 Peter 2:12, the document urged the Christian faithful to "maintain good fellowship among the nations"; moreover, "the Church reproves, as foreign to the mind of Christ, any discrimination against men or harassment of them because of their race, color, condition of life, or religion."[5]

I challenged the participants in the 2009 dialogue meeting to incorporate the positive experiences of living together, in Palestine and elsewhere in the Middle East, into a pedagogical approach designed to ensure that future generations would adopt peace and acceptance of others as a way of thinking and of life. I asked what the contributions of Muslims and Christians were in stopping bloodshed in diverse areas of our world, whether in Palestine,

5. *Nostra Aetate*, 1965. Quoted words are in section 5.

Bosnia, Sudan, or Somalia. If we cannot develop a joint strategy for making peace, then how can we work in parallel to serve peace and justice? What is indeed the responsibility of the religious institution, whether Muslim or Christian or Jewish, in promoting education for peace?

Hence I argued that, as the Rabat Declaration of February 1998 had asserted,[6] there was a need to develop activities directed to youth in order to affect constructively their everyday behavior; activities geared to the rereading of our histories so as to correct the misinterpretations; activities that would examine the way religions are being taught in our schools; and activities aimed at infusing the media with timely and appropriate information in order not to fall prey to stereotyping.

The Rabat Conference was jointly organized by King Hassan II of Morocco and by Federico Mayor, Director-General of UNESCO. It was attended by religious leaders, academics, jurists, and intellectuals from the Middle East and elsewhere, representing Jewish, Christian, and Muslim traditions. The fact that they called for activities to lead to a culture of peace reflected the awareness of the conferees that dialogue meetings cannot be effective if they do not adopt a programmatic approach with specific activities to reach the masses.

I reminded the participants also of the Declaration of Montserrat of 2008, issued in Barcelona by the Conference on Religions and the Building of Peace,[7] which reasserted the Barcelona Declaration of 1994—particularly its call for religions never again to be the origin of confrontation, but rather a source of conciliation. The Declaration of Montserrat emphasized the need to promote committed involvement among the leaders of various religions, as well as those in civil society, to work towards non-violent political solutions to the conflicts in the Middle East and elsewhere in our troubled world. As the Declaration criticized double standards applied by some states that impact the role of religion negatively, it called for religions and civil society to act on political institutions at all levels and to uphold lofty values in a world that is witnessing increasingly unjust economic and social systems. One of the paragraphs of the Declaration of Montserrat highlighted the fact that the meeting took place on the occasion of the sixtieth anniversary of the Universal Declaration of Human Rights (United Nations, 1948) and fully endorsed it. In particular, the Montserrat document expressed respect for the right of freedom of belief, both religious and other, and encouraged dialogue with people of different identities.

6. "Dialogue Between the Three Monotheistic Religions," 1998.
7. "Religions and the Building of Peace," printed in 2010.

The fact that those engaged in dialogue often insist on practical steps to reach the masses or refer to international human rights conventions is to be lauded. In so doing, they place dialogue and encounter groups in context rather than isolating them as mere academic or ivory tower exercises. But I pointed out to the conferees in the 2009 Catholic-Islamic dialogue that often religious leaders who attend such meetings place their signatures with conviction and yet find it difficult to go against the mainstream when they return home to their constituents. Thus the double standards that the Declaration of Montserrat referred to are also applicable to religious leaders. These become enthusiastic supporters in conferences and dialogue meetings of a prominent role for religion in advocating non-violence and condemning violence, irrespective of its source or rationale. Upon arrival at home, however, and upon discovering that advocating the same positions that they upheld in the conferences and dialogue groups may place them in conflict with their constituencies, they retreat into silence, or, worse, they justify the wrong that their group or their government is inflicting on another population. In order for our dialogue to bear fruit, I encouraged the participants in this Islamic-Catholic dialogue to work together to develop educational programs, cultural activities, and youth gatherings, in such a way as to create a concrete reality rather than to waste time in a futile exercise.

The "Final Declaration of the Annual Meeting of the Joint Committee for Dialogue of the Pontifical Council for Interreligious Dialogue (Vatican) and the Permanent Committee of Al-Azhar for Dialogue among the Monotheistic Religions (Cairo, Egypt)," issued at the conclusion of the February 2009 meeting, addressed some of the points discussed and agreed upon during the two-day meeting.[8] The need for peace and security was highlighted with stress on justice and equality. A special responsibility falls on religious leaders, Muslims and Christians alike, to teach and preach the promotion of a culture of peace. School textbooks should be revised so as not to offend the sensitivities of other believers, and the media should become instrumental in working towards respectful and positive interreligious relations. Freedom of conscience and religion falls within the defense of the dignity and rights of the human person and is in keeping with the shared opinion that there can be no peace without the preservation of and respect for human rights. Special attention and care should be given to youth in order to shunt them away from fanaticism and violence and to help them become peace-builders within their societies. Finally, the Declaration, with due respect to the competence of political leaders, asked these leaders to make use of the resources available in international law and through dialogue to solve the unresolved

8. "Final Declaration of the Annual Meeting," 2009.

conflicts in the Middle East. Clearly people come to dialogue and encounter groups because there is something that needs to be changed.

Refugees, Religion, and Reconciliation

At the time of the Arab-Israeli war of 1948, more than 726,000 Palestinians became refugees. Wars always produce victims who bear the wounds of eviction from their homes for generations to come. When in 1948 and 1949 thousands of refugees were housed in temporary, makeshift camps in the vicinity of Jerusalem, three deacons from the Anglican Bishopric of Jerusalem felt that something needed to be done to help these refugees. The winter weather during these years was particularly harsh. I still remember the big snowstorm that hit Palestine when I was six or seven years old. The intervention of the three Anglican deacons started with a letter to the then-Prime Minister of Israel, and its founder, David Ben Gurion. The deacons argued that, in line with the UN General Assembly Resolution 273 of May 11, 1949 (which accepted Israel as a Member State of the United Nations), there was a commitment by Israel in the framework of the Right of Return of Palestinian refugees to accept back 100,000 of them. The Israeli government reneged on its commitment, and hence all refugees were denied return to their original homes.

Of interest for the "dialogue of life" argument, which says that people of different faiths should work together for the good of society—in contrast to exchange and dialogue meetings in closed venues—was the fact that these three deacons contacted local public figures of the various Christian denominations or churches and asked them to join together in a local ecumenical committee with the main purpose of offering needed help to the refugees, mostly Muslims but with some fifty to sixty thousand Palestinian Christians. As an enthusiastic response, a committee was formed that applied to the government of Jordan for a license to serve Palestinian refugees in both the Jerusalem and the Amman areas, or what was referred to then as the West Bank and the East Bank of Jordan, respectively. The example of this committee in Jordan was copied in Lebanon and later on in the Gaza Strip, then under the control of Egypt, and in Israel, specifically in Galilee, where there were hundreds of locally displaced people who had been driven out of their home villages, some of whom ended up in Nazareth and some in Haifa. The committees that were formed in the various localities came to be known as the Department of Service to Palestinian Refugees (DSPR).

In 1997 I learned by chance that the Department was looking for a director. Some of its Board Members encouraged me to apply, and I felt that the position would be one where I could contribute to the work of DSPR and its development. Throughout my years of service in the Department, I have always felt that my colleagues exemplified the Christian spirit of opening up to others, irrespective of religion or other background characteristics. They emphasized that they were part and parcel of their society, the pain and suffering of their people, and the people's expectations and hopes for a dignified life and a better future. Many of the colleagues and staff members of DSPR were themselves refugees and thus knew firsthand the agony of becoming a stranger and a refugee. The services offered included health clinics, vocational training, and educational and cultural activities among others. For decades, those services have reached out to thousands of women, youth, and children. In the Gaza Strip, our largest branch, there were over 110 employees, including one hundred Muslims. There was a handful of Christian Palestinian employees and staff members, who either belonged to the original Christian families of Gaza or were themselves members of refugee families.

A Special Friendship and Witness

In my almost twenty years as the head of the Department of Service to Palestinian Refugees (DSPR), I have been impressed by many of our Western, mostly Protestant partners and supporters, who saw their support for DSPR as support for the indigenous Christians of the Middle East to preserve their roots through service to their fellow citizens, irrespective of religion or other backgrounds. One friendship, however, stands out. It originated with the compassion of an Australian couple, Pat and Harry Wallace, of Scottish origin. They had heard me back in November 2002 when I participated in the launch of the Christmas fund-raising appeal. We were invited, Mary and I, by the National Council of Churches in Australia, a key partner to DSPR and its work for over three decades, to participate in the launch of the appeal by giving talks to Australian audiences and meeting with key politicians to brief them on the work of DSPR and on the overall situation and conditions in the Occupied Palestinian Territory.

During that launch event I was approached by Harry and Pat Wallace for help in locating Palestinian artists who could create paintings for the "Jesus Laughing and Loving" exhibition slated to be opened in 2004 at the famed Greyfriars Kirk in Edinburgh. Zaki Baboun, a Palestinian artist from Bethlehem with whom Mary and I and our two daughters, Margo and Mona, had traveled to Edinburgh, managed to have a couple of his paintings included among the thirty-six paintings representing sixteen countries in the exhibition, although he had struggled with the idea of a happy Jesus living in Palestine, as the Wallaces told us later. The exhibition was an occasion of joy and spiritual growth, and it brought us closer to the Wallaces. It was also the occasion for us to be introduced to Sir Maxwell MacLeod, son of the legendary Sir George MacLeod, who founded the Iona Community in Scotland. A friendship developed with Maxwell and with his sister Mary that has lasted since then.

In July 2006 the Wallaces invited me, both as head of the DSPR and also in my new role as an elected Palestinian legislator (as of January 2006), to be the guest speaker at the Beecroft Forum Dinner, an event organized by the Major Issues and Theology Foundation of Sydney, Australia. Of course they included Mary in the invitation. During our month-long visit to "Down Under" we came to realize that individuals like the Wallaces can make a world of difference with their conviction about the need to extend peace and justice to Palestinians. Three years later, after the Israeli onslaught on Gaza in January 2009, the Wallaces decided to work on yet another painting exhibition. This time they wanted Muslim and Christian children of Gaza to reflect on the grim realities of war and its effects on them. The DSPR Gaza director, Constantine Dabbagh, who is a good friend of mine, helped in contacting schools and adult artists to enable children to participate. The paintings by Gaza children were eventually completed, and we succeeded in getting them out of Gaza and onward to Australia. The collection has been exhibited in Scotland, Australia, and New Zealand. I am told by the Wallaces that selected paintings of the exhibition were used by an Australian Uniting Church minister for the fourteen Stations of the Cross for Holy Week 2017.

The Wallaces invited Constantine Dabbagh from Gaza and his wife Samira in 2010 to travel to Australia as guest speakers for the Beecroft Forum. Constantine used the occasion to inform his audience of the fact that Gaza City was the first-ever Christian city in the world and that the small Christian community there is standing firm together with other Palestinians under very difficult social, economic, and political conditions, due to the ongoing Israeli siege of the Gaza Strip, which started in 2005. He spoke also about DSPR and its work in health, vocational training, and community service. His presentation was warmly received by the audiences with whom he interacted. Recently the Wallaces have been active in supporting Bethlehem University, particularly its Nursing Faculty. The situation of Gaza and its small flock of Christian faithful are also on the Wallaces' minds; in fact, they have collected material for writing and publishing a brochure on "Christians in Gaza"—material that they are sharing with audiences particularly in Australia but also elsewhere worldwide.

Palestinian Christians: An Integral Part of their Society

Palestinian Christians in Gaza and elsewhere in the Middle East always felt that they were an integral part of their societies. Most spoke Arabic as their mother tongue, which in cultural terms made them similar to Muslims. I was amused when a French journalist told me one time, "You indigenous Christians of Palestine are Muslims, except that you go to church on Sunday instead of going to a mosque on Friday." I found his conclusion hilarious, and when I asked him why he thought this way, his answer was that Palestinian Christians had adopted the manners and ways of Muslims, and that even our faith was a communal one rather than an individual one of personal discovery and affirmation. "Besides," he argued, "you pray to Allah in your churches!" I exploded in laughter when he said that because, as I tried to explain to him, <u>Allah is the Arabic word for God</u>. What other word for the Divinity did he want us to use? I asked him to suggest an alternative if he did not want us to use the name Allah.

The conversation with the French journalist revealed the complexity of the misunderstanding that some "informed" Westerners held regarding the relationships between Muslims and Christians throughout the Middle East. But the relationship across religions, in spite of a history of relatively friendly relations between Muslims and Christians in Palestine and elsewhere in the Middle East, had had its ups and downs. Presently, the rise of radical Islamist groups, such as DAESH (or ISIS), which use religion as a pretext to "empty" Muslim lands of historically rooted Christian and other non-Muslim minorities, particularly in Iraq and Syria, has forced many of us, Christians as well as Muslims, to examine our relationships in the various contexts of our co-existence in the different societies of the Middle East.

Thus dialogue is not a luxury but a necessity for many of us in the Middle East. The danger of misunderstanding is the reason why, when there are calls for dialogue, often the people who are engaged in real-life dialogue become a little suspicious. They tend to be apprehensive about the possibility that the recommendations and conclusions of dialogue meetings would appear so harmonious that they would not reflect the realities and the fears on the ground. Much needs to be done on the ground and in the different contexts in which we live in the Middle East to envision together the kind of future and the relationships we want to see developing in our societies. When, as is the reality in the Middle East, religion plays an overall regulatory role in the lives, cultures, and worldviews of people, then the fundamental question becomes this: How can we reconcile different outlooks within society? The terror that struck the churches in Egypt on Palm Sunday 2017 and on Christmas in the previous year also raises the question of what to do with the wounds inflicted on communities that have lost trust in the sincerity of the dominant religious group in a society. Can dialogue, indeed, help to heal intercommunal wounds resulting from terror, discrimination, and an exclusively religious worldview?

With regard to inter-nation or inter-group dialogue, as between Palestinians and Israelis, we need to ask whether reconciliation is possible with separation. Since the beginning in 2002 of the construction of the Israeli Separation Wall dividing Israelis from Palestinians, a marked polarization has taken place between the two groups. This polarization casts serious doubt on the usefulness of dialogue and exchange across Israeli and Palestinian groups pitted against each other in the context of an occupation that refuses to acknowledge the right of the Palestinian people to its own state. (As stipulated in UN Resolution 181 of November 29, 1947, the creation of an Israeli Jewish state would go hand-in-hand with the creation of an Arab Palestinian state.)

Dialogue and exchange activities, however, can be perceived as futile in that they do not usually produce the desired effect, not simply of bringing hearts and minds closer to each other, but also of working together to change the grim realities and to prepare the ground for living and sharing together. So what to do? Some would even go to the extent of criticizing dialogue groups in the Israeli-Palestinian context as attempting to embellish the harsh reality of a continuing Israeli occupation, expropriation of Palestinian lands, and other measures of denial and negation of the political aspirations of Palestinians. Thus more and more Palestinians, particularly women who used to be avowed participants in dialogue meetings, are now refraining from meeting their Israeli counterparts because they sense that dialogue and exchange under the present unequal conditions and amidst the impasse in the political situation can give the false impression that all is well.

With the ongoing Israeli occupation and given the political impasse in finding a just and lasting solution to the Palestinian-Israeli conflict, some tend to see dialogue and encounter groups as "normalization" and as such oppose these efforts. Their argument is that by holding such meetings and other joint activities between Israelis and Palestinians, including business meetings for Information Technology companies and others, the continued occupation and its measures of control are accepted. Unless those who are committed to dialogue are equally committed to work toward ending the Israeli occupation, then the activities that stress exchange and dialogue between the two sides would end up accommodating the difficult realities of a harsh Israeli military occupation on the ground without working to change them.

On the other hand, those who are pro-dialogue and promote contact between the two sides argue that we do need to touch base with each other while not accepting the effects of the continuing Israeli occupation. In their view, Palestinian-Israeli meetings and contacts are essential to lay the basis for a joint undertaking to change the grim realities on the ground. The pro-dialogue and pro-contact position does not necessarily see its practitioners as advocating normalization but as simply creating networks of people on both sides who believe that the situation as is cannot go on. They are accused by some opponents of being simplistic and naïve as their efforts will not result in changing the intricate, structural system of control imposed by the ongoing Israeli occupation.

The Commission for Justice and Peace of the Assembly of Catholic Ordinaries of the Holy Land addressed the topic of "normalization" in a recent statement.[9] "In both societies, Israeli and Palestinian, the life of the Palestinians is far from normal, and acting 'as if' things were normal ignores the violation of fundamental human rights." The statement goes on to say that daily life requires contacts between Palestinians and Israelis but cautions that "all persons and institutions involved in maintaining these relations should be aware that something 'abnormal' needs to be set right rather than allowing the 'abnormal' to become the order of the day." Another Palestinian Christian document, "Kairos Palestine," published in 2009 with the endorsement of thirteen high-ranking church leaders of the Holy Land, addresses Jewish counterparts: "Even though we have fought one another in the recent past and still struggle today, we are able to love and live together. We can organize our political life, with all its complexity, according to the logic of this love and its power, after ending the occupation and establishing justice."[10] Yet another Palestinian Christian document that highlights the importance of justice is "The Jerusalem Sabeel Document," which states: "We can do no other. Justice alone guarantees a peace that will lead to reconciliation and a life of security and prosperity to all the peoples of our land. By standing on the side of justice, we open ourselves to the work of peace; and working for peace makes us children of God."[11]

As a Palestinian Christian I am commanded in the Bible to love my enemy. This love, however, should never be mistaken as a call for normalization and for accepting what is "abnormal." Loving one's enemy does not stop at simple love as it involves also working to change the enemy's heart and

9. "The Question of 'Normalization,'" 2017.

10. "Kairos Palestine," 2009. Quoted words are in paragraph 5.4.2.

11. "The Jerusalem Sabeel Document," 2006. Quoted words appear in the final section.

behavior. Hence if I love the Israelis, according to my Christian religious commandment, then the challenge to me would be how to change their hearts so that they would examine their own stand and their direct and indirect involvement with the continuing occupation of Palestinian land.

I would argue, nevertheless, that enthusiasts who continue to believe in overcoming differences and deep political divisions in order to share the future should also invest in changing attitudes and hearts in their own respective societies. We do not need a "Peace and Dialogue" industry to convince us that we need to work within our respective societies for a different future in which reconciliation can happen. So the task for us Palestinians is to address the challenges waiting for us in our own society: how to educate our youngsters to strive to end the occupation not only nonviolently but with the skills that would allow them to distinguish between "the good, the bad, and the ugly" in the society of the adversary. Many Palestinians, including Christians who read and believe in the Hebrew Scriptures, find themselves at a loss in attempting to understand both Israeli society and Jewish religion. These remain foggy in the minds of many Palestinians, and I am sure that the same phenomenon happens on the other side with respect to Palestinian society and the Holy Writings in which Palestinians believe. An immense amount of work lies before us. Self-congratulations are appropriate when success is achieved in one area of joint undertaking, such as in the treatment of children with cancer or the academic exchanges on water desalination, or when an international gathering that includes Israelis, Jordanians, Palestinians, and others from the Middle East comes up with a joint plan of action on specific matters. The challenge nevertheless is whether we can change hearts and win over minds on both sides, Arab and Israeli alike. It is not constructive when some think that Israeli hearts are already won and we only need to work now on winning Palestinian and Arab hearts! Truly this is a recipe for further failings in our efforts at charting an inclusive course for our future together.

6

Reflections on the Future of Palestine

The Decision to Enter Politics

IN AN AGE OF populism and with the increase of mistrust in politicians as shown in opinion polls in Europe and elsewhere, becoming an elected politician presents many challenges. I was not a born politician, and I always felt that governments have systems of authority that at times become oblivious to the needs of the average citizen. The domineering behaviors that governments exhibit have alienated sizable segments of the population from the exercise of their rights and obligations towards governments, including the right to vote. As a public figure the politician has many partners who follow up on her or his positions as manifested not only in the politician's voting record but also in public utterances on various issues. Personal behavior, including relations within the family and even on social media, becomes a target for gossip, whether attacks or praise, depending on the perspective of the gossiper. Thus a politician is always exposed to a judgmental audience that demands explanations and accountability.

A political career can be an attractive proposition that drives up the adrenaline and puts one at the center of challenging and demanding positions. The successful politician succeeds in managing these positions and finding a compromise that pleases some people for some time, at least. But politics remains a demanding and taxing proposition: the failure of successive generations of politicians to deliver on what is basic and most important for most of the citizens encourages disillusionment and a desire to punish these politicians either by refraining from voting or by adopting populist and various other expressions of disappointment. The power of voting, although hailed as a primary democratic exercise, can also become a punishing tool if politicians do not deliver or if their performance is judged to be dismal. The phenomenon of anti-establishment zeal becomes part of the voting behavior of people disillusioned with the performance of the dominant political elite.

In the Palestinian context, becoming an elected politician, as in the U.S. and other countries, is tied to the political party with which one associates. Personally, I was never a party adherent because I always felt that my status as an academic gave me the freedom to assess political positions and actions on their own merit and not on the basis of party or factional platforms. But it would be misleading if I did not admit that I always wanted to experience politics from the inside.

My venture into politics was tied to my Christian background and my middle-of-the-road political preferences. When in 1996 the newly founded Palestinian National Authority arranged for the presidential and parliamentary elections for the first time, I knew that I did not have a chance and preferred to be an observer. A couple of friends, including lawyer Jonathan Kuttab, a Protestant Palestinian and a firm believer in nonviolent peacemaking who had earned his law degree at the University of Virginia, ran on platforms that promised change and a way forward that would positively impact the lives of Palestinians. Unfortunately for my independent friends, those who won the elections in 1996 were affiliated with the dominant political party, Fatah, as they were assured of the votes of the party's rank and file. The winners represented a spectrum of personalities and public figures, most of whom were endorsed by the leadership that had signed the Oslo Accords in 1993.

Between 1996 and 2006, when the second parliamentary elections took place, I followed the political scene from afar. I heard the growing disillusionment, particularly with the performance of the government. Most of the activities and legislation of the Palestinian parliament were restricted by the Oslo Accords, and hence the parliament could not legislate on matters that pertained to foreign policy or those touching on the negotiations with Israel. This deficiency, nevertheless, was compensated for by the fact that some updating of the antiquated legislation inherited from the time of the British Mandate and the regimes of Jordan, Egypt, and Israel did take place, to the satisfaction of the general population.

Legislation remains an important part of the Palestinian parliament as well as monitoring the government with its various ministries besides approving the annual budget for the country. These are important functions. There could be no democracy without the accountability involved in the dynamic relationship between the executive branch of the government and the Parliament, or the legislative branch. The judicial branch of the government is an essential complement to the function of both the executive and legislative branches. In Palestine we have adopted this trilateral system of governance because we felt it would ensure the checks and balances needed in a democratically run society, even in the contradictory situation of the continuing Israeli occupation.

In 1995, some months before the first presidential and parliamentary elections, I undertook, together with Professor Theodor Hanf, director of the Arnold Bergstraesser Institute in Freiburg, Germany, a field study on the political attitudes of Palestinians. We were pleasantly surprised when our survey concluded that the Palestinians were a nation of democrats. The sample representing Palestinians in both the West Bank and Gaza wanted a government that is accountable; politicians who would deliver on promises and platforms; and a guarantee that freedom of expression would be honored and that negotiation of a peaceful agreement with Israel would not renege on Palestinian political and historical rights, given the transformations that have occurred in Israeli-Palestinian relations since 1948. Palestinians sought a system of governance that would make the government accountable and that would render public figures, including elected legislators, answerable for their behavior, voting records, and performance in public office. While the overall political situation of occupation had hovered over most of the activities of the Palestinian government and its elected officials, Palestinian voters wanted attention to their day-to-day concerns. Palestinians, as our survey showed, were caught between the grim political reality of Israeli occupation with all its restrictions and control measures, on the one hand, and, on the other, the requirements and demands of daily living, such as a good education for their children, decent housing, basic health care, and an overall social environment that would offer a sense of personal security and enable the conduct of everyday activities.

The need for a government in the occupied Palestinian territory was questioned in the first Intifada, which took place between 1988 and 1993. Palestinians were able to organize themselves in peaceful, nonviolent, popular protest against the continuing Israeli occupation and to establish networks of mutual help through which they volunteered for emergency work and other needed services without supervision or instruction by a government. One can argue that the first Palestinian Intifada was some sort of populist movement "of the people, by the people."

I cannot forget an academic friend of mine who, in one of the discussions on the Intifada, mentioned specifically the ability of Palestinians to go on with their lives and to care for various concerns without the interference, or even the presence, of a government. I would argue that the first Intifada encouraged one of the ideas inherent in the model of "town halls," namely, that decisions pertaining to the community were to be taken by the community itself; moreover, the joint struggle against the continuing illegal occupation brought these "town halls" together through networking. This popular process, whereby hundreds of thousands of Palestinians stood by each other and delivered what each could in order to ensure the success of the Intifada, was in fact democracy in action.

When I was a student at Franklin and Marshall College and later on at the University of Virginia, I often questioned the role of the government: is it a reflection of a social contract "by the people and for the people," or is it simply politicians taking over from the people for the inevitable, advantageous benefit of the few as opposed to the majority of people? The mistrust of government is not an innate natural predisposition but simply a reaction to the ways and manners with which governments tend to handle the affairs of citizens and to come up with laws and regulations that are often seen as adding burdens rather than providing comfort to citizens.

I was aware of all these aspects and dilemmas when in 2006 I decided to 2006 run in the elections for the Palestinian Legislative Council or Parliament. In Palestine we have a unique system of elections. Because of the interest of the political establishment in having both women and Christians represented in the Parliament, the election law provides a quota system for the two groups whereby Christians are assured of six seats out of 132 in the Parliament: two Christian representatives from Jerusalem; two from Bethlehem; one from Ramallah; and one from Gaza.[1] For women the quota system specifies that among the first three candidates in any party's list one woman should be included, and among the following six candidates another woman should be added, and so on. In this way the Palestinian parliament is assured of the presence of six Christian parliamentarians and of at least sixteen women.

While the quota system has raised both legal and social questions regarding its "democratic" value, the system assures that women and Christians are represented in the legislative branch in a society that often casts its votes preferentially on the basis of family identity, gender, place of residence, and religious affiliation. While policy platforms are important for electioneering, just as important are the personal backgrounds of the candidates and the numerical strength of their families and broader kinship groups. Christians in Palestine do not have large kinship groups since most Christians are an urban group that tends to have small families. Thus they lack the extensive family and kinship networks that could assure success in elections. Therefore, it was deemed important by Palestinian politicians that Christians should be represented in the Parliament because this would ensure their inclusion in the debates and discussions of concern to the society

---

1. Gaza City is reputed to be the first Christian city in history and has always had a small Christian community, which stands today at around 1,500 Palestinian Christians. For the mass conversion of ancient Majuma, the seaport of Gaza, see Sozomen, *Ecclesiastical History* 2.5. Sozomen was a fifth-century Christian historian.

at large. Neighboring Jordan adopts the same quota system for the same reasons. Without a quota for women and Christians, it would be doubtful if a Christian or a woman would make it on his or her own; the outstanding exception was <u>Hanan Mikhail Ashrawi</u>, who won her seat in both the 1996 and the 2006 elections entirely on her own merit.

Before making the final decision to run, I needed to consult with the Latin (Roman Catholic) Patriarch of Jerusalem, Monsignor Michel Sabbah. Patriarch Sabbah was the chaplain priest of Jeunesse Étudiante Chrétienne, or JEC (Young Christian Students, or YCS), when I was in my last two years at the Frères School at the New Gate of the Old City of Jerusalem. JEC is a Catholic social movement of Christian secondary school students that had its origin in France in the 1930s. As a chaplain to JEC, Father Sabbah instructed us on the method of "See-Judge-Act," which was instrumental in developing our understanding and our course of action with regard to the social, political, economic, and religious environment in which we lived. In each monthly meeting we would select a phenomenon that pertained to our daily living and proceed to scrutinize it on the principle of "See-Judge-Act." The objective of this method was that we should never be observers but we should take part in the affairs of our community and society from a Christian perspective. It was good to be a practicing Catholic, but the Christian life would be augmented by direct involvement in the affairs and concerns of the larger society. The Jeunesse Étudiante Chrétienne (Young Christian Students), or JEC, was a formative movement for us in high school. With readings and reflections on the Bible we addressed the issues and concerns of our environment and discussed how best we could contribute to its welfare.

Father Sabbah was then in charge of Catholic youth movements in Jordan, which covered, besides East Jerusalem and the West Bank, Amman and the East Bank of Jordan until the war of 1967. In addition to summer meetings with similar student movements across the Middle East, mostly in Lebanon, where we joined with sister JEC organizations in the region and reflected together on the challenges facing us and our societies as young people, we had summer sessions in Jordan and monthly meetings that were usually held in the Frères School in Bethlehem, which later became Bethlehem University. Through the work and guidance of Father Sabbah, I became sensitized to the importance of the political role of Christians in Muslim society.

The approach of Father Sabbah was a simple one: we are part and parcel of our society with its problems, hopes, and expectations. We were advised not to withdraw from the responsibilities awaiting us as active citizens, and we had an obligation to serve our country the best way we could.

This instruction provided a sound basis that helped me in my adult life to decide to run for Parliament as a practicing Christian. The message that the leadership of Father Sabbah instilled in us was that we should not be afraid of others and that we should engage them with our religious, social, and political convictions without being apologetic about them.

In an environment that commingled Christians and Muslims, we have to stand on our own ground and be proud of our roots. At the same time we are not strangers to our society, and hence we should be as involved in its affairs as others are. It was this approach, or, if you wish, philosophy of life, that encouraged me to run in the 2006 elections. By then Father Sabbah had become the Patriarch of the Latin (Roman Catholic) Church in the Holy Land. When I consulted with him on whether to run or not, he welcomed the idea but insisted that I would be responsible for running my own campaign without pronounced Church support, either politically or financially. I thought that this was a fair position since it aimed to put the weight of my electoral campaign on my own shoulders, thus ensuring also that the Church could not be reproached for taking positions. I have to acknowledge here that I did receive support and endorsement from various Christian church leaders who trusted me to represent the Palestinian Christian community and its concerns. At least one church leader, however, was opposed to my candidacy because he had hoped that one of his parishioners would win the election. In general, though, strong support was shown to me by the Christian community in Jerusalem—support that stimulated further support from the Muslim community and thus assured my election to the Palestinian Parliament.

The 2006 Elections

Once having received the blessing of Patriarch Sabbah, I made my candidacy known on the Fatah List. My electoral campaign was a team effort in which family and friends became a solid support group with great potential for outreach to a variety of voters. The team that was formed to run this strenuous campaign consisted of my son Zack, then twenty-three years of age, who followed my campaign intensely, offering advice and volunteering to monitor the ballot boxes on my behalf; my brother Maurice, who practiced medicine in the Old City of Jerusalem and knew personally most of the voters who eventually cast ballots in my favor; my friend Hanna, who was the head of the Physics Department at Bethlehem University and worked hard to assure my victory; my brother-in-law Ghassan, who knew some of the inner workings of political factions and their leaders and supporters and thus helped me to map correctly where I could expect the most support. My wife Mary and my sisters Hilda and Therese were always on call for helping out with collecting signatures supporting my candidacy, reaching out to potential voters, preparing electioneering posters, and placing these on designated public boards in the Old City of Jerusalem and its vicinity. I will never forget Clemence, an older neighbor of ours from the Old City, who saw me campaigning one morning at the Damascus Gate, the busiest of the seven gates in the wall of the Old City. She approached me and told me that she had never cast a ballot in her entire life but because of me she would do it for the first time. I was overwhelmed and still remember the incident because of the enthusiastic and unconditional support from this elderly lady, God bless her soul.

The Greek Orthodox Arab Club in Jerusalem, which is a very old and prestigious club, invited all ten Christian candidates from Jerusalem to a debate on what they intended to do for the city and its population if elected. My team of advisors briefed me on how to field difficult questions. My wife and two sisters educated my team and me on the gender perspective and how important it was to include women, not simply in voting but in all aspects of life: economic, social, and political. The public debate was a fun-filled event where two hundred or more of Jerusalem's residents joined the moderator in asking policy questions and inquiring about some personal qualifications that may have had an impact on the parliamentary work expected from the successful candidate.

I did not rely only on my lecturing skills in the debate, as the coaching from my team proved crucial in fielding questions, especially the difficult ones. I thought I did very well in the debate since people congratulated me and some declared that they would give me their votes. In fact, my performance led some of my competitors to argue that the questions had been passed on to me before the debate and thus I knew how to answer. Certainly this was not true. I would not have started my political life with such a questionable exercise.

On Election Day I cast my own ballot in a school near my home. I saw Zack and his friends following up on balloting and ensuring that everything was all right. I visited the polling stations to see for myself how the voting process was going. During these visits I saw teams of international observers, including representatives of the Carter Center, touring the polling stations and recording their observations. Overall the elections went smoothly and democratically, according to the testimony of international observers.

I was elated when I discovered that the constituents casting the 4,030 votes that won me one of the two Christian seats in Jerusalem consisted of equal numbers of Christians and Muslims. Within the walled Old City it was really the work of my brother Maurice and sister Hilda that ensured that most Christians living in the Christian Quarter cast their votes for me. Outside the Old City, two Muslim neighborhoods, Al Tor on the Mount of Olives and Abu Dis close to the Tomb of Lazarus, gave me their unconditional support, which made the difference of five hundred votes in my favor over the votes given to the candidate tailing me. Thus my election was not a strictly Christian affair, as Muslim compatriots cast their votes equally in my favor. Besides, the villages in northwest Jerusalem, beautiful because of their verdant vineyards and located in the vicinity of Qubeibeh, reputed to be the village where Jesus appeared to his disciples following his Resurrection, had also given me significant votes. These are Muslim villages, traditionally in a friendly relationship with both the Franciscan convent and the old age home administered by German nuns, which are hallmarks of the locality. Hence I saw myself as an elected legislator for all Palestinians, irrespective of religion. The general results of the elections were surprising to most secular, center, and independent parties since Hamas, the Islamic resistance movement, won a majority of 76 seats out of the 132 seats, fewer than the 88 seats needed for an absolute majority to change the Basic Law[2] and to modify legislation that requires the absolute two-thirds majority.

Polarization in Palestine

Having won the majority of seats, Hamas was in a position to form the new government and to challenge some of the pragmatic policies concerning Israel held by Mahmoud Abbas, the President of the Palestinian National Authority. For the inauguration of the new government in March of 2006, the new Palestinian Parliament moved to Gaza in order to swear in Mr. Ismail Haniyeh, one of the chief political leaders of Hamas in the Gaza Strip, as the Prime Minister. The government of Mr. Haniyeh was almost unanimously supported by all parliamentarians because it also had members of the other factions and parties serving as ministers.

Following the swearing in of the government, the U.S., Israel, and many European countries boycotted the Palestinian National Authority and withheld financial and other forms of support from Palestinians.

2. The Palestinian Basic Law functions as a temporary constitution for the Palestinian Authority until the establishment of an independent state with a permanent constitution. The Basic Law was passed by the Palestinian Legislative Council in 1997 and ratified by President Yasser Arafat in 2002. It has subsequently been amended twice: in 2003 the political system was changed to introduce a prime minister; and in 2005 it was amended to conform to the new Election Law. See "Palestinian Basic Law" in Sources Cited.

Those boycotting the new government perceived Hamas as a terror-prone organization because of its insistence on the use of armed resistance against the Israeli occupation. Fatah, to which I belonged, adopted in contrast a nonviolent approach and adhered to peaceful political processes to find an exit from the continuing Israeli occupation.

In June 2007 the two differing positions of Hamas and Fatah came to a head-on collision in the Gaza Strip as Hamas took over this area, causing casualties among Fatah supporters and ending the tenure of the Haniyeh administration as a national government for all Palestinians. The Gaza Strip was consequently in the hands of a Hamas-formed government, and the West Bank was run by a new Palestinian government headed by a former World Bank executive, Dr. Salam Fayyad. The division of the Gaza Strip from the rest of the Palestinian Territory meant that in practice Palestinians now had two competing governments—a state of affairs that led to parliamentary paralysis. As a result, the Parliament stopped meeting.

As an elected parliamentarian I had participated in parliamentary sessions during the sixteen-month tenure of the Haniyeh government. I had made some pronouncements on issues and concerns of Palestinians that were appreciated by some of those who saw me on public television, which was broadcasting the parliamentary sessions, live. On one occasion while we were discussing in Parliament our relations with the United States and other Western powers, a leader of Hamas referred to President Bush's statement on the "crusade" against terror, interpreting that remark as if it implied a religious confrontation. I retorted to the Hamas leader that his words showed a lack of respect for Palestinian Christians because he had lumped all Christians together in the "crusade" reference. I reminded him that Palestinian Christians are part and parcel of Palestinian society. I told him that I wished that he had not referred to the statement by President Bush because his comment on it showed lack of sensitivity and confused listeners as to the real issues in contention. My counter-comment pleased the secular and Fatah members of Parliament, and they congratulated me for standing up to the Hamas parliamentarian.

I did not like the dichotomizing or polarization that was dominating Palestinian politics. I believed then as now that, whether we like it or not, Hamas is part of the political scene in Palestine. As such, Hamas is entitled to take part in all democratic processes that would ensure the representation of all Palestinians. My criticism of Hamas, as of other political groups in Palestinian society that believe in armed resistance as a way out, is that, given the imbalance of power, international and regional realities, and the internal situation of polarization among Palestinians, this option would not deliver. In addition, the whole political system practiced by Palestinians in the Occupied Territory is due to the Oslo Accords, which were signed in 1993, and hence Palestinian political factions needed to take a look at their platforms, particularly those of armed resistance, and to opt for new ones that dealt pragmatically with the practical issues of war and peace with Israel. Besides, world public opinion would always favor nonviolence as a means to deal with the question of ending the continuing Israeli occupation.

Many of those Westerners who show understanding and empathy toward the Palestinian plight, including the difficult conditions that Palestinians must endure, often show equal—or even more—empathy toward the Jewish population of Israel. They are caught between condemning the human rights violations committed against Palestinians and wanting to be sure that no harm would come to Israel as a "Jewish state" when a peace deal has been agreed upon by the two sides. I feel that there is always a deep-rooted guilt feeling, particularly among Westerners, about the tragedies inflicted on the Jewish people throughout Western history. This sense of guilt is not helpful to Palestinians, particularly those who believe in armed struggle and martial confrontation. In fact, the biblical narrative that embraces both Judaism and Christianity in the shared Judeo-Christian heritage goes a long way with many groups, evangelicals and others, to incline them toward supporting Israel, irrespective of its punitive measures and control mechanisms that clearly infringe on the human rights of the Palestinian people under its occupation.

For example, a study conducted by Dr. Halla Shoaibi, of the University of Michigan faculty, "estimates that in the period she studied (2000–2007), 10 percent of pregnant Palestinian women were delayed at [Israeli] checkpoints while travelling to hospital to give birth." Sixty-nine babies were born at checkpoints, and thirty-five of these babies as well as five of the mothers died, according to Dr. Shoaibi's findings.[3]

Another example of oppressive measures is the expropriation of Palestinian land. HaMoked, the Center for the Defence of the Individual, which is an Israeli human rights organization, issued a report in 2013 entitled "The Permit Regime: Human Rights Violations in West Bank Areas Known as the 'Seam Zone.'" It refers to the draconian bureaucratic measures imposed by the Israeli military upon Palestinian farmers who, separated from their own agricultural lands by the Israeli Separation Wall (much of which is located inside the West Bank), nevertheless attempt to access their lands. Thousands of Palestinian farmers are affected adversely by this regime which, in the end, bars them from their legally owned lands and crops.[4]

3. "Israeli Checkpoints," *The Electronic Intifada*, 2011.
4. "The Permit Regime," 2013.

Once I argued with a parliamentarian very close to Hamas that if that movement changed its positions and became more pragmatic, it would become credible to and accepted by world powers and would possibly appeal to a wider sympathetic audience worldwide. His counter-argument was that the harsh Israeli policies and the continued military occupation would not be affected positively by nonviolent measures, and that, in fact, Israel would do all in its power to silence nonviolent activism as well. He pointed to the heavy-handed reaction of the Israeli army to the peaceful and nonviolent protests by villagers in Bil'in, a village near Ramallah, and by villagers elsewhere, who were opposing the construction of the Separation Wall on their lands. So the "military" option of Hamas, according to him, was in response to the "military" option of Israeli occupation. If Israel would end its occupation voluntarily, then for sure Hamas would end its insistence on armed resistance, he argued. His response reminded me of the arguments for and against "normalization" of the current relationship with the Israelis.[5] Is it really power and military superiority that would determine outcomes of confrontations, or, in the end, after arms are laid down, would we have to sit down around the negotiation table and discuss terms for ending the conflict?

Because of the division between Hamas in the Gaza Strip and the Palestinian National Authority in the West Bank, the Palestinian Parliament, officially known as the Palestinian Legislative Council, stopped meeting in regular sessions. This created a constitutional problem since the Parliament ceased being the legislating authority and the monitoring body over the executive branch and its administration. In reality, the Palestinian Legislative Council stopped working following the June 2007 rift between Hamas and Fatah.

Aside from the legislative and oversight functions of the Parliament, which were obstructed by the division between the two major Palestinian parties, there are international political ramifications of the internal Palestinian division. Often I am asked whether President Abbas of the Palestinian National Authority can negotiate on behalf of all Palestinians. When I give a positive answer, the next question is this: "What if Hamas rejected the deal that President Abbas would bring about with Israelis?" I argue that the absence of the Palestinian Parliament would make reconciliation between Hamas and Fatah much more difficult and hence would place Hamas in unbridled opposition to any prospects for the peace process. Besides, the tripartite system of governance (legislative, judicial, and executive), which usually acts to support the principle of separation of powers, has received a

5. The topic of normalization was discussed in chapter 5.

serious setback with the inactivity of the Legislative Council. Two different systems of governance operating in the Palestinian Territory, one in Gaza and one in the West Bank, do not add up to safeguarding and advancing the interests of the Palestinian people in general, including the eventual striking of a peace deal with Israel. The Palestinians need to be united and to have a clear, unified vision of what we want.

Personally, I was disappointed by the turn of events with respect to the Legislative Council because I was expecting to be active in legislating for the good of all in my society. The crippling of the Council had left me incapacitated in terms of fulfilling my promises to my electorate because it had discontinued the regular sessions of the Parliament, where I could have presented the concerns of my constituency. I continued to frequent the Parliament and to meet with other members in working groups designed to address pressing social, economic, and governmental public issues. My feeling, though, was that without monitoring and overseeing power over the different ministries of the government, our working groups were chiefly engaged in an intellectual and social exercise. The working groups' meetings enabled us to meet with some of our constituents from across the society, as when we discussed the teachers' strike and their demands for improved working and salary conditions. Some of my colleagues in the working group would follow up on the group's conclusions and accompany constituents to the various ministries in order to bring to the attention of high public officials the demands and needs of our constituents.

One of the primary activities that we continued to undertake was the hosting of parliamentary delegations from abroad, mostly from Europe. The visiting parliamentary delegations can be divided into three categories. The first consists of those delegations who offered unconditional support for us Palestinians; their visits reflected their wish to show their support and to impress upon us the need to persevere. The second category of delegations wanted to understand the situation; often the participants conveyed to us the need to move forward in reconciliation efforts internally and to go on with the peace process with Israel, in spite of the many obstacles facing us. These visitors saw themselves as go-betweens and thus wanted to bridge any gaps, if they could, between Israelis and Palestinians. The third category of visitors had full support and sympathy for Israel; their purpose was to urge us to work harder to come to terms with the Israeli reality, including occupation. They were not interested in seeing an end to the Israeli occupation but rather in normalizing the Israeli position. Specifically, what we Palestinians told these visitors about the difficult living conditions under occupation did not go far with them. One of them—clearly a supporter of Israel—though telling me that what he had heard from Palestinian authorities in Ramallah was merely a banal repetition of long-held positions, nevertheless confided in me his perception that some UN organizations (such as OCHA, the Office for the Coordination of Humanitarian Affairs) are doing impressive work in monitoring the status of human rights and other conditions in the Palestinian territory and calling for closer examination of the situation.

Separation between Palestinians and Israelis

Polarization is counterproductive within a single society as well as between two societies. Within Israeli society the polarization is apparent between the majority on the right of the political spectrum and a smaller group on the left. Polarization between Israeli Jews and Arab citizens of Israel is another concern that should be addressed by Israeli society itself. On the Palestinian side, the polarization between the secular political groups, such as Fatah and the left-leaning factions, on the one hand, and Hamas, the religiously based party, on the other, is practically dividing the society into two separate governments: one in Gaza and one in the West Bank. Polarization in any society means that there is no consensus on the vision and on the way in which the society at large should identify, prioritize, and engage with its various challenges.

In the Palestinian-Israeli context, however, polarization is both concrete and cognitive. The Separation Wall divides Israelis from Palestinians and makes Israelis feel that they are safe and secure in their part of the country. The Palestinians, in reaction to the Separation Wall, have developed what I term as "cognitive separation." The moment that Palestinians pass the many Israeli checkpoints and other security measures that are intended to contain their lives and restrict their movements, they start pretending that the Israelis do not exist. They go on with their lives in spite of the many impositions on them. Some of my constituents confided in me that this was the way they were able to feel liberated from the yoke of Israeli occupation: by distancing Israelis from their cognitive map, at least for a while. Thus separation is not only physical and concrete, but also psychological and cognitive, and, as a Canadian theologian pointed out to me, neither concrete nor cognitive separation is a venue for healing and reconciliation. This Canadian friend told me, "You are a traumatized people, and accordingly your attempt at 'cognitive separation' is an affirmation of this traumatization."

The "World Happiness Report," issued yearly by the UN since 2012, reveals that the Israelis are much happier than we Palestinians are. Israel's ranking of happiness between 2014 and 2016 was "11" (eleventh highest), in contrast to our own ranking, which stood at "103" for the same period out of a total of 155 countries ranked.[6] This could be an indicator of our traumatization. I am not surprised by Palestine's ranking on the "World Happiness Report," as every time I speak to fellow Palestinians, irrespective of social standing or geographic residence, I sense their feeling of frustration and disappointment. In fact, at certain times I have concluded that we Palestinians are suffering from mass depression.

A majority of Israelis on the other hand, especially the Jews among them, feel that their state is providing them with the essential services that make their lives comfortable. With the "security-added" construction of the Separation Wall setting them apart from us Palestinians, their neighbors, the resulting sense of protection, although an illusion in my view, could also contribute to their feeling of happiness. The essential question is whether two peoples, one happy and one unhappy, can make peace with each other.

The Challenge of Nonviolence

Visits of delegations became more frequent following periods of confrontation between Palestinians and Israelis, such as military actions and incursions into Gaza. I recall a leading Socialist Italian parliamentarian urging us, after one of the Gaza wars, to adopt an absolutely nonviolent approach. He said that our best strategy as Palestinians would be strictly nonviolent behavior vis-à-vis the Israeli military, without even a stone thrown at them. This way, he assured us, you would be able to win hearts and support in Europe and elsewhere. I asked him if he wanted us to be saints in light of the harsh realities of occupation. He took my question seriously: if you would act like saints, he responded, no one would be ethically or morally justified in failing to support you and identify with your cause. When I spoke to Patriarch Sabbah about the position of this Italian Socialist parliamentarian, he concurred with it.

At the present time Patriarch Michel Sabbah is a retired head of church. In a conversation regarding the current political impasse, he told me that our first objective as Palestinians should be to disarm the Israelis. We cannot do this without being absolutely nonviolent: not a stone, not a gunshot, not a knife. This way, no one can accuse us of violence or, worse, terrorism. Israel uses any attack on its military or civilians to label Palestinians as terrorists intent on destroying the democratic State of Israel and its basically Western values. History is ignored, and the human rights infractions against Palestinians—such as the expropriation of their land to build settlements for Jews only and such as their confinement in their villages,

6. "World Happiness Report," 2017, Statistical Appendix.

towns, and the bigger open prison of Gaza—are all forgotten when an act
of violence is committed by a Palestinian. The cause behind the act is overlooked while the act itself is judged to be horrendous. Accordingly, if we
adopt the nonviolent approach and stick to it in a disciplined manner, then
we can approach Israelis, Westerners, and others with our just cause and
work with them to end occupation. This is what Patriarch Emeritus Sabbah
means when he insists on the nonviolent approach as the necessary means
to disarm the Israelis. Clearly the absolute nonviolence that the Italian
parliamentarian and Monsignor Sabbah were advocating is an enormously
challenging proposition. Can we procure our political rights through the
nonviolent approach, as South Africa and Gandhi's India did?

When I relay conversations like these to my constituents, some retort
that the Palestinian Authority, which was established by the Oslo Accords
in 1993, has been pursuing nonviolent peaceful negotiation with the Israelis for the last twenty-four years and this has taken us nowhere. "So, Mr.
Sabella," they tell me, "if you would subscribe to the views of your Italian
visitor and Monsignor Sabbah, then be cautioned that it would take another
hundred years to achieve the kind of peace that all of us desire." In response,
I point out to my constituents that we Palestinians, both politicians and civil
society activists, have failed to develop the kind of strategy that would succeed in conveying to a broader Israeli and international audience the harsh
realities caused by occupation and in convincing them to work with us to
end the occupation. Some of my constituents would argue back that they
have tried it, as I did myself for over twenty years, and nothing dramatic has
evolved out of the contacts with our well-meaning Israeli and international
counterparts.

In fact, some of the Israelis with whom we have had contact have always felt that we Palestinians were the foreigners and they were the owners
of the land in the first place. I will never forget a young Israeli interlocutor
who told me once in a panel discussion that the land was Jewish from eter-
nity and that the Palestinians who lived on it were there merely to hold it in
safekeeping for the Jewish people. Now that the Jewish people have gathered
on the land with the establishment of Israel in 1948, the Palestinians have
to acknowledge that the land has returned to its historically lawful owners
and determine which of two possible courses of action they will take: either
to leave the country or to live with full acknowledgment of Jewish control
over the land. This, to me, amounted not only to disrespect for Palestinian
feelings, aspirations, rights, and history but also was intended to delegiti-
mize the Palestinian presence on the land, which goes back for centuries.
The Jewish extremist position seeks to invalidate any significant Palestinian
association with the land beyond considering Palestinians as shepherds, not

owners, of the land—shepherds whose task was to care for the land tempo-
rarily while awaiting the Jewish return.

The far-right Israeli ideology of settling the land and denying the national rights of Palestinians harms those on the Palestinian side who are
working hard to impress on their people the need to arrive at a historic
compromise that would be beneficial to the two peoples sharing the land.
There are anger and frustration among Palestinians who see that the settlement expansion, the disregard for the basic human rights of their people,
and the policies that aim at fragmenting and encircling Palestinians in their
cities, towns, and villages, without free movement, all add up to casting
doubt on the utility of pressing for a political solution. By means of land and
water expropriation as well as severe restrictions on Palestinians' mobility
and economic progress, Israel is creating facts on the ground. Some in the
international community want the Palestinians to accept these facts as legal
and to negotiate on the basis of such normalization. This situation not only
weakens the likes of President Abbas, who insists on a nonviolent political
solution, but creates the impression among the Palestinians and others in
the region that Western powers are not fair because they opt for double
standards when it comes to Israel.

My own worry about the continuing conflict with Israel is that it encourages all kinds of extremist groups to claim that their violence against
Israel and the West is rooted in the historic injustice inflicted on the Palestinian people in 1948. Hence this injustice justifies in their own eyes all
acts of violence directed against Israel and the West. Besides, the positions
of Western powers, in particular of the successive U.S. administrations, on
the Palestinian-Israeli conflict have mostly been one-sided and have never
convinced the masses in the Arab and Muslim worlds that fairness has been
exercised in dealing with the injustices suffered by the Palestinian people as
a result of the creation of Israel in 1948 and its continuing occupation of Palestinian land since 1967. Accordingly, if we were to arrive at a genuine peace
solution with Israel that would end the Palestinian-Israeli conflict once and
for all, this achievement would subtract one factor from the multitude of factors that complicate the relationships between the Arab and Muslim worlds
and the West in general, including Israel. But the conflict is a primary source
of mistrust and dissension, and in the medium run, if a solution is achieved,
its results may not be all apparent. In the long run, however, such a solution
would usher the Middle East, particularly the States of Jordan, Syria, Lebanon, and Israel, into an era of possible economic, political, and social stability and a vision of working together for the good of all. Some may describe
this position as too naïve, simplistic, and visionary; the alternative, however,

is one that would see the continuation of conflict, the costs of which would be too exorbitant for Israelis, Palestinians, and Arabs alike.

I cannot think of any solution to the Palestinian-Israeli conflict other than through peaceful means. Yes, I agree with those who argue that we Palestinians are in a position of political weakness because of our internal division, the preoccupations of the Arab states elsewhere, the unconditional support for Israel from U.S. administrations and the Congress, and Europe as disabled politically as it has ever been. In spite of the odds against us, we remain, despite our weakness, in a strong position because Israel needs our recognition and it can never be at peace without conciliation with us. I do not think that acts of violence, irrespective of how costly they are in terms of human and other sacrifices, would persuade the Israelis to come to the negotiation table in good faith. I am convinced that we Palestinians need to develop a strategy of peace with its core in nonviolence.

As I am asking my people to develop a vision for a nonviolent approach to the resolution of the conflict with Israel, so I am equally adamant that the Israelis, especially their political leaders, could do much more to advance peaceful prospects with us. The Israelis, considered to possess one of the world's mightiest armies, have a special responsibility to use their power with mature self-restraint and to see to it that they do not continue to provoke Palestinian sensitivities, religious or secular. Such provocation would result in new cycles of violence to the detriment of all.

Even if the Israelis fail to develop a genuine approach to peace negotiations, we Palestinians should continue to insist on our nonviolent preference. From the experience of my parents, who became refugees in 1948 and had to deal with the consequences of their refugee status throughout their lives, and from the pain and tears that they have shed as they have spoken of their lost home and experience of exile, I have come to realize that the only way out is through adopting a nonviolent approach. The process of making peace is a painful one; pain, nevertheless, should not cause us to give up and opt for further violence and confrontation.

Demography and Conflict

With my background in sociology, when I consider the population statistics of Palestinians and Israelis, I am struck by the fact that already on this holy stretch of land, the size of Rhode Island, there are over 12.5 million inhabitants, half of whom are Jews and the other half Arabs. About twenty to twenty-five years from now, if current trends continue, the population will double; so we will have close to twenty-five million people inhabiting Israel and the Palestinian Territory.[7] How might this statistical projection affect the politics of the conflict and the prospects for a solution that would start readying the ground for this population explosion?

Some in Israel would argue that this demographic situation has never been a serious concern because Israel has the security means to contain the Palestinian population. Besides, the essential and existential questions are not those of population and numbers, according to these Israelis, but those of the importance of the land for the Jewish people. Therefore, the continued settlement in the West Bank, the hermetic closure of the Gaza Strip, and the refusal to acknowledge the right of Palestinians to a state of their own are all essential to safeguard the Jewishness of the place. An Israeli acquaintance of mine, a professor of renown in an Israeli university, told me that Israeli politicians do not even consider the demographic dimension. They deal with the moment, and they could not care less about the problematic aspects of the future.

I am concerned about this myopia as an elected member of the Palestinian Parliament and as an avowed believer that only a political solution will invite a future vision of shared living in the Holy Land for Palestinians and Israelis. In my talks with American groups visiting Jerusalem, I highlight the fact that the population of the Gaza Strip today is close to two million, of whom almost one million are below the age of fifteen years, while over 75 percent of the population is aged thirty years or less. When we consider that the unemployment rate is close to 50 percent and that Gazans are not allowed freedom to leave the Strip, which is 212 square miles, then the question becomes: what future can there be for children and youth? And how would the enormous difficulties of life faced by Gazans be resolved in order not to exacerbate the situation and to drive hundreds of thousands of young people into despair? Hermetic closure of the Gaza Strip and other security measures in the West Bank can work for some time but not for all time; accordingly, without finding a solution for the overall situation, uncertainty will persist as to how developments could affect the future of both Israelis and Palestinians.

We Palestinians bear a responsibility to ease the conditions of life for our own people, especially in Gaza. While occupation is an ill that must be addressed by Palestinians, Israelis, and all concerned, Hamas in Gaza has a special responsibility to ensure that its military actions against Israel will not result in harm to the entire population of the Gaza Strip. Israel has also a primary responsibility to avoid hurting the civilian population when it responds with its military might to the actions of Hamas or when Israel

7. "Palestinian Population to Pass Jews," 2016.

initiates "preventive" military operations against targets in Gaza. The Palestinian population of the Gaza Strip is caught in between while the political pressure applied to Hamas by Israel, the Palestinian Authority, and Egypt, which shares a border with the Gaza Strip, ends up inadvertently punishing the civilian population and curtailing its basic human rights. These powers cannot hold the population of the Gaza Strip hostage to their politics; war follows war between Israel and Hamas, and after each of these limited wars a truce is usually negotiated by Egypt that returns the situation to its previous status. At one time, when the Oslo Accords were signed back in 1993, some planners spoke of the Gaza Strip becoming the Palestinian Singapore (tiny but prosperous). At present, however, UN organizations caution that the Gaza Strip will not be inhabitable less than ten years from now.

SHORT-SIGHTED RESPONSES

My concern for the Gaza Strip and its inhabitants is heightened by the fact that I am a Palestinian parliamentarian representing all Palestinians. It pains me as a human being to see that the Gaza Strip has become a virtual open-air prison. When I speak to American visitors, I ask them if some ranches in Texas are larger than the entire Gaza Strip. Their affirmative answers tend to drive home the appalling tragedy that Gazans endure.

A related topic that is close to my heart is the dwindling number of Palestinian Christians in the Gaza Strip: a Christian friend of mine, a distinguished heart surgeon who lives in Gaza, recently informed me that in ten years' time there will be no Christian living in Gaza. This is indeed sad since the small Christian community of Gaza has always been known for its contributions in commerce and artisanship among other areas of expertise. At the present time the Christian population in the Gaza Strip is nearly 1,250 people; this number, however, is diminished when Christian youngsters leave to study elsewhere in the Arab world, Europe, or the United States because they usually do not come back. The grim realities in the Gaza Strip make it unlikely that young people, whether Christian or Muslim, will return.

The pressing humanitarian situation and other issues that affect people's lives make it imperative that both Palestinians and Israelis move to a middle ground in order to find practical solutions that would create a different environment where the two peoples can live side-by-side in relative harmony and a sense of overall security. This goal necessitates that Israeli and Palestinian leaders start thinking about the future jointly rather than separately. Today there are many who believe that the two-state solution is no longer possible given the fact that Israel's settlements in the West Bank (which are illegal under international law) are always expanding and the expectation is that within less than a decade the number of settlers living in these settlements will reach one million. The map of the West Bank with its numerous scattered settlement blocs resembles Swiss cheese with its many holes. The settlements are interspersed among Palestinian villages, towns, and agricultural lands, and the Israeli authorities have budgeted millions of U.S. dollars over the years in order to create the roads, electricity, and other essential infrastructure designated primarily for the use of settlers. The *de facto* reality of the settlements means that Israel has virtually annexed large parts of the West Bank. It is unlikely that Israel would give up these settlements even if a peace deal is struck with the Palestinians. I sense a great uncertainty about the future of relations between the Palestinians and the Israeli settlers in the West Bank. Without a political solution accepted by the two sides, these relations would most likely be entangled in occasional confrontations, resulting in victims on both sides and a heavy price paid by us all.

Some of my constituents would argue that the pacifist approach that I am advocating would end up accepting as normal all the illegal measures that Israel and the settlers have imposed on the Palestinian population since 1967. My response is that the pacifist approach is to find a way out that would enable our people to ascertain and exercise our political rights to a state of our own that would ensure our continuity with dignity on our own land, even though the territory on which we would eventually set our state is less than 22 percent of historic Palestine. Yes, the Israeli counterparts would consider this nonviolent approach as a sign of weakness and would persist in grabbing the land and building settlements illegally, in making Jerusalem an exclusively Jewish city, and in denying our rights. We Palestinians would face a test of our perseverance in insisting upon our rights, and we would have to advocate tirelessly and nonviolently for these rights. It would be imperative to aim at developing the kind of mass support for our nonviolent position that the South Africans and the Indians under Gandhi succeeded in eliciting.

When I speak of the failure of Palestinian factions and leaders in developing a vision, I am precisely addressing the vision of nonviolence. Our Palestinian cause is a just cause, but when we adopt a violent approach, or even hostile language, we provide ammunition to our Israeli and other detractors who quickly label us as inciters or, worse, as terrorists and thus invalidate our cause. On the other hand, we lose world public opinion when we insist that those who adopt the military option against Israel are freedom fighters, as if those who opt for the nonviolent approach are not. In an age when terrorism is seen as threatening to Western countries, it becomes easy for many to perceive violent acts of Palestinians as falling in the same category. But aside from worry over world public opinion, the fact that violence does not pay in the end is a lesson that we Palestinians should take to heart. Our culture has beautiful traditions of making peace, such as *Sulha*, and of finding reconciliation among families and neighborhoods after long periods of conflict; we should use these to come to terms with our pain and to move forward in order to end the conflict with the Israelis.

Sulha is a Palestinian cultural tradition that brings warring parties within the society to peace and reconciliation. In Arabic *Sulh or Sulha* means striking a peace accord where two families or two communities have had a long bout with enmity and conflict. When we speak of *Sulha* in our Palestinian society, we usually imply that the *Sulha* or peace takes place between families that have known each other for a long time and that, because of a particular incident or dispute, have ended up at loggerheads with each other. Strikingly, some authors refer to the Palestinian-Israeli conflict as one between cousins, and when we do not want to use the word "Israelis" in a conversation, it becomes expedient to refer to Israelis simply as "our cousins."

Why should we Palestinians so easily put aside such inspiring traditions of peacemaking and reconciliation in our own culture and not elaborate on how we can use this rich cultural legacy in order to work out the complex conflict with the Israelis? Again, I may be accused of naïveté and of overlooking the concept that what is applicable and successful within one culture cannot, in the case of our conflict with Israelis, succeed across cultures. My response is that we have our own inventory of methods for dealing with conflict in order to promote peace and reconciliation. Accordingly we should not wait for "experts" on conflict resolution, peace, and reconciliation to provide inspiration for us.

Holy Sites and Conflict

One source of consternation involving religious and political sensitivities is the fact that Muslims and Jews share the same holy sites across the land. Both Judaism and Islam venerate many of the same ancient prophets, such as Abraham, and revere the sites associated with these prophets. While Muslims and Arabs refer to the compound in Jerusalem that contains the Dome of the Rock and the third holiest mosque in Islam, Al Aqsa Mosque, as Al Haram Al Sharif compound, Jews, on the other hand, refer to it as the Temple Mount. Some religious Jews want to share the compound so that they could have certain hours in which to enter and pray freely. This would mean that part of the compound would have to be given to Jewish worshipers, as happened in the Ibrahimi Mosque in Hebron. Muslims and Arabs view these designs as changing the official Status Quo of the compound and warn that provocative visits by Jewish worshipers to the compound would stir up the feelings of Muslims and would invite violence. Most sensible individuals and governments, like that of Jordan, the Heads of Churches in Jerusalem, and UN organizations are calling on Israel to respect the Status Quo and not to provoke hatred by allowing religious Jews freedom of access to the site and by eventually giving them a place of prayer inside the compound. Israeli politicians and some in the religious right are usually indifferent to these calls, categorizing them as efforts to deny the Jewish people its right to the holy place where the Third Temple once stood. On the other hand, Jews refuse to allow Muslims to pray at Rachel's Tomb in Bethlehem or at the Western Wall in Jerusalem, both of which sites are holy to Muslims as well.

This religious complexity of shared holy sites is a potential threat to the peace of Palestinians and Israelis alike. In fact, this conflict over the holy sites may draw hundreds of millions of Muslims worldwide into the political struggle with Israel, and this, in the end, is far from helpful for either Palestinians or Israelis, for either Muslims or Jews. The Status Quo of the holy sites, particularly those shared by Islam and Judaism, should be respected by all. If we fail to defuse the cause of tension concerning these shared religious sites, we will unfortunately continue to witness incidents injurious to both Palestinians and Israelis.

On Friday, July 14, 2017, as I was writing this chapter, an incident occurred that involved three Palestinian youngsters who gunned down two Israeli policemen on guard at the holy compound; consequently they themselves were shot down. This tragedy makes me shudder about future prospects for relations on this and other holy sites. Wisdom and respect for the sensitivities of the three principal religions in the Holy Land are urgently called for. Those on the Israeli side who argue that now Israel is a sovereign power in the Land and should accordingly exercise this sovereignty, irrespective of what Muslims and others think, are inviting the Jewish state to accelerate the cycles of mistrust and confrontation between the two peoples and the three religions of the land.

Following the July fourteenth incident Israel decided to introduce magnetic inspection gates and installed screening cameras at two gates of the sacred compound that would have obliged Muslim faithful to pass through them. For two weeks there was a standoff between Israeli policemen and thousands of Muslim faithful who refused to enter the compound to pray. Instead, Muslims surrounded the Mosque from the outside and exercised their right to pray on the streets and pavements leading to the compound. In one incident, which went viral on the social media, one young Palestinian Christian wearing a cross and holding his Bible open was

seen praying side-by-side with Muslim youth. This was a reflection of the
Christian Palestinian position that the Status Quo for the Mosque should be
preserved, as it is a place of worship and veneration for Muslims.

Seeing the thousands of Palestinian Muslims, at some point estimated
at thirty thousand, who have insisted on praying outside the Mosque compound until all cameras and electronic gates are removed made me think of
the complexity of the quest for a peaceful solution to the Palestinian-Israeli
conflict. There was a time when a telephone call from the President of the
United States would have been enough to convince Israeli and Arab leaders to take the needed steps to calm a volatile situation or prevent it from
escalation. Nowadays, with social media and with means of speedy communication available to all, political decisions and processes cannot ignore
what the masses think and what would move them to become an active
factor in processes of confrontation and reconciliation. The people cannot
be ignored any more, and even when we think that the average person pays
attention only to his or her daily upkeep and living concerns, this person
and hundreds and thousands of likeminded people in similar conditions
could all rise together to make their voices heard on issues pertaining not
only to religion but to politics as well. It was due to the massive outpouring
and display of togetherness by the Palestinians that the Israeli authorities
finally agreed to remove the cameras and the electronic gates. We cannot,
nevertheless, discount the accompanying diplomatic and political efforts
exerted by King Abdullah of Jordan and by the Palestinian President Abbas
in helping to resolve this conflict.

Life is not easy in the Holy Land. Whenever I address groups of visitors
and pilgrims in Jerusalem, I tell them that people here often refer to biblical
and Qur'anic figures, like King David, Jesus, or the Prophet Mohammed,
as if they were still with us, engaged in their lordly activities and sermons
in the next room. In fact, we carry these sacred figures within us, and they
shape our worldview and our interactions with others, which at times are
not at all conducive to feelings of empathy and understanding. The curse of
exclusivity could prevent us from seeing and feeling the sensitivities of others and hence would lock us inside our own self-centered bubbles. Religion
to people in the Middle East remains an important component of identity.
Without it they would feel at a loss. Can religion help us to transcend ourselves in recognizing the other and accepting her or him as created in the
image of God?

Europe and Palestine

Amidst all these complexities, I have come since 2011 to represent Palestine 2011
in the Council of Europe in Strasbourg with its Parliamentary Assembly
of forty-seven European countries. The Council of Europe in 2009 set up
its program of Partners for Democracy with the idea of inviting national
parliaments of neighboring regions, such as the Middle East and North Africa, to send delegations as non-member states. The primary requirement
for joining is to "embrace the values of the Council of Europe, which are
pluralist and gender parity-based democracy, the rule of law and respect for
human rights and fundamental freedoms."[8] The Council of Europe insists
on the partnership model and refrains from relationships that would distort
this image by making the Council appear as the teacher, and the partners for
democracy as the students.

The idea of accompanying countries such as Morocco (the first to join,
in 2011), Palestine, Jordan, and Kyrgyzstan as they maneuver their way to
democracy is a laudable one. At the same time, the fact that delegations of
these countries can attend all plenary sessions, make statements, and give
presentations, without voting, on all issues of the agenda is an added advantage. This provision gives us the opportunity not only to air our views
on subjects related to the Palestinian-Israeli conflict but, as important, to
participate in discussions on issues such as refugees and migrants in Europe
as well as to sensitize European parliamentarians on perspectives usually
not considered in their presentations.

The Israeli delegates from the Knesset, Israel's parliament, are there,
representing their country as an Observer State. The presence of Palestinian
and Israeli parliamentarians together in the same hall has the potential for
stimulating discussions on issues of mutual concern. In fact, we have spoken
on issues pertaining to water-sharing, and at one time, prior to our official
joining, on the "cemetery of numbers," the practice by the Israeli authorities
of keeping the bodies of Palestinians—those who had been killed during
confrontations—in a cemetery that assigned numbers, instead of names,
to the buried. No spectacular success has ever come out of these contacts,
but it must be noted that throughout my involvement with the Council of
Europe there have been Israeli Knesset members who felt, as we did, the
need for a two-state solution and an expeditious political process shared
by our two peoples. Unfortunately of late, the Israeli Knesset members are
not showing up so often, since they feel that the Parliamentary Assembly of
the Council of Europe undertakes reporting on human rights and on other

8. Resolution 1680 (2009) of the Parliamentary Assembly.

developments in the Occupied Palestinian Territory that is not to their liking; besides, they think that attendance at the four yearly sessions of the
Parliamentary Assembly could be a waste of their precious time.

We in the Palestinian delegation have opted for full commitment to
attending all the sessions of the Parliamentary Assembly even when the
agenda does not refer to the Palestinian-Israeli conflict. We have also insisted on preregistering our delegates' inputs and contributions to debates
and on inclusion in question-and-answer sessions with prominent speakers. When David Cameron, Prime Minister of Britain, delivered a speech
to the Assembly, a colleague of mine asked him about what measures his
country would adopt in order to promote a peaceful solution to the Palestinian-Israeli conflict. His response was that he was pleased to see that both
Israel and Palestine had representatives in the hall and that he believed that
the two peoples should be working together to find the appropriate solution. One other question, which I myself addressed to President Hollande
of France, concerned his initiative to hold an international conference in
Paris to help advance the political peace process between Palestinians and
Israelis. His response was that we should do everything possible to promote
a peaceful resolution to the conflict in the Middle East. He thanked me especially because I addressed my question to him in French.

As a delegation, we have conscientiously participated in committee
meetings; personally, I rarely miss a meeting of the Committee on Political
Affairs and Democracy, which is considered one of the major committees of
the Parliamentary Assembly. My colleagues usually attend one of the other
five committees and alert other members of the delegation to relevant topics
of discussion and to events that require our attendance. One such meeting
in a recent session took place in the Committee on Legal Affairs and Human Rights, which was considering preparing a report on "Detention of
Palestinian Minors in Israeli Prisons." In this specific meeting an Israeli parliamentarian was present, and on listening to the discussion on this planned
report, she said that she would make sure that Israel would not cooperate
with the designated rapporteur because the Parliamentary Assembly of the
Council of Europe usually comes up with reports that are biased against Israel. She said, among other things, that the minors whom the report would
defend had committed serious crimes. Some European parliamentarians
insisted in response that the report was not intended to justify criminal acts
of Palestinian youngsters but to highlight that the prison conditions of these
youngsters are contrary to the standards expected from an Observer State
such as Israel on legal and human rights of minor detainees.

Our active participation in the Parliamentary Assembly of the Council
of Europe has earned us recognition by the presidents of countries and others

in the council. In fact, in one of the visits to Palestine of the rapporteur on the status of our partnership, he praised the work of our delegation in front of President Abbas of the Palestinian National Authority; he mentioned to him that the Palestinian Delegation was exemplary in its commitment to attending the sessions and the meetings of the various committees and in fact would be a model to some European delegations.

My own take on our participation in the Council of Europe is that it is beneficial for us to be sensitized to the issues and challenges of Europe. Often the interventions, reports, and discussions that go on in the Hemicycle (the hall where the Parliamentary Assembly of the Council of Europe holds its meetings) and in the committee meetings pertain to contemporary issues of concern to Europe as a continent and to the different countries represented. I have felt that since 2011 a change has taken place in Europe, judging from the positions of the various delegations, with regard to their focus on the Palestinian-Israeli conflict. Nowadays many of the delegations are concentrating on what is happening in Europe with migrants and refugees, terror attacks, and the need to coordinate and cooperate in order to preempt future attacks. Apparently attempts at developing joint positions on the various topics of discussion meet with dissension among some who perceive their priorities as different from what is being proposed in the Council. Moreover, without specifying nationalities, I can state that some delegations are so obsessed with their own conflicts with other delegations that their delegates use any speaking opportunity to characterize the actions of their adversaries as contrary to the principles and values of the Council of Europe. Certainly they do not discern their own infractions—in contrast to our own balanced position, whereby we do not highlight the conflict with Israel every time we intervene (speak). We stand ready, nevertheless, to respond whenever distortions are implicit in interventions of others, including our Israeli counterparts.

Europe is facing problems. While I felt in the past that Europe could come up with joint positions on a multitude of issues, both internal and international, I am not so sure of this after participating in the meetings of the Council of Europe for over six years. But from my perspective as a neighbor of Europe, I believe that we need a united Europe not simply to stand in opposition to certain others but to provide a model in which national states cooperate for the good of all. Confronting the conflicts in the Middle East and those in Europe itself, we have an increased need for an active, united Europe. In the matter of the Palestinian-Israeli conflict, I feel that Europe has not done enough to promote the end of conflict and to expedite the political process between Palestinians and Israelis. In fact, I perceive that there is some retreat from this issue by many European statesmen as they

deal with immediately pressing issues in their various countries. This is unfortunate since it maintains the status quo in Israel and Palestine and makes
the quest for a political solution more difficult in the long run.

Xenophobia, Islamophobia, and other phobias are sure to withdraw
Europeans inward and to make them hesitant to accept others. On the other
hand, the flow of migrants and refugees from Africa and the Middle East
must be addressed and a long-term strategy adopted. In a recent meeting
of the Committee on Political Affairs and Democracy held in Denmark, the
Finance Minister of Denmark proposed that his own and other European
countries should develop, together with African countries, strategies that
would create millions of new jobs for young people in Africa. Otherwise, he
said, some of these millions of young Africans will be working to make their
way eventually to Europe instead of helping to develop their own countries.
I concur completely with his position, and I would say also that Europe
should adopt and extend this kind of policy to the Arab world, where in the
next two to three decades we will need millions of new jobs.

Besides, the current situation of conflict in Syria, Yemen, and Libya,
in addition to the instability in Iraq, does not promise to stem the tide of
potential immigrants and refugees soon. I do believe that the phenomenon
of DAESH (or ISIS) and other extremist groups has also influenced Europe's
position on relations with the Arab world and specifically on the Palestinian-Israeli conflict. Security concerns have become the top priority, and no
one can blame the Europeans for wanting Arab states to cooperate with
them on this topic. With the terror attacks in the heart of Europe, it is easy
for Europeans to regard any violence happening in Israel as part of a general phenomenon that must be confronted. For this reason, together with
the preoccupations with internal domestic matters, many European states
refrain from taking time and energy to advance peace prospects between
Israelis and Palestinians. But, as I have many times reminded the respected
parliamentarians in the Parliamentary Assembly of the Council of Europe,
Europe should be more assertive in promoting peaceful solutions to the ongoing conflicts, whether in Syria, Yemen, Libya, or Palestine and Israel. We
need to look for the causes of Europe's instability also in developments in
the neighboring southern Mediterranean countries in North Africa and the
Middle East region and to decide on how we should all treat the causes of
our joint discontent. Europe cannot handle its own security concerns without addressing broader issues of development, economic prosperity, and an
end of conflicts among its southern neighbors.

One good thing about our partnership with the Parliamentary Assembly of the Council of Europe is the constant reminder we receive on the
need to hold parliamentary elections and the insistence that we should work

diligently to abolish the death penalty. Every time Hamas in Gaza carries out the death penalty, we are contacted by the Council with expressions of condemnation and a request for our opinion on these executions. Our position is very clear, as President Abbas has declared a moratorium on the implementation of death sentences. We expect the Gaza authorities to comply with this position, especially since any execution throughout the Palestinian Territory needs the signature of President Abbas personally. Hence executions carried out by Hamas in Gaza are illegal and should be stopped.

We are adamant in our position that we want to continue with our Partner for Democracy status; we also want to use "the expertise of the European Commission for Democracy through Law (Venice Commission) in our institutional and legislative work."[9] In spite of the disengagement that I personally perceive on the part of Europe with respect to the Palestinian issue and the resolution of the conflict with Israel, I remain hopeful that our work with the Parliamentary Assembly of the Council of Europe will eventually bear the desired fruits. It is not simply that I want Palestine to be on the map of European institutions, but I also want my country and people to be active participants in working towards a future of harmony, peace, and stability.

Jerusalem

As a representative of East Jerusalem in the Palestinian parliament, I am often asked to present papers or deliver lectures on the conditions of life in Jerusalem for its Arab Palestinian inhabitants. The Jerusalem Institute for Policy Research, which is an Israeli organization that publishes the Statistical Yearbook for the Municipality of Jerusalem, places the overall population of the city in 2015 at 866,000, of whom 63.6 percent are Jews and "Others" and 37.4 percent are Arabs, both Muslims and Christians. The Christian Arab population of the city is estimated at some 12,000-plus inhabitants with some additional 3,000 expatriate Christians from various countries, living or working in convents, monasteries, and other Christian institutions.[10]

The conditions of life for the Arab residents of the city are dismal. A visitor to the city would quickly see that we are talking about two different cities, in terms of road and service infrastructures, and not about a unified city. The Association for Civil Rights in Israel (ACRI), again an Israeli organization, reports that in 2015 75.4 percent of all Palestinian residents in East Jerusalem and 83.9 percent of Palestinian children in the city lived below

9. Document 12711 (2011) of the Parliamentary Assembly.
10. "Statistical Yearbook, 2017 Edition."

the poverty line. This report clarifies the extent of the ills suffered by its population, including the Separation Wall and the disruption it has caused for over a quarter of the Palestinian population of the city.[11]

The claim that Jerusalem is a united city is countered by the discriminatory practices of Israeli public institutions in charge of the welfare and development of the entire city. Jerusalem's Palestinian inhabitants are permanent residents according to Israeli law; they hold Israeli identity cards and are entitled to vote in the municipality's elections and to receive public services as citizens do. They do not vote for Israeli Knesset members because they are not citizens with Israeli passports that entitle their holders to vote in national parliamentary elections. When Palestinians from East Jerusalem travel abroad, they use either Israeli-issued travel documents or their Jordanian travel documents. In the first case, they can travel via Ben Gurion Airport in Tel Aviv; in the second, they have to travel across a bridge to Jordan.

In the Oslo Accords it was agreed that the issue of Jerusalem would be left for negotiations at a later stage, when the other issues have been resolved. The Israelis have used this agreement to argue that the Palestinian National Authority cannot operate in the city and that any activity it conducts, including cultural ones, are considered illegal by the Israeli authorities. Institutions that are supported by the Palestinian Authority have been closed, including sports clubs, the chamber of commerce, and educational and research institutions, among others.

These closures have left a vacuum in the cultural, commercial, and financial life of East Jerusalem and have contributed to a perception among the population that the Palestinian Authority does not care about the city with its problems and challenges. At one point in a conference on the city in 2017 on the occasion of fifty years of Israeli occupation, a speaker compared the feelings of the city's residents to the African American hymn "Sometimes I Feel like a Motherless Child," and argued that Jerusalem's Palestinians feel like orphans without a mother or a father because nobody cares about their city and the transformations taking place in it that leave them at a great disadvantage.

In the Jordan-Israel peace agreement of 1994 there was a clause on the special role of Jordan in maintaining the Muslim shrines in Jerusalem and the commitment by Israel to give high priority to Jordan's historic role regarding these shrines when negotiations on their permanent status take place.[12] The special relationship of Jordan to these shrines has proven to

11. "East Jerusalem 2015."
12. *Treaty of Peace*, 1994.

be helpful particularly in times of crisis when events and developments at Al Haram Al Sharif (called the Temple Mount by the Israelis) necessitate the intervention of Jordan to contain further infringements or violence on the compound. The Israeli authorities, nevertheless, have taken various measures to drive home to Palestinians and others that virtual control of Al Haram Al Sharif compound is in Israeli hands and accordingly Israeli Jewish religious claims should be exercised. This makes the sacred compound a spawning ground for increased mistrust, mutual recriminations among Jews and Muslims, and sporadic confrontations in which loss of life is unavoidable.

Roman Catholic Patriarch Emeritus Michel Sabbah and Lutheran Bishop Munib Younan of Jerusalem both argue that Jerusalem is the key to peace between Israelis and Palestinians. Jerusalem, according to them, should be shared, and freedom of religious practice in line with the Status Quo of the holy places should be respected by all. If there is a will, then there is a way to make Jerusalem a habitable city for its two nationalities and its three religious groups. No one, including the Palestinian Authority, is calling for a re-division of Jerusalem. The insistence is that both Israelis and Palestinians should develop systems that could make the city operate like Brussels with its multi-national and ethnic groups or like Vatican City as an enclave within Rome. Agreements on the hotly contested topics can be negotiated, and access to the city for the believers of the three faiths can be accordingly guaranteed. In a situation of peace for Jerusalem, cooperation between Palestinians and Israelis would become a must. Municipal and judicial authority and even policing and law enforcement would have to be shared. The ingenuity of both Israelis and Palestinians would come into play to create an environment where different groups in the city can rub elbows with each other while going on with their daily lives and religious rituals.

Nothing is impossible, not even in Jerusalem. I do subscribe to this vision of one Jerusalem, which would promote harmonious acceptance of each other and of the different traditions and beliefs with which we order our lives from our own vantage points. We cannot continue in Jerusalem in the way we have been operating for the last fifty years. Every time there is an incident at Al Haram Al Sharif compound, I am saddened because it is usually a reprise of previous incidents in which confrontations were the order of the day. If no agreed-upon vision for Jerusalem is found that brings Palestinians and Israelis together, then for sure the future will not be a promising one, particularly if tensions and religious sensitivities drive young people to vent their anger through violent actions.

Diaspora Communities

In my work as a parliamentarian I have often questioned the role of the Palestinian Diaspora abroad, particularly the Christian Palestinian immigrants who comprise over 70 percent of the entire Palestinian Christian population worldwide. When I was elected in January 2006, I received an invitation from my friend Harry Wallace in Australia for a speaking tour. The occasion was also used to meet with the Palestinian community "down under." What I observed was that these Diaspora Palestinians, having relocated the culture and societal structures inherited from their original place of birth, lacked the ability to organize on a modern basis in support of their homeland. In response to a Palestinian friend who asked me whether I was coming to Australia to fundraise, I responded that this was not my purpose for the visit and that if the Australian Palestinians wanted to contribute to the development of their country of origin, then it was their responsibility to organize to do so.

The question of Palestinian Diaspora communities and their failure to play a more significant role in the rebirth of Palestine is one that should be explored. We have significant Palestinian communities in Central and South America. In Chile, some statistics speak of over three hundred thousand Chileans of Palestinian descent, most of whom are Christians, including some affluent and enterprising bankers and financiers. In the U.S. two-thirds of Palestinian and Jordanian Americans are Christians, according to the U.S. census statistics. In Australia there are more Christian Palestinians in Sydney than there are in Jerusalem. It is clear to me that there is a lot of potential for organizing these communities to support the development of Palestinian society and to help in finding an exit strategy out of the impasse in the political process. If we want to see a future Palestine that is at peace with itself and its neighbors, then we need more efforts from all Palestinians, particularly the Palestinian communities in the Diaspora.

What Does the Future Hold?

At the time of writing, we are promised by President Donald Trump that the Palestinian-Israeli conflict will be resolved and that an "ultimate deal" between the two sides will be forthcoming. The Palestinian Authority is doing all in its power to facilitate such a deal; for example, it has relinquished all preconditions for the restart of the negotiations with Israel, letting go of its earlier insistence that no negotiations can take place while Israel is constructing new illegal settlements and expanding old ones on occupied

Palestinian land. The hard work of John Kerry, Secretary of State under President Obama, with his frequent travels to Israel and Palestine to reignite the peace process, has come to naught, due primarily to Israel's unwillingness to move forward on the peace process. The question asked by Palestinians now is whether President Trump can succeed where his predecessors in the White House have not.

Some in Palestine—and I share their worry—are concerned that the American position has never been favorable to the rights of Palestinians because the U.S. preoccupation has always been with how to support Israel and provide it with a military and political edge. Even when the U.S. offers economic help and support to us Palestinians, the objective for improving our living conditions is an agenda that encourages accommodation to Israel's goals and policies in the Occupied Territories. Thus Israel's interest appears to Palestinians as the primary factor in the U.S. approach to the ongoing conflict and its resolution. More concessions will be expected from us, the weaker side, if the ultimate deal is to be struck.

I feel that we are in a "Catch-22" situation: damned if we do and damned if we don't. This feeling is troublesome because the settlers' demographic aspiration to reach the one million mark in the Occupied Palestinian Territory by 2020 and the heightened religious animosity over Al Haram Al Sharif/the Temple Mount compound prevent a promising future for either side. One wonders how an "ultimate deal" could materialize under these conditions. When I asked some Israeli acquaintances what they thought of Mr. Trump's promise of an ultimate deal, one of them pointed out that unpredictability is a trait that may divert the whole process and render it impossible to strike any deal between Israelis and Palestinians. Let us hope that these acquaintances will be proven wrong.

In the Israeli-Palestinian conflict both sides see themselves as victims. On the Israeli side the victimhood goes back to the anti-Semitism of Europe and the tragedies that have befallen the Jews throughout centuries. Some Israeli politicians apply the label "anti-Semitism" widely and inappropriately. Those Israeli politicians and even some in academia would like to imprint on people's minds that any criticism of the Israeli occupation, of the policies whereby Israel retains its grip on the Palestinian territories, or of the harm that Israel inflicts on the Palestinian people is a new version of anti-Semitism. Accordingly, the Israeli self-perception of victimhood gives them a sense of freedom to engage in any practice deemed convenient to retain their political and military superiority over Palestinians and to gain a feeling of security.

On the Palestinian side, the pervasive pessimism of most Palestinians keeps anger simmering below the surface. Anger channels itself into feelings of victimization. The injured feeling of victimhood can fuel behavior that is self-destructive even when targeting others, and it can be seen as justification for committing acts that are unacceptable by any moral or ethical standard, acts that negate and hurt others. The sense of victimhood sways Palestinians' feelings against the West and against Israel and intensifies their emotional reactions to events and developments concerning the conflict with Israel.

Both Israeli and Palestinian "victims" feel that there can be no middle ground on which to stand and to acknowledge each other. A sense of victimhood bars the path to solutions that would require the development of a common vision for the future. The challenge for all of us is to shed our victimhood mentality and liberate ourselves from its yoke, rather than perpetuating destructive perceptions.

In my regular talks to American groups visiting the Holy Land, I am always asked what average Americans can do. I am convinced, I tell my American friends, that even as individuals we can make a difference. If we see something wrong—as when a Christian pastor told me about her shock when seeing the Separation Wall around Bethlehem—then we should communicate with our elected representatives and with those who have the power to make a difference.

I always remind American visitors that at a certain point in Palestinian history, back in the early twenties of the last century, when the Mandate system was being discussed, Palestinians were requesting that the U.S., rather than Great Britain, become the Mandate power in Palestine. The reason for their preference for the U.S. was that it had never been perceived as a colonial power in the Middle East region and had never been known for taking advantage of other peoples and their resources. I also remind my interlocutors of the fact that the Quakers, Mennonites, and other religious groups in American society were the first to support Palestinians when they became refugees after the 1948 war. Mainstream churches, including the Catholic, Evangelical Lutheran, Episcopal, Presbyterian, and United Methodist Churches, the Disciples of Christ, and the United Church of Christ, among others, have stood by the Palestinian people in their plight. The U.S. government remains one of the largest contributors to UNRWA, the United Nations Relief and Works Agency, which specializes in serving and educating Palestinian refugees and their children. So, in spite of political disagreement with the U.S. administrations over their support for Israel, it must be admitted that Americans and their government have been sensitive to the conditions and tribulations of Palestinians. My advice to my American friends—both visitors to the Holy Land and those living in the "good ole USA"—is that they should persevere in insisting that their voice for peace with justice in Palestine must be heard. We need American support because without the involvement of average Americans we cannot reach out to those who make policy and determine the national interest of the United States. I am of the belief that the national interest of the U.S. in the long run is in facilitating a just and lasting solution to the Palestinian-Israeli conflict. There will never be full justice to my Palestinian people; but without even the relative justice that will come to us if a viable solution is found, the prospects for the future will appear menacing for all in the Holy Land.

Epilogue

As the family grows and as each of the younger members searches for the way forward, the environment of continuing political conflict affects the prospects for individuals and communities alike. The search for a just and lasting solution to the Israeli-Palestinian conflict should not be abandoned. An end to the conflict will not only herald political stability, but, as important, it will offer opportunities for individuals, families, and the two national communities to fulfill themselves in mutual acknowledgment and harmony. On the other hand, concrete walls that promote polarization between groups will continue to detract from long-term beneficial prospects that can result from a genuine and lasting peace accord. Politicians are particularly responsible for developing an inclusive vision for the future that can help to accommodate the two national narratives in Israel and Palestine and can acknowledge and respect the three religious traditions of Judaism, Christianity, and Islam.

The situation of the Christian and other minorities in the Middle East will continue to be cause for concern. Current civil strife in Syria and the instability experienced in Iraqi society have made it quite difficult for many Christians and members of other minority groups in these two countries to feel at home. The development of DAESH (ISIS) with the destruction that it has wrought points, among other things, to the need to create an educational system that seeks to sensitize our children to the presence of others in society. Such an education would help the children to see the differences of race, religion, ethnicity, language, and cultural traditions as positive factors contributing to an inclusive, open, multicultural society.

While education and its curricula are the concern for local educators, the role of international politics and the ill-advised interventionist decisions in Iraq and elsewhere in the Middle East should not be discounted as contributing significantly to the disintegration of Arab states that has promoted the development of extremist and fanatic groups such as DAESH.

The challenge today for all those who care about the future of the Middle East is how to work together in order to create societies that are open to all their citizens and encourage the notion of citizenship over particularistic traits and characteristics that divide one group from other groups.

For a Christian Palestinian, telling one's personal story, which includes the family's story with its particular history and traditions, is an expression of hope—the hope that those Christian Palestinians, the living stones, will persevere as they stay put in their ancestral homes in spite of all odds. This message of hope is not only intended to provide inspiration for the self-preservation of the community, but it is also addressed to those in the West and elsewhere, including those in the Arab world itself, who have never realized that there has always been a presence of indigenous Arab Christians in the Middle East, in fact for nearly seven centuries before the rise of Islam. This message of hope is also intended to convey to the Palestinian Christian Diasporas, estimated at three-quarters of all Palestinian Christians worldwide, that their brothers and sisters in the Holy Land need their accompaniment and partnership.

Photographs

Wedding of Zachariah and Marguerite Sabella, 1939

The Sabella family home in Qatamon, early 1940s; on the steps:
Bernard's father, Cousin Joseph, Aunt Leonie

Bernard Sabella, First Communion, 1956

Street scene at the "Dar"

Palm Sunday, 1958: Bernard's mother, Marguerite Sabella, with six of her eight children (left to right, Hilda, Bernadette, Abel, Maurice, Tony, Bernard)

High school graduation, 1964, the Frères School, Old City Jerusalem, Jordan,
with Brother Felix and the Mayor of East Jerusalem. Bernard is in the front row, the
first on the right.

Christmas, mid-1960s, left to right: Bernard's father and mother;
his siblings Abel, Therese, Daoud, Hilda, Tony; and Aunt Mary

The First Communion of Bernard and Mary's oldest child, Margo;
little brother Zack being held by his father

Bernard and Mary with Zack (age 6), Margo (age 14),
and Mona (age 1 year), in 1989

A session of the Palestinian Legislative Council (Parliament), Ramallah, 2006;
Bernard Sabella in front row, second from right

In the Parliamentary Assembly of the Council of Europe, Strasbourg;
Bernard Sabella with Azzam Al Ahmad and Ibrahim Khreisheh

Sources Cited

Arnold, Thomas, and Alfred Guillaume, eds. *The Legacy of Islam*. Oxford: Oxford University Press, 1931. Full text available at https://archive.org/stream/legacyofislam032426mbp/legacyofislam032426mbp_djvu.txt.

Census of Palestine 1931. Volume 2. Part 2. Tables by E. Mills, Assistant Chief Secretary Superintendent of Census. Alexandria, Egypt: Messrs. Whitehead, Morris, Limited, 1933. http://users.cecs.anu.edu.au/~bdm/yabber/census/PalestineCensus1931vol2.pdf.

"Declaration on the Role of Religion in the Promotion of a Culture of Peace." Participants in the 1994 UNESCO conference, Barcelona, Spain. http://www.unesco.org/webworld/peace_library/UNESCO/HRIGHTS/362-365.HTM.

"Dialogue Between the Three Monotheistic Religions: Towards a Culture of Peace." UNESCO, 1998. http://unesdoc.unesco.org/images/0011/001183/118310Mo.pdf.

Document 12711. "Request for Partner for Democracy status with the Parliamentary Assembly submitted by the Palestinian National Council." Parliamentary Assembly of the Council of Europe, September 2011. https://unispal.un.org/DPA/DPR/unispal.nsf/0/7A1043D1D6F8BF2A8525791F0067D2B9.

"East Jerusalem 2015: Facts and Figures." Association for Civil Rights in Israel. May 12, 2015. http://www.acri.org.il/en/wp-content/uploads/2015/05/EJ-Facts-and-Figures-2015.pdf.

"Final Declaration of the Annual Meeting of the Joint Committee for Dialogue of the Pontifical Council for Interreligious Dialogue (Vatican) and the Permanent Committee of Al-Azhar for Dialogue among the Monotheistic Religions (Cairo, Egypt)." Vatican City: Pontifical Council for Interreligious Dialogue, 2009. http://www.vatican.va/roman_curia/pontifical_councils/interelg/documents/rc_pc_interelg_doc_20090225_final-decl-rome_en.html.

✓ Fox, Edward. "The Mysterious Death of Dr. Glock." *The Guardian*, June 2, 2001. https://www.theguardian.com/education/2001/jun/02/highereducation.uk.

"Israeli Checkpoints Kill Women in Childbirth, Says New Study." *The Electronic Intifada*. 6 July 2011. https://electronicintifada.net/content/israeli-checkpoints-kill-women-childbirth-says-new-study/10145.

"The Jerusalem Sabeel Document: Principles for Just Peace in Palestine-Israel." Jerusalem: Sabeel Ecumenical Liberation Theology Center, 2006. https://www.fosna.org/content/jerusalem-sabeel-document-principles-just-peace-palestine-israel.

Jerusalem University College website. "Alumni & Donors" page: "President of JUC: Dr. Paul Wright." https://www.juc.edu/alumni/director.asp.

Jerusalem University College website. "Return Home" page: "Location Makes All the Difference!" https://www.juc.edu/index.html.

✓ "Kairos Palestine: A Moment of Truth." December 2009. Printed and distributed by Friends of Sabeel-North America, P.O. Box 9186, Portland, OR 97207. http:// www.kairospalestine.ps/sites/default/Documents/English.pdf. Also available with accompanying documents and a Presbyterian study guide at https://www. pcusa.org/site_media/media/uploads/oga/pdf/kairos-palestinestudy-guide-final-6-14-11.pdf.

Nostra Aetate (*Declaration on the Relation of the Church to Non-Christian Religions*). Proclaimed by His Holiness Pope Paul VI, October 28, 1965. Vatican City. http:// www.vatican.va/archive/hist_councils/ii_vatican_council/documents/vat-ii_ decl_19651028_nostra-aetate_en.html.

"The Palestinian Basic Law." http://www.palestinianbasiclaw.org.

"Palestinian Population To Pass Jews by 2017 in Israel and Territories." *Haaretz*, January 2, 2016. Reproduced by *The Forward* at http://forward.com/news/ breaking-news/328404/palestinian-population-to-pass-jews-by-2017-in-israel-and-territories/.

"The Permit Regime: Human Rights Violations in West Bank Areas Known as the 'Seam Zone.'" Research and writing by Adv. Aelad Cahana and Yonatan Kanonich. Jerusalem: HaMoked, March 2013. http://www.hamoked.org/files/2013/1157660_ eng.pdf.

"The Question of 'Normalization.'" Commission for Justice and Peace, Assembly of Catholic Ordinaries of the Holy Land. Jerusalem, 2017. https://zenit.org/articles/ commission-for-justice-and-peace-the-question-of-normalization/.

"Religions and the Building of Peace: The Encounter and Declaration of Montserrat." Barcelona: Foundation for a Culture of Peace, printed in 2010. http://fund-culturadepaz.org/BarnaDOC/llibre_montserrat_eng.pdf.

Resolution 1680 (2009). "Establishment of a 'partner for democracy' status with the Parliamentary Assembly." Parliamentary Assembly of the Council of Europe, June 2009. http://assembly.coe.int/nw/xml/XRef/Xref-XML2HTML-en.asp?fileid =17764&lang=en.

Sabella, Bernard. "Christian Contributions to Art, Culture and Literature in the Arab-Islamic World." Presentation at Villanova University conference "Christians in the Contemporary Middle East." Villanova, Pennsylvania, December 5, 2016. Video at http://www1.villanova.edu/villanova/publications/jsames/conference/resources. html.

"The Significance of Jerusalem for Christians." Patriarchs and Heads of Christian Communities in Jerusalem. November 23, 1994. *Dialogika*. Philadelphia: Saint Joseph's University Institute for Jewish-Catholic Relations. Copyright, Council of Centers on Jewish-Christian Relations, 2014. http://www.ccjr.us/ dialogika-resources/documents-and-statements/ecumenical-christian/730-chrjeru94nov23.

Sozomen, *Ecclesiastical History* 2.5, Nicene and Post-Nicene Fathers, 2nd Series, 2:262, available online at http://www.ccel.org/ccel/schaff/npnf202.iii.vii.v.html.

"Statistical Yearbook, 2017 Edition." Chapter III/1. Jerusalem Institute for Policy Research. http://www.jerusaleminstitute.org.il/.upload/yearbook/2017/shnaton_Co117.pdf.

Treaty of Peace Between the Hashemite Kingdom of Jordan and the State of Israel. October 26, 1994. http://www.kinghussein.gov.jo/peacetreaty.html.

"World Happiness Report." United Nations, 2017. http://worldhappiness.report/wp-content/uploads/sites/2/2017/03/StatisticalAppendixWHR2017.pdf.